AMERICAN
ELOQUENCE

AMERICAN ELOQUENCE

LANGUAGE AND LEADERSHIP IN THE TWENTIETH CENTURY

RODERICK P. HART

Columbia University Press
New York

Columbia University Press
Publishers Since 1893
New York   Chichester, West Sussex
cup.columbia.edu

Copyright © 2023 Columbia University Press

Cataloging-in-Publication Data available from the Library
of Congress.

ISBN 978-0-231-20906-9 (cloth)
ISBN 978-0-231-20907-6 (paper)
ISBN 978-0-231-55777-1 (ebook)

LCCN 2022023409

Columbia University Press books are printed on permanent
and durable acid-free paper.
Printed in the United States of America

Cover image: © Bridgeman Images
Cover design: Chang Jae Lee

To

Richard B. Gregg and George A. Borden

Mentors, colleagues, friends

For Sherrie:
How fortunate you are to have had Roselee and George as your parents. How lucky I am to have them embedded so deeply in my memory.

Rod

CONTENTS

1. Eloquence: Why? 1

2. Eloquence: When and Where? 16

3. Eloquence: How? 36

4. Cultural Resonance 56

5. Personal Investment 93

6. Poetic Imagination 123

7. Eloquence Assessed 155

8. Eloquence Tomorrow 191

   Appendix: "Importance" Versus "Eloquence" Rankings for Twentieth-Century Speeches 211
   Acknowledgments 217
   Notes 221
   Index 261

AMERICAN ELOQUENCE

1

ELOQUENCE: WHY?

Eloquence is an old and fusty word, perhaps an old and fusty concept as well. Who needs eloquence in the world of Twitter, a world in which Donald Trump's ALL CAPITAL LETTERS tell you exactly what he's feeling—in real time and with gusto? Who needs eloquence when Zoom can make us look professional when attired in a crisp white shirt and pajama bottoms? Who needs eloquence when podcasts can teach us, when Instagram can socialize us, when Netflix can titillate us, and when cable news can deliver new attitudes to us just as Amazon Prime delivers our running shoes? Eloquence makes us pause, but who can pause in a world that never stops?

Yet some persist: "We need from our candidates today a thoughtfulness that finally expresses itself in words that can arrest us with their eloquence, that can connect us to a vision that is finally poetic even if couched in terms of policy and practicalities."[1] A fine sentiment; an earnest sentiment. But there is also a certain triteness here, an "Oh that again?" quality. Is this an eighteenth-century complaint or one penned yesterday? Is this an American prayer or one uttered in Bolivia? Does the statement solicit a Republican salute or one from a Democrat? Besides, who needs more talk from a line of work that so often makes truth a shambles? Would a new eloquence help us forget Watergate or the Clinton scandals or the murder of George Floyd? Surely only silence can stave off the jangling fates that await.

Cyprian Soarez, a sixteenth-century Jesuit, says otherwise: "What can be more wondrous," asks Soarez, than "for speech to pass into the minds of other people through very delicate passages of our ears, designed in such a unique and skillful manner, and to imprint its mark so perfectly and so fixedly on them that it comforts the sorrowful, arouses the languid, reanimates the discouraged, [and] restrains those who have been carried away by empty pleas?"[2] Father Soarez imagines a grand something here, but what? Is there still room for eloquence in a society driven by what David Hume called "ministerial maneuvering" and the "interplay of factions"?[3] Can eloquence still usher "a unified nation into existence," or did John Adams mislead us when saying so?[4] Is eloquence still a signatory to public virtue? Can it send us off on a grand trek? Can it draw us together, found cities, make laws, and invent new arts as Isocrates would have it? Can eloquence exalt us in our brittle, anomic present?

This book takes eloquence seriously but not obeisantly. It notes that eloquence can make us think deeper thoughts, draw us closer to our fellow citizens, and energize us when we feel bereft or disconsolate. By going beyond the ordinary, eloquence can make us feel less ordinary—deeper, truer, more richly emotional. The eloquent eulogist puts us in touch with those who can no longer be touched, tapping into feelings we have felt but cannot speak. Eloquence is "a hedge against arrogance and indifference," say Theodore Glasser and James Ettema, and a hedge, too, against random thoughts and cheap emotions.[5] Eloquence is us at our finest.

This book interrogates the nation's history of eloquence. It surveys a wide swath of political discourse—some old and some contemporary—and, in doing so, calls on the best of the American tradition. To give up on eloquence, I shall argue, is to give up on political hope and the possibilities of human language. By demanding change, eloquence keeps us from getting trapped in our historical selves or from betraying a common future. Admittedly, politics can be a sordid business, a way of rationalizing war, poverty, social injustice, and human disregard. "We have art in order not to die of the truth," says Nietzsche, and eloquence can keep us from dying that death. To give up on eloquence is to give up on ourselves.

This book offers a new way of thinking about eloquence. Others have tried such things before, and I shall draw on their wisdom. But I will also follow my own lead by offering a new way of defining and measuring eloquence. For me, this is not an exercise in mad accountancy but an attempt to explain what makes great speech great and why it is still needed. Focusing mainly on twentieth-century oratory, I will argue that eloquence is the byproduct of *cultural resonance*, when a speaker makes us feel known, at home; *personal investment*, when a speaker honors us with personal disclosures; and *poetic imagination*, when a speaker helps us conceive the hard to conceive. There are other ways of gauging eloquence, but these are my ways.

I shall also argue that, at its best, eloquence becomes the servant of nationhood, cultivating truth for communal ends. Eloquence preserves our common memories, reminding us where we have been and to what we are destined. But before getting into such matters, we need to think harder about why such a hoary concept deserves consideration in an age of driverless cars and trips to Mars. Surely by now we have outgrown the rhetorical arts. Surely the fractious politics of the day have worn away all hope for a commonweal. Surely by now *Wall Street Journal* editorials and hip-hop lyrics provide all the verbal resources needed for a fulfilled life. Or perhaps not.

JUDGING ELOQUENCE

Even though eloquence is devilishly hard to understand, two things seem true: first, people know it when they hear it, and second, they are willing to fight about it. Figure 1.1 tells a curious story.

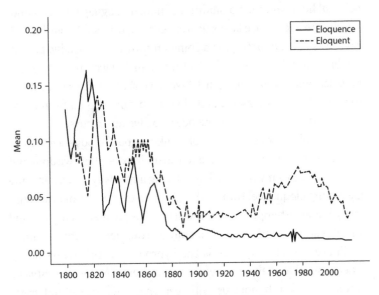

FIGURE 1.1 References to *eloquence* versus *eloquent* over time

As expected, references to *eloquence*—the concept—have dropped off dramatically since the dawn of the nineteenth century. Despite the increasing availability of mass communication—or perhaps because of it—eloquence is no longer discussed as often as before. On the other hand, judgments of who is *eloquent* continue to be a popular sport. Even a casual internet search finds all manner of people declared eloquent: John F. Kennedy, of course, but also Prime Minister Jacinda Ardern of New Zealand. Judith of biblical fame has been judged far more eloquent than Rebekah, also of biblical fame. The Indian cricketer Mansur Ali Kahn Pataudi has been deemed eloquent, but so too has Doug Baldwin of the Seattle Seahawks. The right side of the brain has labeled *Something Like Avalanches* eloquent (in a postrock sense) while the left side of the brain finds APL an eloquent programming language.

What do such judgments tell us? What is *at stake* when people argue about who uses language well? Is it animated by their intellectual commitments? their political truths? their cultural identities?

Why argue about such stuff? And why so confidently? CNN's Anderson Cooper is a case in point. He disliked Donald Trump to the core and often took it out on the former president's language. Said Cooper on one occasion: "We listened to this man muse and meander, rant and regurgitate the same tired tropes and untruthful claims. We watch him boast and brag and preen and do that odd thing with his nose when he sucks in air very loudly and none of it surprises us. That's how far we have fallen."[6]

Cooper's list of indictments here is a mottled one. Like any good news commentator, he is upset by Trump's misstatements of fact, but he is especially bothered by his style—his boasts, his rants, his repetitions—things that might be forgiven in one's neighbor at a cookout after the beer has been poured. Cooper also attacks Trump's imagery, as if the president of the United States were required to ape T. S. Eliot or Emily Dickinson. Cooper is especially put off by Trump's body, particularly his breathing apparatus, which he connects to his overall perfidy. We, too, are caught in Cooper's dragnet, and his final judgment is apocalyptic: we and Trump are cast out of Eden, the second great fall of humankind.

Other judgments of Trump's rhetoric have been less harsh. Simon Montefiore calls Trump "bombastic" and "unconventional" but also notes that his improvised, "meandering speeches" often "delighted rallies of his supporters." While his fans could not recall what Trump said, the impression he left was "authentic and unforgettable" says Montefiore.[7] Barack Obama was another matter entirely. As we see in figure 1.2, Obama was universally declared eloquent during his presidency. Obama treated language as a treasure, and he carefully meted it out. People were often transfixed by Obama, who could not only share a narrative but also perform it while speaking. An interior person comfortable with himself and his manuscripts, Obama could dazzle people in public when required to do so.

Donald Trump hates Barack Obama, and he especially hates Obama's eloquence. Once when talking to a reporter, Trump noted that, upon their first meeting, Obama "was very nice to me but after that we had some difficulties." But "it doesn't matter," said

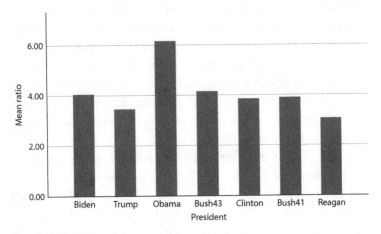

FIGURE 1.2 Ratio of *eloquent* to *glib* references for recent presidents

Note: First-year references found via NexiUni database searches

Trump, "words are less important to me than deeds."[8] "Trump hates Obama," said a former Trump adviser, "he used to go around calling Obama a child."[9] Said another observer: Trump "cannot shake President Obama from his head."[10] And another: "Trump is obsessed with Obama. Obama haunts Trump's dreams."[11]

The antinomies here are striking—words versus deeds, adults versus children, interiors versus exteriors, dreams versus realities—all of which point to eloquence. The eloquent speaker makes words act. The eloquent speaker reaches within us while reaching outside of us. The eloquent speaker appeals to our innocence as well as our collective dreams. Barack Obama did all these things instinctively; he was born to eloquence. For that reason, and for the first time in recent presidential history, Donald Trump was not to be seen when his predecessor's formal portrait was unveiled at the White House.

Eloquence mystifies Donald Trump because he finds words to be such a waste of time. While always ready to express his own emotions, Trumps finds the emotions of others a mystery and, really, an irrelevance. Trump is a linear man, a man without curvatures. Once, when standing at Mount Rushmore, he variously declared that "Lincoln won the Civil War" and then "we are building the wall." When reaching out to the assembled moms and dads, he took a moment to declare that "our children are taught in school to hate their own country." Inspired by the four presidents towering above him, Trump reminded people what a really great construction project can do for a nation: "We are the people who dreamed a spectacular dream—it was called Las Vegas in the Nevada desert—who built up Miami from the Florida marsh."[12] Donald Trump is an empiricist to the core. While Barack Obama is a man whose head and heart are fused, Trump treats head and heart as mere body parts. For that reason, Trump's greatest enemy— COVID-19—was his undoing. When the nation needed a president who cared, a president who could weep, Donald Trump was on the fifteenth fairway.[13]

RESISTING ELOQUENCE

Donald Trump is not alone in being suspicious of eloquence. Modernism, too, has found it wanting. In James Joyce's Ireland, says Matthew Bevis, "oratory was a national obsession as well as a family hand me down," but the times have changed.[14] Today, people no longer congregate for political discussions as they once did, and churches are finding fewer people in their pews. In the courtrooms, reports Marcus Priest, "excitement and colour are now lacking," with barristers having been "replaced by movie stars, musicians, and journalists" as admirable "public people."[15] In addition, eloquence places cognitive demands on us, and that can prove difficult for people accustomed to short-order arguments. Because of the internet, "almost anyone can produce and author content," reports Danielle Pye, and "blogging has made it easy to be a publisher." Meanwhile, digital cameras have "democratized photography," turning everyone into a rhetorical animal.[16] In short, changing tastes, changing technologies, and neoliberalism have left little room for eloquence.

But eloquence faces older foes as well. Petrarch once warned that eloquence and cosmopolitanism are a dangerous combination, sure to lead astray the humble peasant within us. "It is a peculiar characteristic of orators that they take pleasure in large cities and in the press of the crowd," says Petrarch, and "they curse solitude and hate and oppose silence where decisions are [best] made."[17] Urbanity links eloquence to ignorance, says Petrarch, and, more dangerously, eloquence links ignorance to power. Three hundred years later, Giambattista Vico echoed Petrarch's concerns, noting how dangerous eloquence could be if unattended by a rich education. When asked by King James for his advice on starting a new university, Francis Bacon "insisted that young scholars should not be admitted to the study of eloquence unless they had previously studied their way through the whole curriculum of learning."[18]

For many thinkers in the Western tradition, eloquence is dangerous because it leads to falsehoods. John Locke, a contemporary of Vico, made the case plainly: "All the artificial and figurative application of words eloquence has invented are for nothing else but to insinuate wrong ideas and move the passions, and thereby mislead the judgment, and so indeed are perfect cheats."[19] Here, Locke puts his finger on eloquence's carnal danger: its tendency to traffic in human emotions, which leads to an even more basic problem: women. "Through Eve's open mouth," says Lynda Boose, "sin and disorder entered the world." "Through the employment of her tongue," Boose continues, Eve "is imagined as the usurpation of the male phallic instrument and the male signifier of language." The result: "Perpetually guilty, perpetually disorderly, perpetually seductive, Eve and her descendants become the problem that society must control."[20] The inevitable result: Alexandria Ocasio-Cortez and Marjorie Taylor Greene.

This notion of eloquence as a moral liability has not abated. Martin Luther King Jr. attracted a cadre of clandestine FBI agents because of his eloquence; later, Barack Obama was viewed by some as the devil incarnate for the same reason. That both men were African Americans—men unwilling to apologize for their emotions—only added to Eve's malefactions. But it gets worse. God, says Philip Arrington, has also had to find a way of keeping up with the eloquences of the day. What began "as a limited circula-tion of hand-written scrolls and codices, or narratives embedded in stained-glass cathedral windows, soon became a printing indus-try all to itself that extended far beyond mere copies of the Bible." As the years unfolded, Arrington observes, "all kinds of technolog-ical modes of delivering and distributing what God is thought to have said" were invented. "Through loudspeakers, pamphlets and fliers of biblical commentaries, radio, televised evangelists, and films," says Arrington, and then via "the countless proliferation of religious websites," the Lord was forced to adjust to the times.[21] Although accurate figures are hard to come by, televangelism bud-gets in the United States now run into the hundreds of millions of dollars a year.

Quentin Skinner notes that eloquence is often seen as a physical force and that only adds to the worries it inspires. "We still refer to the capacity of eloquent speakers to *seize* the attention of their audi-ence," Skinner notes, and "*hold* them in the palm of the hand; we also speak of the power of the eloquent speech to *sway* us, to *transport* us, to *carry* us away."[22] These are metaphors, of course, but Thomas Hobbes sees the inevitable outcome: "There can be no author of rebellion that is not an eloquent and powerful speaker" and also "a man of little wisdom."[23] Here, Hobbes puts his finger on elo-quence's serial conflations: falsehood plus disorder plus passion plus power. "Eloquence may set fire to reason," Oliver Wendell Holmes famously declared, a worry that has not abated to this day.

Eloquence leaves a trail of mistrust because it calls to mind what we humans fear most, our ability to influence one another—which, among other things, can inspire uprisings in the nation's streets or hateful screeds on the nation's websites.[24] While it is true, says the classicist Hannah Gray, that "truth would be mute without eloquence," without the ability to take what is "at hand and to make it generally intelligible and useful," it is also true that feelings sent aloft often descend on those least able to prudently judge their consequences, as the events of January 6, 2021, surely showed.[25] Eloquence is a wondrous thing, except when it is not.

FINDING ELOQUENCE

Everyone knows what eloquence is until they are asked what eloquence is. When pressed on such matters, when asked how they
know eloquence when they hear it, people's voices typically trail off,
which is not to say that all are bereft of opinions:

- Ben Johnson: "A fool may talk, but a wise man speaks."
- George Santayana: "Eloquence is a republican art, as conversation is
  an aristocratic one."
- Augustine: "Wisdom without eloquence is of small avail to a country."
- Pascal: "Continuous eloquence wearies."
- Emerson: "Eloquence is the best speech of the best soul."

Why is it easy to wax philosophical about eloquence but hard
to define it? What logic did Ben Johnson use when distinguishing foolishness from wisdom? Did George Santayana really mean
that everyday folks cannot be eloquent at home or that despots'
harangues cannot be propulsive? A kindred question for Saint
Augustine: Could a country not succeed if guided by a quiet leader
who mixes easily with people, who carefully monitors the national
economy, and who refuses to send young men off to old men's wars?
Must all leaders talk, talk, talk, and, if so, would that not inevitably
lead to Pascal's fate? Emerson may be right that eloquence is the
best speech of the best soul, but how—by what methodology—did
the great transcendentalist measure the souls he encountered on
the streets of Boston?

The linguist David Crystal claims that people "seem to recognize
eloquence when they hear it," a claim that, to the best of my knowledge, has never been tested.[26] I have no doubt, though, that most
people have an inkling about eloquence. One rarely hears phrases
like "rather eloquent" or "passingly eloquent." People are usually all
in or all out when it comes to eloquence. That is especially true if
you are Irish, or so said the *Treasury of Eloquence* in 1882. "The voice
of eloquence is sweeter than the voice of song," stated its preface,

quickly followed by a description of eloquence as "an art, heavenly in the magic of its inspiration, superior to music's charms in thrilling the ear, and privileged to sway by conviction the reason of the soul."[27] There is something here, but what?

I am after more definitive answers in this book, less lyrical outcomes. But I also want to take people's *feelings* about eloquence seriously because they reveal much about their cultural moorings. The ancient Greeks meant something, after all, when noting that eloquence was the main thing distinguishing human beings from animals; they meant something different when worshipping Hermes, "the god of thieves and public speakers."[28] Today, some people find eloquence in Ted Cruz and others in Nicki Minaj, and those feelings, too, mean something. We must ask why eloquence compels us, says the rhetorical scholar Davis Houck, because doing so makes us confront the taken-for-granted, our assumptions about what is good and bad.[29]

But interrogating eloquence is hard because it is suffused by the inchoate. For some people, eloquence is a blinding force, felt but unexplainable. For others, today's eloquence is but a pale imitation of its former self. Still others see traditional notions of eloquence as impossibly gendered and impossibly racist, cultural outcroppings of a white, Western patriarchy. Class affects our perceptions of eloquence as well. Hugh Blair noted in the 1800s that many of his fellow citizens regarded eloquence as "a trick of speech, the art of varnishing weak arguments plausibly, or of speaking so as to please and tickle the ear."[30] The attitudes Blair described can be found elsewhere: "Many words, little sense" (Japan); "Talk does not cook rice" (China); "Fair words butter no parsnips" (United Kingdom).[31]

People know what they know about eloquence, but the concept ought not be dismissed outright. "The biggest problem in America, the biggest problem in any modern industrialized society," says the former speechwriter Peggy Noonan, "is loneliness." "A great speech from a leader to the people," says Noonan, "eases our isolation, breaks down the walls, includes people. It takes them inside a spinning thing and makes them part of the gravity."[32] Noonan is eloquent here, but we need to know more. Eloquence is sometimes elitist, but can it also be pedestrian? If eloquence is now in short supply, can it be remanufactured? We also need to know more about people's standards for eloquence—those that are idiosyncratic and those popularly shared. Some say that eloquence colonizes the public sphere; others, that it advances public virtue.[33] Who is correct? And what about this matter of loneliness?

This book cannot answer all of these questions, but it can make a start. When searching for eloquence, though, I will tack to a different wind. I will not, for example, examine the literary manifestations of eloquence or how poetry works its magic. I will also not look at the physicality of eloquence, how vocalics and meter and gesture contribute to a speaker's impact. Instead, I will focus on the most primitive dimension of language—word choice—ignoring morphology, phonology, syntax, and much else. Worst of all, I will use a computer program to help me understand eloquence, thereby doing violence to the pantheon of orators in one fell swoop.

My search for eloquence is thus a primitive one. I will use my computer program to plow through tens of thousands of texts, looking for language patterns not easily discerned by the average person. While Churchill and Lincoln and Hemingway were more than the words they used, they used some words more than others, and I will ask why. They used certain words with some audiences and other words with other audiences, and again I will ask why. When making these inspections, I will operate on the imperfect assumption that people were affected by the words Churchill and Lincoln and Hemingway used but were unaware of those influences. Word choices, I will argue, build up slowly in a speech, ultimately creating a certain "tone." Eloquence is the product of these mixings and minglings. While examinations like these cannot tell us everything we need to know, it can chip away at our ignorance. Eloquence is a great gift, and I will work hard not to abuse it when putting it under the microscope.

This book will survey eloquence broadly, focusing on what seems unique to the American polity. But America is a complex place.

Its land mass is large; its demography, diverse; and its tastes, multiform. While politics has been a white man's province for most of its history, things began to change in the twentieth century, and I will feature those changes in this book. Is the American community still a community? When judged by certain standards, it is. Football is popular with most of its citizens; they watch sitcoms and reality shows regularly; and almost anyone wearing jeans can still be seated in most U.S. restaurants. Americans are more religious than people in other parts of the world; they like their public schools and libraries; and almost all of them want a four-day workweek. Americans are especially fond of their toys—their cars, their smartphones, their microwave ovens, their designer glasses. Americans are also noisy. They are quick to pronounce their (multiple) ideologies, and they are especially given to adjectival constructions—*bigger, better, stronger, smarter, prettier.* Americans are not a contemplative people, and they act quickly, definitively, especially when there is a buck to be made.

But America is also many nations, and that presents a problem for eloquence. How should a leader address a country in which 350 different languages are spoken, in which 200 brands of Protestantism are practiced, and in which the various cable news stations report widely different takes on the news each evening? How can a leader reach out to citizens who have become shockingly partisan, when evangelicals have learned to fear multiculturalists, when white feminists and Black feminists cannot make common cause, when some citizens love their police departments while others revile them, and when different brands of replacement theory and critical race theory are pronounced each week? What reservoir of hope can feed eloquence during such tumultuous times?

I know of no easy answer to these questions, but I do believe that the past has lessons to teach. My hope in this book is to examine how eloquence has been used to manage previous political conflicts and to see what lessons it still retains for us. True, Americans in the 2020s are in a fitful state. They have been dogged by an endless pandemic, by the deleterious effects of climate change, and by ever-more-sophisticated brands of cyberterrorism. Some politicians shrink from these challenges, letting themselves be intimidated into silence. Where did leaders in the past find their courage? What caused them to speak out? What did they say? How did they say it? And why did the citizenry suddenly rally round, sidelining their prejudices because they sensed a salvific change afoot? Can that happen again? Do today's Americans still harbor a shared America? If so, can eloquence draw it forth?[34]

CONCLUSION

Eloquence is strange. People seem to want it—yet not too much of it—but they cannot really tell you what it is. Most agree that Barack Obama had a lot of it, whatever it is, and that Donald Trump had little of it, even though he got 74 million votes in 2020. For many Americans, to call our leaders eloquent is to say "I like the way they talk" and nothing more. For them, eloquence is a style, an attitude, a posture, a pacing that triggers certain feelings in them. Eloquence also has something to do with ideas—big ideas that dwarf us, small ideas we had forgotten. When encountered in history class, "old eloquence" typically embarrasses us by being too doctrinal, too oracular. Today, we want something snappier, something au courant. Nonetheless, we all want eloquence, whatever it is, at our funerals.

Four hundred years ago, George Puttenham said that the point of eloquence is not to confirm our place in the world but to give us the illusion of leaving it.[35] Easily said, perhaps easily done, but how? This book answers that question by defining eloquence in a specific, operational way and then applying it to a large body of texts. Chapter 2 commences that journey by surveying the many different ways eloquence has been defined before, while chapter 3 lays out my way of assessing that shimmering, elusive construct. Chapters 4 through 6 present my three-pronged approach to eloquence—cultural resonance, personal investment, and poetic imagination—and use it to probe a large and diverse corpus. Chapter 7 goes one step further, folding these individual estimates into an overall measurement of eloquence and then applying it to what are allegedly the hundred most important speeches of the twentieth century. When doing so, I will not rely solely on numbers but will reach deeply into the rhetoric itself, showing what "computational eloquence" looks like when manifested. Chapter 8 will review the implications of these studies for a nation steadfastly ambivalent about eloquence.

Catherine Nicholson has said that "to speak English eloquently" is "to speak it strangely."[36] I will take Nicholson literally here. To say that something is "strange," I shall argue, is to make a mathematical assertion, a statement claiming that a given text deviates in important ways from a cache of other texts. All critics in that sense are scientists, people who use normative understandings to spot new phenomena. We know eloquence when we hear it because it stands apart from what we have heard before. Something suddenly "breaks" in the flow of life, revealing things we hadn't noticed previously. We often react emotionally during such moments, as a speaker taps into old beliefs that suddenly, magically, rush to the surface. These moments are rare, just as eloquence is rare. We need to understand such moments.

2

ELOQUENCE: WHEN AND WHERE?

Susan Sontag, a gifted writer, philosopher, and cultural commentator, once said that "it's not 'natural' to speak well, eloquently, in an interesting articulate way. People living in groups, families, communes say little—have few verbal means. Eloquence—thinking in words—is a byproduct of solitude, deracination, a heightened painful individuality."[1] Here, Sontag offers a lofty, even magisterial, view of eloquence: Eloquence is rare and precious because it is rare. Meg Ryan, an actor who lives several suburbs away from the literati, takes things less seriously: "When I wear high heels I have a great vocabulary and I speak in paragraphs. I'm more eloquent. I plan to wear them more often."[2] Meg-the-American: Eloquence is nice, but don't get carried away with it. Former president George H. W. Bush agrees: "I may not be the most eloquent, but I learned early that eloquence won't draw oil from the ground."[3] The children's author E. B. White splits the difference. Eloquence has its place, says White, but one must acknowledge its infinite variety: "A despot doesn't fear eloquent writers preaching freedom—he fears a drunken poet may crack a joke that will take hold."[4]

Americans have been ambivalent about eloquence since the nation's founding. There is a certain ostentatiousness to it, they reason, so one must guard against being hoodwinked by spellbinders. Because of their medium of choice, writers like Susan Sontag can craft prose alone in their garrets and thus be worshipful of eloquence. Political speechmaking, in contrast, is always somewhat meddlesome. When speaking, after all, one stands apart from one's audience even while soliciting their favor, and that can make speech feel intrusive, an interruption of daily life. In contrast, people *choose* to consume literature on their own schedules and so have some right to expect—even demand—eloquence. Speech, alternatively, frequently comes to us unbidden, making eloquence something of a surprise when we encounter it.

Speech that smells too much of the lamp, that seems too practiced, usually cannot be rescued by a palpable sincerity. "By saying something," the sociologist Erving Goffman once observed, "the speaker opens himself up to the possibility that the intended recipients will affront him by not listening or will think him forward, foolish, or offensive in what he has said."[5] The rejected poet can die a quiet agony, but the rejected speaker—because of mass mediation, because of politics' visibility—can die a thousand deaths on the way to the grave.

Because there are real differences between written and oral modalities, this chapter examines what an American brand of spoken eloquence might look like. Eloquence, I shall argue, is a function of the unique "speech culture" in which one finds oneself. Norms for eloquence change from era to era and are also affected by social mores. "You must speak straight so that your words may go as sunlight into our hearts" said Cochise, the Apache chief.[6] We see here the directness of a preindustrial leader. There is no verbal excess here, making Cochise seem charming but out of synch with a modern, capitalist sensibility. We talk differently today. Our metaphors are more brocaded, and we are more sardonic. Even though Cochise may speak the truth here, it seems too true a truth, causing us to avert our gaze.

To understand eloquence, one must therefore understand the sociology of spoken discourse. Unlike written documents, for example, speech is always *situated*. Speech happens in front of others, thereby posing an existential risk to the speaker. We "stand with" our remarks when speaking, says Carroll Arnold, so it is not surprising that speech contains more personal pronouns and indigenous language than do written remarks.[7] Speech is also *transitory*. It comes into existence and then, through "rapid fading," immediately goes away, condemning a speaker to what he or she has said, with no ability to unsay it. Given these encumbrances, speakers use more repetitions and interjections than do writers, more verbs than nouns as well. Speech, in this sense, is always "busy." Finally, speech is also *leaner* than writing, deploying more monosyllabic than polysyllabic words, more concrete than abstract nouns, and more repetitions as well. While poets can reflect on their emotions in tranquility, speakers are rarely granted that indulgence given the pressures of the moment.[8]

Spoken eloquence, in short, is complicated. Speakers are forced to reckon with what others have said in similar circumstances, with long-standing cultural traditions, with their listeners' changing preferences (the language they like, the arguments they cannot abide), and with their audience's evanescent attention to the matters being discussed. Writers must also reckon with these factors, but they can do so in seclusion and without their readers shifting uncomfortably across the table from them. While these bounties do not accrue to most speakers, some argue that, theoretically at least, eloquence is available to all. Donald Trump may well be the exception. In his defense, Mr. Trump might plead that he has chosen to speak for a living rather than write and that that has made life difficult. Expectations for eloquence, he might add, make life even harder.

ELOQUENCE THEN

In 1868, Thomas Wentworth Higginson described speech as "the poorer work" but quickly added that speech also "yields such moments of inspiration as make all writing seem cold."[9] Easily said, but how to identify such moments? By looking broadly, says Ralph Waldo Emerson, since "the conditions for eloquence always exist.

It is always dying out of famous places and appearing in corners."[10] But where to find such corners? Start by consulting the past, says Alfred North Whitehead, looking at classic texts that are "patient of interpretation."[11] Yes, but what makes a classic a classic, and isn't there something of a circular logic here—stipulating ahead of time what one hopes to find? Denis Donoghue describes the most diffi- cult problem of all: "How to distinguish eloquence from its strutting cousins—grandiloquence, magniloquence, bombast, cant."[12] With people's tastes changing so much from age to age, can the past truly tell us what eloquence should look like today?

When examining traditional understandings of rhetoric, three criteria for eloquence stand out:

* *Natural simplicity*: Eloquence is perfection "originating in nature," says Quintilian; eloquence involves a "natural power" to affect us and give us pleasure, says Cicero, a power that is lost when discourse departs "from the language of ordinary life."[13] For Jean- Jacques Rousseau, eloquence is best captured by "the utopian image of peasants governing themselves by gathering under an oak tree."[14] For naturalists like Rousseau, pursuing eloquence avidly is to miss the mark. Far better, they advise, to grow a local conversation into something larger, something more encompassing, even while pre- serving its humble roots—Jimmy Carter, not Donald Trump.

* *Disciplined emotions*: For Homer, eloquence requires the mas- tering of our feelings, "tender and vehement alike."[15] For Aristotle, it requires "looking for deliberative pathways" so that logic and emo- tion become fused.[16] For François Fénelon, "logic alone doesn't have the power to move or persuade listeners," but gaudy ornamentation must also be considered an unworthy indulgence.[17] Because elo- quence is the means "by which men operate on the minds of others," said George Campbell in the eighteenth century, it requires thinking the best thoughts possible while bridling mere sentimentality.[18]

* *Moral refinement*: Samuel Taylor Coleridge argues that the major function of the artist is to "bring the whole soul of man into activity."[19] A tall order, that, but Immanuel Kant asks for even more, including "a cultured moral sense" and a discourse that seeks not to

deceive "by means of beautiful illusion" but uses the instruments of rhetoric noninstrumentally.[20] "Moral beauty" is the only rhetorical force Kant allows, says philosopher Lars Leeten, with intentional deception being "the greatest violation of a human being's duty to himself."[21] Rhetoric is dangerous, said Kant, and eloquent rhetoric even more dangerous when it confuses ends and means or substitutes personal betterment for public virtue.

Natural simplicity, disciplined emotions, moral refinement—venerable language to be sure. But even with these safeguards, Thomas Hobbes was a backbencher, one who believed that citizens could "trust neither their senses nor their passions to give them information about the outside world," that "long debates" were a sure sign of civic corruption, and that citizens needed to be immunized "against the alluring but politically destabilizing rhetoric of false prophets."[22] Hobbes was not alone; eloquence has always had its trust problems. Philosophers and theologians have been especially suspicious of it, but so, too, were those concerned with the social compact, who believed in people's capacities to reason together. James Madison put a sharper point on it in *Federalist 10*, where he declared that there are really only two ways of dealing with demagogy: "the one, by destroying the liberty which is essential to its existence; the other by giving to every citizen the same opinions, the same passions, and the same interests."[23] Madison proves quite the modernist here. While embracing classical standards of rhetoric, he also knew that democracies must tend themselves, that the times would change and that standards for eloquence would change as well. And so they did, and so they have.

ELOQUENCE NOW

Denis Donoghue has called eloquence "speech in excess of expectation," but what can that mean in a world where our expectations for everything—cheap plane fares, plentiful mobile hotspots—are constantly on the rise?[24] Today, time itself seems to have vanished, with everything happening at once, leaving little time for deep reflection. Given that condition, many people step back, resisting social involvement lest they be declared persons-out-of-time. "Now and again," says the rhetorical scholar Thomas Farrell, "the ineffable qualities of insight and the occasional demands for utterance are gathered together in one luminous moment," a moment of eloquence.[25] But who can wait for that to happen? The information scientists Olivier Morin and Alberto Acerbi have identified what they call "the birth of the cool," an era in which emotional words in published books having declined precipitously over time.[26] Quick, factual bursts of information constantly descend upon us, leaving little time for one of Farrell's moments. We hear things but do not dwell on them, hence eloquence has a harder time finding us.

In such an era, the entire concept of eloquence needs to be rethought. With more and more time to speak and less and less time for listening, what chance does public language have to arrest our thoughts and emotions? I see three features that make doing so problematic:

- *Utilitarian appropriateness*: It is too brazen to suggest that eloquence is now "manufactured," but that is not completely off the mark. The long speeches of yesteryear are rarely delivered today and, if delivered, come to us in shards—contextless pieces of discourse picked up by the press and redistributed by marketers on the internet for mass audiences. Eloquence has become "fractal" in these ways, as slogans (versus complete thoughts) that register well with focus groups often win the day.[27] Not surprisingly, scholars find that the language of togetherness ("we Americans," "the German people") increased throughout the twentieth century, with rhetoric looking for a place to comfortably reside.[28] Eloquence is like hang gliding, says Denis Donoghue, "an activity between sky and earth that, if done at all, should be done well."[29] Doing so becomes precarious in a hurry-up world where one of eloquence's old pals—memorability—becomes almost laughable.[30]

- *Technological appropriateness*: In a fine piece of work, Kathleen Hall Jamieson describes the special "intimacy" required of public discourse in the television era.[31] Rhetoric that formerly "overpowered" an audience with an "onslaught of evidence" and "fiery oratory" has given way to conversational motifs and visual dramatizations. Jamieson says that this new, "effeminate" style prizes narrative over statistics and self-disclosure over historical allusions, resulting in a televised version of the fireside chat. For Jamieson, Ronald Reagan epitomized this new style. Reagan was masterful when using the extended example and when humanizing the inhumane (war, poverty, disease, etc.). Reagan's thoughts were rarely deep, but his emotional touch was usually spot-on. Ironically, says Jamieson, Ronald Reagan, an ideological conservative, pioneered a revolution in televised communication that advanced "women's participation in politics on their own terms."[32]

- *Vernacular appropriateness*: Eloquence has never been just one thing. The Western rhetorical tradition has embraced some common standards (natural simplicity, disciplined emotions, and moral refinement) but those standards have admitted to considerable variation over the years. That is even truer today. The English language is diversifying, says Peter Elbow, because "the majority of speakers of English in the world are [now] African and Asian."[33] In such a world, says Celeste Condit, "we can reduce hierarchy by recognizing a broader set of ingredients for eloquence."[34] "Dichotomy feminists" and "diversity feminists" may fashion language differently, says Condit, but "the need for human cooperation makes eloquence indispensable if humans" are to "prosper as a species."[35] Racial differences, too, call for more diverse notions of eloquence. Julius Lester notes, for example, that Malcolm X used clear, uncomplicated words to "cut through the chains on black minds like a giant blowtorch," thereby transforming "polite" versions of eloquence into something revolutionary.[36] In short, being able to imagine different instantiations of eloquence is now an imperative.

This hasty overview of how eloquence has been envisioned over the years shows, if nothing else, how difficult it is to reliably capture its various manifestations today. Nonetheless, I shall persist. My hope is to draw on these multiple standards when fashioning a tool to assess modern eloquence in a thoughtful, demonstrable, way. Eloquence, says Robert Casiero, produces reflections "that are both enduring and provisional, that are broad enough to advance specific notions of the public good, to enforce "powerfully imaginable" ideas, and to meet the needs of diverse audiences.[37] In chapter 3, I will offer my own way of making such assessments, but first let us examine how different cultures have conceived of eloquence and how their insights might inform a contemporary, U.S.-based examination.

ELOQUENCE THERE

In the late 1700s, Hugh Blair declared that "an English sermon seldom rises beyond the strain of dry and correct reasoning" while "a French sermon is, for the most part, a warm and animated exhortation" that addresses "the imagination and the emotions."[38] Presuming that Blair was correct, how do such things happen? Why can one find clear rhetorical differences in countries sitting just across a narrow channel from one another? Is "taste" an assembly-line product, churned out distinctively in schools of theology? Or do different parishioners in different boroughs demand something unique on Sunday mornings? Does French blood really course faster in French veins, thereby requiring passion in the pulpit? Is British modesty now so severe that clergy dare not engage the sentiments lest people's feelings spill over, God forbid, into the bedroom?

Early in my career, I read a book, *Political Language and Oratory in Traditional Society*, edited by Maurice Bloch, that changed how I saw the world.[39] Bloch's is a marvelous work containing ten sumptuous essays written by cultural anthropologists who traversed the globe asking what political speechmaking looked like in such places as Bali, Madagascar, Kenya, and the island of Tikopia. They attended political rituals among the Mursi of East Africa, the Maori of New Zealand, and the Melpa of Papua New Guinea. Bloch's book shows how formalization of speech can become an adjunct to power and how language codes can strangle social relations, but also how subtle rhetorical cues can signal shifting power dynamics. Political ceremonies in particular, say Bloch and his colleagues, are used to ward off alternative forms of expertise and to keep political rivals in their places. But reinvention can also happen if the time is right and if rhetorical innovations happen incrementally.

These were exotic tales for me, forcing me to ask new questions about something I thought I already understood: political discourse in the United States. There are many different political eloquences, I came to understand, outcroppings of deep-seated cultural structures. To examine these structures is to discover where power resides; to study eloquence is to examine societies during some of their best moments—which is not to say, of course, that unbridled eloquence cannot lead a society astray when used in service of racism, sexism, and their several desultory cousins. When functioning optimally, though, eloquence does four things that are especially important:

- *Achieving personal influence.* Nothing could seem clearer: to have power, you must speak powerfully. But that is not true in Uzbekistan: "No matter how eloquent you may be, keep yourself inferior to those who know you, so that you will not become idle in the time of knowledge."[40] In other words, undue self-attention can blind leaders to the incipient political forces around them. For the Tswana of South Africa, it therefore becomes wise to "restate the values" associated with one's office rather than attempt too much virtuosity, a tactic that blends "restricted" with "elaborated" codes.[41] The advice is slightly different for the Maori in New Zealand. Rhetorical distinctiveness can be helpful ("a skilled orator does not speak by rote"), but a play for prestige ("signaled by some departure from the expected forms") can lead one astray.[42] In short, power comes to those who pursue it without appearing to have done so.

- *Celebrating social harmony.* Throughout her writing, Hannah Arendt championed "representative thinking," imagining "how I would feel and think if I were in" another's place.[43] Translated into rhetoric, such advice results in "veiled speech," according to the Melpa of Papua New Guinea, letting speakers preserve social relationships even while allowing "their dissatisfactions to pass over to their hearers."[44] A similar kind of diplomacy can be found in Egyptians' "wisdom literature," which encouraged combining in one's discourse ancient and modern truths as well as the lessons of daily life and divine teachings.[45] "Encompassing" discourse of this sort is also emphasized by the Maori of New Zealand, especially when addressing new members of a given community.[46] If done well, this sort of blended rhetoric provokes "a smile of acknowledgment rather than a shudder of revulsion," says Rob Goodman, resulting in a "kind of surplus," the "art of saying more than we mean" or, as I would have it, of sharing only those meanings we can wisely share under the circumstances.[47]

• *Reinforcing existing hierarchies.* For most Americans, political power is most easily witnessed when a sitting president speaks from the Oval Office or when major candidates slug it out under the klieg lights during a political debate. Maurice Bloch urges us to look further, to the quieter forms of influence found in political rituals. He notes, for example, that when the Merina of Madagascar use "elaborate forms of speechmaking," "fixed formal styles," and "endless quotations," power goes underground, thereby becoming an unseen but constraining social force.[48] Under these circumstances, says Bloch, a speaker "implies his last words by his first" by following a priori assumptions of what can and cannot be said, thereby costing him his individuality.[49] Such "coded" or "imitative" speech has an efficiency to it, but it also becomes a limiting device as speakers and listeners come together in the presence of their ancestors and of the rule-governed performances they have shared in the past. As a result, power circulating during these ritualistic moments is often recursive.

• *Disrupting political hegemony.* Ronald Greene tells us that a rhetoric of consensus often results in "the exclusion and/or normalization of those who do not consent," but he also reminds us that the sword cuts both ways.[50] While establishment leaders have more opportunities for public engagement and message recirculation, subaltern voices also have their influences. Thus, the rhetorical canon (especially in democratic nations) contains both privileged and disruptive voices. David Coplan provides an interesting example in his examination of migrants' rhetoric in Lesotho, a nation economically dependent on neighboring South Africa. Migrants, who often spend 35 percent of their time laboring in South Africa, use song, poetry, and quasi-public performances to protest "exploitative and disintegrative social conditions" and to create for themselves "a sense of personal autonomy from within which they may truly act." The "sefela poet" becomes, says Coplan, both a "cultural hero" and a "marginal man." This marbled identity makes him problematic for those in charge.[51]

Rhetoric-and-place helps us geolocate. We are tribal in that way, instinctively returning to the places of our youth, to our schooltime haunts, to adventures we have had and ceremonies we have witnessed—graduations, weddings, funerals. In the best of all worlds, these moments of demarcation would be attended by eloquence, making the life course smoother, more understandable, more memorable. Foreign travel does something similar, showing us how others live their lives but also calling forth understanding of the spaces we already inhabit. Rhetoric operates similarly; it is a reconnoitering device—it tells us where we live, what seems comfortable, and what seems a place too far.

ELOQUENCE HERE

In many ways, this book attempts the impossible—measuring eloquence in a way that respects the phenomenological experiences of most Americans. As we have seen in the foregoing, the very concept of eloquence has changed from age to age and from culture to culture, which prompts the question: What does eloquence look like in the United States at the dawn of the twenty-first century?

Do "natural simplicity" and "moral refinement" still mean what they formerly meant? Do media technologies still determine how public discourse operates? Is eloquence merely a quest for "personal influence" and a way of "reinforcing existing hierarchies," or is it something larger, grander? Has everything changed over time? Has nothing changed?

Table 2.1 does not really answer those questions. Worse, it poses more questions. The table is a random tour of public personalities who have been deemed eloquent by one or more news outlets. The table shows at least two things: (1) that the term *eloquence* is used liberally and (2) that it features human qualities that are otherwise hard to describe. Ostensibly, to be eloquent in the United States is to be brave, precocious, candid, angry, or to have some other socially redeeming feature. In that sense, eloquence seems little more than an award we bestow on others for some set of reasons.

Table 2.2 flips the script by looking at those found lacking in eloquence. When that happens, being diligent, sincere, or inspiring works well enough if you're a politician, and being humble or funny works just as well. Whether present or absent, then, eloquence is viewed more as a characterological quality than as something linguistic, which makes it even harder to measure. Perhaps, then, the ghost should be given up entirely. Perhaps only the fantasy writer Sam Sykes has the answer: "Half-drunken poetry is the most honest kind of poetry; too slurred to be eloquent, not slurred enough to be witless."[52]

Given eloquence's appeal but also its opacity, what is one to do? Chapter 3 presents my answer to that question. It describes a tripartite way of measuring eloquence in a reasonably practical way. The eloquence I describe will necessarily be time bound and place bound, reflecting the experience of a scholar born in the middle of the twentieth century in the United States of America. I will describe the importance of *cultural resonance*, which in the United States means a blending of pragmatic and transcendent themes. The "sentimental style" of the 1800s, a style that sought "total control of consciousness" by using what Richard Weaver has called "spacious"

TABLE 2.1 ATTRIBUTIONS OF *ELOQUENCE* PROVIDED IN NEWS REPORTS

SPEAKER	TOPIC/ OCCASION	BOUNTY PROVIDED	STATEMENT	SOURCE
Meghan Markle (UK royalty)	Growing up (middle-school graduation)	Precocity	"Two years ago, we came here as young girls—a bit frightened and overwhelmed and filled with wonder and anticipation about our new school and what our future would bring."	*The Sun*, September 21, 2018
Gloria Carter (Jay-Z's mom)	Coming out (GLAAD Awards)	Bravery	"Here I am. I'm loving, I'm respectful, I'm productive, and I'm a human being who has a right to love who I love."	*Billboard.com*, May 6, 2018
Panti Bliss (drag queen)	Social prejudice (talk show)	Introspection	"I do sometimes hate myself . . . and sometimes I hate you for doing that to me."	*Postmedia Breaking News*, February 11, 2014
Killer Mike (American rapper)	Urban riots (press conference)	Candor	"That's why you burn down your own community, not because you want to burn down your own community, but because you feel like nobody gives a shit."	*The Guardian*, June 1, 2020

SPEAKER	TOPIC/ OCCASION	BOUNTY PROVIDED	STATEMENT	SOURCE
Megan Rapinoe (soccer player)	Identity bias (FIFA Best Awards)	Resolve	"Going through all of the backlash and the craziness and the hatred, that only solidified my understanding of myself and the power in my voice."	*The Times*, December 30, 2019
Michelle Williams (American actress)	Gender inequality (Emmy Awards)	Autonomy	"[This is] what is possible when a woman is trusted to discern her own needs, feel safe enough to voice them, and respected enough that they'll be heard."	*University Wire*, September 25, 2019
Mitt Romney (U.S. senator)	Impeachment (U.S. Congress)	Fury	"Corrupting an election to keep oneself in office is perhaps the most abusive and destructive violation of one's oath of office that I can imagine."	*New Yorker*, February 17, 2020

TABLE 2.2 ALTERNATIVES TO *ELOQUENCE* PROVIDED IN NEWS REPORTS

POLITICAL CANDIDATE	RECOMPENSE PROVIDED	PRESS COMMENTARY	SOURCE
Bob Dole	Humor	"Bob Dole is a man of few words, most of them *not eloquent*, but he is in possession of one of the finest, quickest wits in Washington."	CNN News, October 4, 1996
John McCain	Inspiration	"I think McCain's life speaks for itself, and the eloquence at the end of the speech was *not eloquent* in a way. It was just the facts of what had happened, narrated by McCain in a pretty straightforward way."	FOX News, September 4, 2008
Mitt Romney	Sincerity	"People understand that he may be a lot of things, but he is not mean spirited. He is not nasty. He does not come across that way. He comes across as an occasional bumbler. He is *not eloquent*. He is quite the opposite. And I think people will accept that."	*Bloomberg News*, February 2, 2012
Donald Trump	Efficiency	"Yes, he's *not eloquent* in the way he says certain things but they think that it doesn't matter. That he's going to get into the White House and he's going to be able to change the course of this country and put it back on track according to them."	MSNBC, September 14, 2015

POLITICAL CANDIDATE	RECOMPENSE PROVIDED	PRESS COMMENTARY	SOURCE
George W. Bush	Diligence	"The left has always said that Bush was stupid. You don't go to Yale and become a fighter pilot and be stupid. He was *not eloquent*, I'll give you that. But Bush was a doer and not a talker. He didn't jet all over the world spending millions partying with communists and celebrities."	*Minority Report,* December 15, 2015
Lindsey Graham	Integrity	"Graham's outburst was *not eloquent*, but he expressed what I regarded at the time . . . as the searingly obvious truth that the Democrats on the committee were happy to destroy a decent and accomplished man in order to prevent a 5–4 conservative majority on the Court."	*Weekly Standard,* October 15, 2018
Mike DeWine	Humility	"Mr. DeWine is *not eloquent* like Churchill or Lincoln or FDR. He does not marshal language or wit for battle. And no one would call him charismatic. He is homespun and humble, and as likely to push his chief public health adviser, Dr. Amy Acton, into the spotlight as to claim it for himself."	*Pittsburgh Post-Gazette,* April 26, 2020

or ruminative language, continues to be used in contemporary times, but it is almost always balanced by a more sober and probative discourse.[53]

This combination of facts and values, science and aesthetics, data and doctrine, accountancy and axiology, proofs and mystery, expertise and prayerfulness is not uniquely American, but it is fully American. It is a way of saying to an audience: "I understand the trek you're on as well as its promises and problems, but I also understand your dreams of a more satisfying life." This blending of the pragmatic and the transcendent lets a speaker say what listeners themselves cannot say but which they still feel. "Eloquence is against dullness, dryness, routine, habit, 'the malady of the quotidian,'" says Denis Donoghue, but it is also against bloated, overly romantic language that departs from the facts at hand.[54]

According to Kenneth Cmiel, Henry Ward Beecher was quintessentially American in this sense. He sought not to "prove things too much" by adding "passions verging on the evangelical" to his remarks.[55] Beecher "conjured up a democratic version of the sublime," says Cmiel, "by merging the lofty with the rustic" to enlist an audience's sympathy.[56] This "middling style" took hold in the nineteenth century in "political oratory, popular preaching, and daily conversation," says Cmiel, but it was really the popular press that turned it into a daily occurrence.[57] Today, of course, the pragmatic and the transcendent are blended more subtly, but they still work together to give American rhetoric a distinctive sound.

Another part of that sound is *personal investment*, a willingness to open oneself up to one's listeners. As mentioned earlier, this tendency to self-disclose was enhanced by television's demands for intimacy, and it is now a make-or-break proposition for politicians. Richard Nixon paved the way with his famed apologia in 1952 (now known as the Checkers Speech). Charged with misappropriating funds, Nixon talked his way back onto the Republican ticket by presenting a fervid, but banal, rendition of his family's finances. Nixon's disclosures "became the antidote" to his political crisis, says Edwin Black, "the sole and urgently prescribed corrective to the political toxicity of secrecy."[58] Throughout his career, says Black, Nixon situated himself "on the very boundary between narrative and drama," reaching inside while reaching outside.[59]

Because of people like Nixon, revealing one's ontological self has become a constant command. "Why is the bill important to you, Senator?" "What makes you a fan of the space program?" "Did you play with rocket ships as a child?" "Did you enter the science fair in the ninth grade?" "Are you friendly with certain astronauts?" "Will your state profit from the NASA budget?" As I have argued elsewhere, *motive* has become central to politics in the United States, largely because of its rhetorical attractiveness.[60] For one thing, motives cannot be seen and, hence, admit to a variety of imaginings, embellishments, and contradictions. Too, if charged with having false motives, one can never fully establish one's innocence, so politicians get ahead of the game protectively by opening themselves up to prying eyes. That is awkward for them, never mind for their loved ones, but personal disclosure has nevertheless become a political commandment. Richard Nixon can be thanked for that.

The third dimension of eloquence is *poetic imagination*, the ability to go beyond the facts on the ground by envisioning what the world would look like if reconceived. I measure that quality by cataloguing the various "metaphorical families" a speaker employs. Imagery, I argue, invites us to create "assemblages" of ideas as, say, when love is described as an expedition or when death is described as one's last dance. Metaphors are designed to "upset" our usual ways of configuring the world and to make life more mysterious ("How long will love's expedition last?" "Can I choose when to dance my death?"). Metaphors open up closed worlds, giving us new things to think about (e.g., Proust's conception of friends as "gardeners who make our souls blossom") and by combining the familiar with the strange (e.g., Picasso's "art washes away the dust of everyday life"). Metaphors also delight in the unexpected (e.g., Orwell's "advertising is the rattling of a stick inside a swill bucket") and the outrageous (e.g., Groucho's Marx's "a hospital bed is a parked taxi with the meter running"). Metaphors come and go in popularity, telling us how old we are ("that outfit is fire" for millennials, "that album is groovy" for boomers).[61]

Compared to Proust and Groucho, politicians are not overly athletic with their metaphors, but they use them nonetheless. When effective, political metaphors are "adhesive," attaching us to new ideas (e.g., JFK's "America is tossing its cap over the wall of space") or old prejudices (e.g., Donald Trump's "let's drain the swamp in Washington"). Metaphors arrest the decomposition of memory, giving us a handy peg on which to hang ideas (e.g., "America as a melting pot") and events (e.g., "big stick diplomacy"). Metaphors that contribute to eloquence, says Edwin Black, "balance withholding and disbursing to the point that they beget mystery. Enough is disclosed to license the authenticity of the rhetor, but that same disclosure signals its own fractionality, leaving the audience aware that what it has come to know is not all there is to be known."[62]

The premise of this book is that eloquence occurs when the pragmatic and the transcendent are happily combined, when speakers disclose enough to make themselves seem trustworthy, and when imagery is used to bring ideas to life, to make us wonder anew. These three features draw on the wisdom of the past but also have distinctly Western, distinctly modernist overtones and undertones. There is nothing formulaic about them, however. Eloquence is too demanding a chef to be guided by mere recipe. But this three-part approach helps me sort out a text, identifying what works and what doesn't, so it is offered here as a guide to eloquence in action.

CONCLUSION

One might think that eloquence is an unalloyed trait, but sometimes it is quite alloyed. A Barack Obama speech, for example, has been described as "eloquent but flawed."[63] The proposal for an unmanned aircraft system was found to be "eloquent but wrong-headed."[64] A book by the political activist Barbara Ehrenreich was thought to be "eloquent but crabby,"[65] while online pension scammers have been described as "eloquent but malevolent."[66] If we are to believe the news, British pop rock is occasionally "eloquent but inarticulate,"[67] a memoir by Sven Birkerts "eloquent but pointless,"[68] and a Bruce Cockburn album "eloquent but voiceless."[69] And here is the cruelest cut of all: a church sermon by the Rev. Dr. Calvin O. Butts that is "eloquent but protracted."[70] Eloquence, it seems, is rarely found alone.

One has to be impressed by the confidence with which the foregoing statements have been made. The commentators seem to know eloquence when they hear it and still have time left to find something else. How do they make such discriminations? What helps them distinguish 100 percent eloquence from the 75 percent version? Do they draw upon all of their rhetorical history, or only some of it, when making these discriminations? Do their political biases, their cultural predispositions, ever get in the way? Are they as good at spotting eloquence on Friday afternoon as they are on Monday morning?

Because these kinds of questions vex me, I shall proceed cautiously. I will examine a large body of political discourse and ask of each document: Is this statement culturally resonant? Does it show signs of personal investment? Has the speaker applied his or her imagination to the topic at hand? This approach will not capture everything that needs to be known because eloquence is always a puzzle. Thus, as with any puzzle, I will begin by identifying the edges and then work my way inward. Computers can help in that regard by isolating rhetorical patterns within a text. While it is rather impertinent to ask a machine to find the edges of eloquence, there is much to be gained by asking a small number of questions clearly and consistently for a very long time and by keeping a careful log when so doing. The following chapter reports how I have done so.

3

ELOQUENCE: HOW?

Frank Lloyd Wright was surely the greatest architect born on American soil. During his career, Wright designed more than a thousand original structures on paper, over half of which were actually built. Among the most iconic are Fallingwater in Mill Run, Pennsylvania; the Guggenheim Museum in New York City; Taliesin West in Scottsdale, Arizona; the Robie House in Chicago; and the Hollyhock House in Los Angeles. Looking at one of Wright's structures provides a feast for the eyes: magnificent shafts of interior light, rooms separated by grand supplies of openness, and oddly cantilevered wings mysteriously joined to the heart of the building.

Living in one of Wright's houses was another matter entirely. "It takes a brave soul to buy one of Wright's houses," says the Chicago-based architect John Eifler.[1] Because form superseded function for Wright, his creations often developed structural problems. Fallingwater, for example, almost fell into the river, and his clever roof designs let water seep into his structures' interiors. Keeping his homes warm during the winter was also difficult because of their airiness. Tiny kitchens, built-in furniture that could not be relocated, insufficient closet space, nonexistent basements, carports instead of garages—all these features made renovating one of Wright's homes more expensive than the original sale price. Yet Frank Lloyd Wright's homes were elegant.

This book examines the rhetorical counterpart to Wright's buildings: American oratory at its best, which is also a matter of form and function. Eloquence is an aesthetic thing, a blending of ideas and memories and beliefs and emotions. But eloquence is also the result of language that can be measured, just as Frank Lloyd Wright's use of concrete can be measured (he didn't use enough) and just as his roofs can be measured (they were sometimes too large). To measure eloquence is not to diminish it but to understand it more fully.

Figure 3.1 shows what happens when a computer program has its way with Martin Luther King Jr.'s "I Have a Dream" speech, his Fallingwater. The figure compares King's remarks to campaign speeches, religious sermons, and protest speeches—logical complements to his magnificent oration. When texts like these are positioned side by side, they call our attention to things we half-know and to things we thought we knew but did not. Dr. King was, for example, a preacher by trade, but his famous speech at the Lincoln Memorial was more realistic (practical, tangible) than sermonic. King's was not a campaign speech, but it was still a political document—although few politicians can afford to be as certain, as canonical, as King was. King clearly protested things on August 28, 1963, but because he was a man of the cloth, he was more optimistic than most protesters.

But perhaps the two most interesting things about King's speech involved his avoidance of commonality (you-and-me language) and activity (words describing motion). While we think of King's speech as inspiring, his inspiration was not purchased at the cost of honesty. His low commonality scores call attention to the clear societal tensions he described—"whirlwinds of revolt," "horrors of police brutality," "trials and tribulations," "the heat of injustice." But King's is also a passive, contemplative speech in which he ruminates

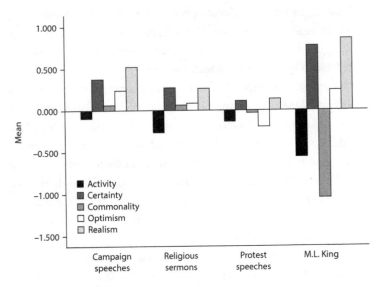

FIGURE 3.1 Martin Luther King Jr.'s "I Have a Dream" speech versus other genres

on ineffable things—"the content of their character," "the sunlit path of racial justice," "the true meaning of its creed," "your quest for freedom."[2]

Have we done violence to Dr. King by turning his words into numbers? I argue that we have not. A quantitative analysis like this makes his speech "productively odd," shedding new light on its rhetorical brilliance. King's speech is its own separate thing; its complications attest to its majesty. When King's crowd left him that day, they could not say exactly what had happened, but they knew that their lives had been newly complicated. King pulled no punches, yet he uplifted them. As Celeste Condit says, "Eloquence well performed helps people understand their experiences in new ways . . . and to coordinate their behavior around these understandings."[3]

"The presidency," said Franklin Roosevelt, "is more than an engineering job, efficient or inefficient. It is preeminently a place of moral leadership."[4] Yes, but it is also an engineering job, so it behooves us to understand the tools of leadership. Eloquence may be "a less verifiable category than wealth," as Denis Donoghue says, but that does not mean it is totally unverifiable.[5] By comparing texts to one another and by asking specific questions of them, we can learn interesting things we had not imagined. Eloquence like King's, says the rhetorical scholar Nathan Crick, "makes one feel part of the movements of history—of being part of a community that is only now unfolding itself into the world."[6] This chapter describes how such unfoldings can be measured.

ELOQUENCE AT A DISTANCE

Simon Sebag Montefiore makes eloquence a simple matter. "You want to know the rules of great oratory?" he asks. Montefiore answers clearly, definitively: "It must be short without glibness; substantial without ennui; powerful without haughtiness; dramatic without contrivance; confident without bombast; intimate without condescension; emotional without melodrama; courageous without bravado; beautiful without artifice; passionate without posturing; poignant without plangency; honest without vanity; world-historical without grandiloquence."[7] It is hard to disagree with Montefiore, but it is also hard to know exactly what he is saying. Assessing such qualities as "ennui," "contrivance," "vanity," or "bravado" might be possible on our best days but not on every day. Sometimes, rhetoric just draws us in, leaving us with no way of explaining what has just happened.

For reasons such as these, it is helpful to get some distance on rhetoric. My way of doing so is by using DICTION, a computer program that breaks a text into its component parts and then compares them to a set of preprocessed norms to see what makes the text distinctive. When doing so, DICTION reports how often a passage dips into fifty or more dictionaries (word lists). To date, the program has been deployed in some seven hundred scholarly studies across the humanities and social sciences—in psychology, sociology, rhetoric and composition, political science, communication, management, finance, etc.[8]

But why would anyone who loves language want to tear it apart? Why use such tools after hearing the novelist John Barth declare that the computer "could not act on a hunch or brilliant impulse; it had no intuitions or exaltations; it could request but not yearn; indicate, but not insinuate or exhort; command but not care. It had no sense of style or grasp of the ineffable; its correlations were exact, but its metaphors wretched; it could play chess, but not poker."[9] Stephen March piles on: "Literature cannot meaningfully be treated as data. The problem is essential rather than superficial. Literature is not data. Literature is the opposite of data."[10] Using a computer to study discourse, says Timothy Brennan, is like watching "a weightlifter doing a pirouette" and erroneously "treating information as knowledge."[11]

Scholars in the digital humanities disagree. Like it or not, they say, literature only happens when words work themselves out in certain ways, just as Frank Lloyd Wright's buildings only happened if wooden joists were available for construction. Refusing to assess verbal proportions is like decrying autopsies because they defile the human body or refusing to operate on a nun's gall bladder because it violates her purity. Like it or not, autopsies and surgeries teach us what is true and what is not true. So let it be with lexical analysis. Watching how words mix and mingle (sometimes dismissed as a "bag of words approach") is an abomination only if scholars are unimaginative when doing their reconnaissance.

Consider, for example, the following words at play:

- "Don't judge each day by the harvest you reap but by the seeds that you plant." (Robert Louis Stevenson)
- "Do not go where the path may lead, go instead where there is no path and leave a trail." (Ralph Waldo Emerson)
- "When you reach the end of your rope, tie a knot in it and hang on." (Franklin D. Roosevelt)
- "Spread love everywhere you go. Let no one ever come to you without leaving happier." (Mother Teresa)
- "The greatest glory in living lies not in never falling, but in rising every time we fall." (Nelson Mandela)

These statements give us a kind of internal peace by exalting the unhurried life. But there is also a darkness here—paths that mislead us, ropes that are too short, happiness not guaranteed. There is also a certain contemplativeness, but it is juxtaposed to human action. Much doing is being done—judging, reaping, planting, leaving, hanging on, spreading, rising, falling—actions with a decidedly modernist thrust. We find no thinking or accepting, no calming or considering. Thus, if the statements leave us at peace, they do so only because we have triumphed over the forces of "active darkness." To miss the imbalance between dark and light is to miss the authors' rhetorical dexterity.

It is for reasons such as these that quantitative studies of textual data have increased during the past thirty years. The project goes by different names—automated lexical analysis, corpus linguistics, computational social science, sentiment analysis—but all such studies focus on pattern recognition, which, says Laurens Bod, has always been "part and parcel of humanistic practice."[12] The online availability of texts has advanced such work, but "distant reading" (as Stanford's Franco Moretti calls it) has its theoretical justification as well—the need to radically interrogate conventional wisdom. For example, Moretti and his colleagues find that book titles began sporting more metaphors at the end of the eighteenth century (e.g., *The Belly of Paris, Heart of Darkness*) in an attempt to puzzle readers and challenge them. Proper names also increased in the titles (*Emily, Henry, Georgina*) to broaden the marketplace for popular reading. Titles became shorter and adjectives became more common, with authors becoming bolder, as the trappings of the eighteenth century were being discarded. Our cultural yearnings and social uncertainties are embedded in book titles, says Moretti, private matters for all to see.[13]

Digital scholarship continues to make inroads into such areas as genre study,[14] technical and managerial reports,[15] political history,[16] classroom interactions,[17] and news coverage.[18] Scholars working with textual data have found that some financial managers base their investment decisions on blog content,[19] that fame is short-lived today (judged by Wikipedia entries),[20] that male and female authors are no longer as different as they once were,[21] that churchgoers live longer lives than secularists (judging by published obituaries),[22] and that social media content containing a high emotional charge is shared more often than more sober postings.[23]

These are miscellaneous findings, but digital study need not be a miscellaneous practice. While computers can map "the overall data landscape of a text," says Lev Manovich, they can also examine more nuanced matters.[24] Tracking key phrases over time, says Eric Slauter, lets scholars "write more inclusive histories of political thought," identifying, for example, the transition from hierarchical to egalitarian modes of thought in the West.[25] Sometimes, say Dana Boyd and Kate Crawford, Big Data scholars can become lost in "apophenia," identifying patterns where none exist, but that happens with students of little data too.[26]

Those who oppose automated language analysis presume that all readers are "close readers," but that assumption is surely wrong. We "graze" over thousands of words each day, paying them little heed and habitually ignoring the context in which the words are uttered. We take in great gulps of texts, both oral and written, remembering very little of what we read or hear. We humans are destructive creatures in these ways, abandoning much of what we consume, which brings us back to eloquence. Eloquence "arrests" these destructive tendencies, making us linger over new thoughts or luxuriating in old thoughts newly conceived. Eloquence shocks us into fresh realizations.

Computer-based studies require us to precisely define what we are looking for, to do so in detail, and to invite others to corroborate our findings. Traditional humanists are often bored by this issue of corroboration, says Franco Moretti, which is unfortunate because a knotty concept like eloquence needs all hands on deck to be understood.[27] Ultimately, though, the great advantage of digital studies lies not in their scientific validity but in their ability to introduce new questions. Perhaps it is scandalous to reduce eloquence to word counts, but if so, is it a scandal that teaches us something important?

If pattern seeking is a natural human endeavor, would not *systematic* pattern seeking make things even better?

"Over the years," says the literary scholar Stephen Ramsay, "my work has become a quest for meaningful astonishment."[28] That seems a worthy goal for the study of eloquence. After all, say David Kaufer and Robert Hariman, a message is "a large, multivariate space of micro-rhetorical options"; given that complexity, wouldn't a computer come in handy for identifying small matters leading to larger ones?[29] Because "the tone of a text, may be as influential as its substantive content," say Lori Young and Stuart Soroka, and because tone is the byproduct of interlocking rhetorical decisions, computers can force us to slow down when making our way through a text (or through a body of texts).[30] By arraying textual elements side by side and end to end, computers ask the best question of all: "How do I know what I know?" Sometimes the cost of asking that question is an increased supply of humility.

ELOQUENCE BY THE NUMBERS

My approach to studying eloquence has been guided by six key assumptions: (1) speakers use words to do things; (2) they use them in varying proportions; (3) speakers are rarely aware of having done so; (4) audiences often don't notice the words being used but (5) still respond to them; and (6) eloquence occurs when these decisions are made wisely. Principles like these make us read texts differently. Denied the comforts of context, one is invited to study the "lexical layers" of a text, noting how words of a certain type (for example, Active words) lay atop words of a different sort (say, Optimistic words), thereby creating a distinctive "tone" (e.g., a coach's half-time speech or a political rally in Omaha). Such Active-Optimistic speeches "drown for the moment all reflection whatsoever," causing audiences to react with their viscera.[31]

By tracking word proportions, the computer brings granularity to the study of spoken discourse.[32] Because programs like DICTION attack a text from so many different angles, each separate reading becomes a mutually implicative reading, telling the user when a text conforms to or deviates from a given set of norms. DICTION uses some ten thousand search words to analyze a text, none of which is duplicated in its various dictionaries, thereby providing an unusually rich understanding of the passage in question.

Programs like DICTION violate context, the text as created. But this is not to say that the text as created is the text as received. "Context" vanishes the moment it comes into being. Audiences are "gist processors," say the psychologists Charles Brainerd and Valerie Reyna, taking what they need from a text and leaving the rest behind.[33] They become the victims of "spreading activation," argue Robert Boynton and Milton Lodge, overwhelmed by the sudden associations a text triggers in their minds.[34] Thus, while DICTION cannot distinguish between a sentence like "the dog bit the man" and "the man bit the dog," it notices the *topical similarities* between the sentences while ignoring the business of who did what to whom.

When computers were first introduced to the humanities, the possibilities seemed endless: concordances of great literary works; authorship studies to discover how many Shakespeares were housed in Shakespeare; stylistic maps tracking the arc of Western thought; lexicographies following the migration of words from culture to culture. All such studies have been done, many to good effect. But overreactions have also occurred. Too often, says Susan Wittig, computer users have turned words into numbers and then forsaken the text completely.[35] Some social scientists, in their rush to get on with the mathematical modeling, fail to provide examples of what they have found, as if heuristic redemption of their findings was unimportant. "Only the presence of critical judgment," says Rosanne Potter, "saves the research from veering off into number juggling."[36] "If I read a paragraph and come to a conclusion about that paragraph's meaning," says Michael Gavin, "no statistical analysis is going to change my mind." Nevertheless, he adds, "my belief is this: Counting words is interesting."[37]

Wittig, Potter, and Gavin reflect my own beliefs—that a text becomes especially meaningful in light of other texts. But too many studies, says Notre Dame's Nan Da, produce this conundrum: What is robust is obvious, and what is not obvious is not robust.[38] Usually that happens when researchers force computers to do all the work. The better alternative is to "retreat to the text" after the numbers have been gathered to see what they look like in real life. Ultimately, it is the questions, always the questions, that justify studies in this area: Have detective stories changed over time, and if so, what do they say about us? Did Augustine's rhetoric change after his theological conversion? Is gender "constructed" differently by men and women today?[39] If computers can reliably "cue" us to the internal workings of a text, what could possibly go wrong?

This book calls into question three common assumptions: first, that eloquence is so obvious that it need not be defined precisely; second, that eloquence is so idiosyncratic that no generalizations are possible; and finally, that eloquence is so mystical that everyone is correct when discussing it. I find these assumptions to be specious, so I have come to define eloquence in a tripartite way.

CULTURAL RESONANCE

The rhetorical scholar Walter Fisher has argued that there are two frequently competing myths embedded in the American dream: a materialistic myth rooted in the Puritan work ethic—taking initiative, solving problems, achieving success—and a moralistic myth featuring human dignity, social responsibility, and obedience to God.[40] Carroll Arnold agrees, arguing that we have a Bill of Rights because the highly transcendent U.S. Constitution needed a pragmatic booster to ensure clear, specific, and binding rules for the citizenry.[41] Woodrow Wilson could not sell the League of Nations, says Arnold, because he was overly theoretical, while Jesse Jackson, a preacher by trade, effectively mixed idealism with proceduralism to distinguish himself from the more doctrinaire elements in the clergy. This tension between transcendence and pragmatism, says

Arnold, can be found in American public discourse throughout history; it is the successful balancing of these tendencies, he claims, that make for rhetorical success.

Cultural resonance occurs when a speaker shows an understanding of people's everyday experiences while also endorsing their root values. Talk that is too airy or too expedient usually fails in the United States, at least with most audiences on most days. "A politics that brackets morality and religion too completely," says Michael Sandel, "soon generates its own disenchantment."[42] Not surprisingly in such a diverse nation, transcendent overindulgences sometimes occur, resulting in the popularity of Jonathan Edwards, John Wesley, Billy James Hargis, Jimmy Swaggart, Joel Osteen, and countless others—also the Ku Klux Klan, the John Birch Society, the New Left, the Tea Party, radical environmentalism, Antifa. Of ideology the United States has had more than its share.

But it is also true, says George Core, that a writer can produce an "eloquence of fact" by laying out "a detailed scene, fact after glorious fact, with no real ideological commentary."[43] For Thoreau, says Lee Campbell, "eloquent prose hugs the ground of the lived-through, sensuous world."[44] Thoreau felt that "a sentence should read as if its author had held a plough instead of a pen, could have drawn a furrow deep and straight to the end."[45] But when either ideological or technical discourse become imperious, says Kenneth Cmiel, a natural distrust develops.[46] On most days in most situations, the American people want equal shares of transcendence and pragmatism.

My way of measuring cultural resonance is straightforward. Using word lists built into DICTION, I created two indicators by standardizing scores for individual components and then adding a score of ten (to eliminate negative numbers). The formulas are as follows:

- Transcendence = Inspiration + Praise + Satisfaction + Religious Terms + Patriotic Terms + Embellishment (heavy use of adjectives)
- Pragmatism = Concreteness + Numerical Terms + Temporal References + Spatial References + Past References + People References + Insistence Scores (a measure of verbal repetition)

My studies show a strong negative correlation (-.376) between Transcendence and Pragmatism for some ten thousand passages. In other words, when most speakers come to the fork in the road, they pick either Pragmatism (corporate employees, scientists, economists, financial reporters) or Transcendence (preachers, socialists, archconservatives, identitarians). Individual speakers, of course, will respond individually—some low on both scores, some high on both, with the rest vacillating in between. Political parties, too, make different choices from time to time and from genre to genre, as do social activists. Establishment figures, though, normally hearken to both strains of the American political vernacular. This book is animated by that presumption.

PERSONAL INVESTMENT

Personal investment is a straightforward measure: a simple count of how often first-person pronouns are used (as coded by DICTION). In a database consisting of some sixty thousand texts, an average of 12.5 self-references is used in a 500-word passage, although 25 percent of the speakers or authors never refer to themselves. Politicians do so regularly (sixteen times in the average passage), but reporters seldom do (fewer than three times in print news, five times in a press conference, seven in broadcast coverage). Preachers and entertainers refer to themselves with some frequency, but corporate spokespersons and scholars rarely do.

Referring to oneself is a mixed blessing. Doing so adds a subjective dimension to a text, thereby drawing in listeners (especially when combined with a personal narrative). We humans are intrigued by one another; we also want to know everyone else's business. Sometimes, though, self-references bring up questions of trust ("Why is she revealing so much?") and egomania ("Why should I care about your trip to Canada?"). Authenticity can be signaled by self-references ("He's done the same things I have done," "She really cares about this topic"), while too few self-references can make a speaker seem diffident. Sometimes, though, an impersonal tone can be helpful. Legal documents and scientific reports, for example, gain credibility by removing all human touches, thereby producing a tone of protective generality.

Sandra Gustafson reports how revolutionary self-references occasionally become. Anne Hutchison, a Puritan reformer, spiritual leader, social activist, and key figure in the Antinomian movement in seventeenth-century America, spoke her mind—often quite personally—when confronting the theological establishment of her day, "refusing to submit to the discipline of scriptural text and the associated linguistic and interpretive skills that bore with them the weight of social and gender hierarchies."[47] Although it takes a leap to get from Anne Hutchison to Donald Trump, he, too, revolutionized things with his incessant focus on himself, his family, his biases, his experiences, and his supreme knowledge of all things—from beauty pageants and NFL football to nuclear arms treaties and, of course, COVID. Trump used more self-references during his press conferences than any of his predecessors, and his stump speeches only ended when he finally got tired of talking about himself. Trump proved that self-references are a mixed blessing indeed.[48]

POETIC IMAGINATION

Neera Tanden, former head of the Center for American Progress, a longtime campaign adviser for Michael Dukakis and Bill and Hillary Clinton, and, more recently, an adviser to President Joe Biden, wanted to be Biden's director of the Office of Management and Budget. Metaphors got in her way. During a short but rough patch of time, Tanden referred to the majority leader of the U.S. Senate as "Moscow Mitch"; said that a vampire had more heart than Senator Ted Cruz; observed that another senator, Lisa Murkowski, was "high on her own supply"; and declared that a fourth member of the Senate, Susan Collins, was "criminally ignorant" and that her political rival was one of Tanden's "long-lost relatives." While metaphors can be charming, a break from everyday tedium, Neera Tanden's images were often seen as mean-spirited and overwrought.

Perhaps the most telling thing about Tanden's rhetoric was the *range* of her metaphors. In the examples above, Tanden combined subversive, demonic, pharmacological, felonious, and familial metaphors in one mad rampage. This lack of synchrony showed her to be too greedy for the spotlight and spending too much time sculpting her craft. If rhetoric were a crime, Neera Tanden would have been tried for premeditated murder rather than manslaughter.

Paying attention to metaphorical families, then, can tell us a good deal. Accurately coding metaphors is hard, though. Using multiple coders and formal content-analytic procedures can help, but even then, slippage can occur because metaphors are, well, slippery. Demanding though metaphors are, we dare not abandon them. As scholars have shown, it makes a real difference whether we think of politics as an occupation or a contest,[49] ethnicity as a heritage or an infestation,[50] war as an infirmity or a chess match,[51] Europe as a polyglot or a unity,[52] the world as a lifeboat or a spaceship.[53]

Metaphors are more than just colorful; they also structure thought. One who thinks of politics as a game, for example, is likely to engage in gamelike behavior: scoring points on the opposition rather than reasoning coolly. Metaphors are "disciplinary" in these ways, superintending what thoughts can be thought. Too, metaphors can lead us by the nose, driving our emotions one way, our thoughts another way (e.g., "Obama is on a charm offensive"). Metaphors can provide cognitive shortcuts, making it easier to access certain ideas (e.g., Ben Franklin's "A good conscience is a continual Christmas"). Metaphors can also habituate us to a distinct cultural bias (e.g., "Americans have always been pioneers").[54]

The following text box lays out the metaphorical families examined here. Coding metaphors, it must be made clear, is not a project for the faint of heart. After many years of working in this area, I have concluded that achieving high reliability among multiple coders when tagging metaphors is largely impossible unless one wants a mechanical result—an unacceptable choice when studying eloquence. The main problem, of course, is that metaphors are multidimensional. Take, for example, a metaphor like this: "Biden is the grandfather from hell—cranky, corny, spacy, and afraid of his smartphone." How shall we code this? Is the metaphor Communal ("grandfather"), Conflictual ("cranky"), Utilitarian ("phone"), Empowered ("*smart*phone"), Moral ("hell"), Diminished ("afraid," "spacy"), or Natural ("spacy" again, "corny" too)? Clearly, the metaphor is all of these things, perhaps more as well.

1. Diminished
   Quantity: scanty, poor, cheap, worthless
   Quality: old, weak, exiled, burdened
   Feelings: shame, pain, sadness, anonymity
   Result: fear, isolation, defeat darkness

2. Empowered
   Goal: control, size, influence, dominance
   Capacity: muscular, vigorous, solved, authoritative
   Feelings: new, fresh, strong, permanent
   Result: courageous, elite, rewarded, defended

3. Utilitarian
   Entities: building, clothes, era, kitchen
   Qualities: reliable, organized, practical, timely
   Skills: weights, measures, analytics, calculate
   Tools: machine, clock, automobile, electronics

4. Liberating
   Activities: proclaim, release, create, invent, question
   Feelings: passion, revolution, excitement, surprise
   Tools: art, poetry, plans, propaganda, entertainment
   Result: dreams, magic, charm, vision, phantoms

5. Communal
   Loving: friendly, familial, patriotic, protective
   Generous: join, help, participate, neighborly
   Pedagogical: guide, teach, lead, empathize
   Cooperative: partners, citizenry, peace, harmony

6. Conflictual
   Physical: struggle, fight, react, ambush, attack
   Verbal: argue, confront, reject, debate
   Occasions: war, skirmish, feud, battle
   Tools: weapon, explosion, soldier, gun
7. Bodily
   Entities: man, woman, child, humanity
   Physical: heart, hand, back, viscera
   Sensory: hear, see, taste, feel, touch
   Nourishment: food, bread, meat, fruit
8. Natural
   Entities: fish, mammals, trees, land, city
   Heights: sky, heavens, mountains, sun
   Depths: farms, pathways, sea, valleys, road
   Events: trip, rain, heat, nighttime, journey
9. Industrious
   Pursue: seek, achieve, work, guide, exchange
   Transact: earn, deposit, invest, credit, profit
   Qualities: busy, determined, lazy, apathetic, urgent
   Outcome: wealth, progress, debt, costs, products
10. Moral
   Entities: God, history, spirit, law, policies
   Beliefs: truth, democracy, dignity, faith, mission
   Bounties: hope, justice, trust, patriotism, rights
   Liabilities: evil, crime, sin, disgrace, racism

The four thousand or so metaphors coded in this study were coded exclusively by me. Metaphors, I have come to believe, are delicate creatures, too delicate to be attacked by a gaggle of graduate students, even well-trained graduate students. Extended metaphors—like the one about Biden as grandfather—are particularly tricky, sending off multiple associations simultaneously.

Fortunately, while extended metaphors are common in literature, they are comparatively rare in political discourse because they call so much attention to themselves.

My operating assumption is that metaphors are comparative devices containing two independent axes ("live," "wire") which are then joined together to create something new ("A.O.C. is a livewire"). When coding, my approach was to identify a metaphor's first two axes and then assign each to one of the families listed in the text box. So, in the Biden example, *grandfather* and *hell* were the first concepts identified and thence labeled Communal/Moral. Such a stripped-down approach is reductionistic, to be sure, but three factors recommended it: (1) most of the images identified in my study contained only two metaphorical axes; (2) with such a large corpus of images (n = 3,795), a few miscodings could not possibly disturb the overall trends reported; and (3) the patterns identified in the early stages remained constant throughout the coding process. My estimate is that this bare-bones approach let me capture 80 percent of the metaphors used, with the remaining 20 percent consisting of repeated or redundant metaphors.

In short, because metaphors are so bewitching, it takes discipline to make them stand still. As we will see in chapter 6, the overall trends identified are really quite hearty, with some metaphorical families being used consistently more often than others. From a social scientific perspective, metaphors introduce "noise" into the coding process, but "noise," of course, is exactly what makes metaphors compelling. Things would be neater if metaphors did less work than they do, but, stubbornly, they decline that option.

ELOQUENCE ON OCCASION

Two preeminent rhetorical scholars, John Murphy and David Zarefsky, are troubled by the kind of work being done here. "Rhetorical practice," says Murphy, "is too messy for generalization. We warp rhetoric when it becomes an 'object' of scientific study." Worse, says Murphy, such attempts disengage "critics from political and moral responsibilities inherent in the activity."[55] For Zarefsky, rhetorical analysis is best when a critic pores through a text line by line, with full attention to its historical circumstance and resisting "the impulse to generalize or to make predictions."[56] Similarly, Stanley Fish decries those who would "dress up garden variety literary intuition in numbers" or who fail to feature "context, intention, literary history, the idea of literature itself" in their analyses.[57] Above all, said Carl Bridenbaugh back in 1963, historians must never "worship at the shrine of that Bitch-goddess, quantification."[58]

With all due respect to the aforementioned, my study analyzes some sixty thousand passages, with an exclusive focus on their lexical properties and with special attention to the cultural resonance, personal investment, and poetic imagination evidenced within them. My goal was to produce a "midrange" analysis that reports numerical trends but also features the texts as produced. Hopefully, standing back from the discourse will let me examine cultural forces while getting close will show why audiences responded as they did.

The empiricists Daniel O'Connell and Sabine Kowal have argued that "one looks in vain for a clear set of criteria to set apart empirically the best presidential speeches from the worst."[59] I address that challenge here by deploying a number of different datasets:

- Campaign Mapping Corpus: This is a large collection (over sixty thousand 500-word passages) constructed at the University of Texas at Austin that puts U.S. presidential campaigns in historical perspective. The project contains a searchable text base drawn from speeches, debates, ads, print coverage, broadcast transcripts, letters to the editor, polling interviews, and social media exchanges between 1948 and 2020. To date, the project has produced eight books and more than two hundred journal articles, scholarly papers, and graduate theses and dissertations.[60]
- Classic Oratory Corpus: This is a small collection (30 speeches, 154 passages) consisting of major speeches delivered during

the eighteenth and nineteenth centuries in the United States. The collection includes addresses by John Hancock, Patrick Henry, Sojourner Truth, Susan B. Anthony, Abraham Lincoln, William Jennings Bryan, and other famous statespersons.

• American Fiction Corpus: Rhetoric and literature are different matters, but eloquence applies to both, albeit in different ways. To examine those intersections, portions of one hundred major literary works (833 passages) were selected, including works by Jane Austen, Robert Browning, Lewis Carroll, Willa Cather, Ralph Waldo Emerson, Zane Grey, Aldous Huxley, D. H. Lawrence, and others. The data set contains serious works as well as popular fiction from the eighteenth through twentieth centuries.

• Lucas-Medhurst Corpus: This grouping contains what are alleged to be the hundred most prominent speeches of the twentieth century (655 passages) as judged by 137 scholars in a national survey. The speakers are a diverse lot, including sitting presidents (Theodore Roosevelt through Bill Clinton), losing candidates for that office (Eugene Debs through Teddy Kennedy), social activists (Carrie Chapman Catt and Margaret Sanger through Mary Fisher and Elizabeth Glaser), famous attorneys (Emma Goldman, Clarence Darrow, Joseph Welch, Anita Hill), writers and intellectuals (Elie Wiesel, Newton Minow, Ursula Le Guin), and other noteworthy personalities (Russell Conwell, Douglas MacArthur, Lou Gehrig).[61] Chapter 7 of this book provides added detail about this study.

Examining historical materials through contemporary eyes can produce a certain strangeness, causing some questions to edge out others. As one group of digital humanists has observed, literature is "a historical record of the evolution of culture"; if that is true, rhetoric becomes a way of managing culture—intellectually, politically, and socially—thereby revealing what eloquence looks like when fully formed.[62]

CONCLUSION

In some ways, eloquence is an answer to a question, to several questions. How can something new be said when the same old problems—war, injustice—stalk us constantly? How can long-standing ideals be refashioned when modern audiences bore so easily? Great challenges call for great responses, but where can one find greatness when politics seems so craven? Can words still touch the souls of others? Can they summon forth a people? Eloquence is an answer to these questions, but it is not an obvious answer. "The world is not clear," says Richard Lanham; only through rhetoric "is it *made* clear."[63] Yes, but how?

"Twist a radio dial or rustle a newspaper," says John Peters, and you will encounter bits of discourse that never quite connect."[64] We need eloquence to make such connections. "Memorable language does not necessarily mean elevated thought," says James Fallows.[65] We need eloquence to thrust us higher. Conversation rarely strays "beyond the conventions of politeness," says Thomas Farrell.[66] We need eloquence to make us bolder. In the following pages, I will ask if eloquence can still do these things.

4

CULTURAL RESONANCE

John Jay was a man of many parts—one of the nation's founders and, later, a diplomat, an abolitionist, the second governor of New York, and the first chief justice of the United States. He was not, however, a sociologist, or at least not a very good one. Jay wrote in the *Federalist* in 1787: "Providence has been pleased to give this one connected country, to one united people, a people descended from the same ancestors, speaking the same language, professing the same religion, attached to the same principles of government, very similar manners and customs, and who, by their joint counsels, arms and efforts, fighting side by side throughout a long and bloody war, have nobly established their general Liberty and Independence."[1]

It is hard to know where to begin here. Almost nothing John Jay said is true—not of the British colonies nor of the nation that followed them. Given the difficulties of transportation in the 1700s, for example, the colonies were largely disconnected from one another and would remain that way for years to come. While the colonists did manage to stave off the British militarily, thus establishing their independence, loyalties to King George III of England hardly evaporated overnight. In addition, the colonists' ancestry was a mottled one, consisting of Europeans, for the most part, but Europeans of Scotch and Irish descent as well as Swedes, Finns, French Huguenots, immigrants from the Rhine Valley, along with distrustful Presbyterians and Puritans in New England; Quakers, Catholics, and Lutherans in the middle colonies; and Baptists and (many) Anglicans in the south. Living as they were in these cultural enclaves, many colonists retained their native tongues, and those who did speak English still clung to their ethnic and class-based traditions.[2] It would take many years for the nation to become a nation, many more for people to feel organically connected to it (a project still underway during the era of MeToo and Black Lives Matter).

It is hard to know if John Jay fully believed what he said because, like all the founders, he had the heart of a politician. He knew that imagining a cohesive nation was a prerequisite to establishing one. Like his contemporary Benjamin Rush, Jay knew that schools needed to teach "the art of forgetting"—forgetting the enmities the colonists brought with them from the old country.[3] The resulting rhetoric, says Christopher Looby, became a mixture of Protestant millennialism, apocalyptic Machiavellianism, Calvinist Whiggism, classic republicanism, and civil religion.[4] This awkward blend did not produce consensus overnight, but it did give the nation the "energy" it needed to eventually replace "Puritan industriousness" with "capitalist striving."[5]

According to no less an authority than Daniel Webster, Patrick Henry epitomized this new, energetic discourse. Henry's "eloquence was peculiar," says Webster, "impressive and sublime beyond what can be imagined." Henry's voice "never exceeded or fell short of the occasion," Webster continued, and "was at all times perfectly under his command." And yet, says Webster of Henry: "it was difficult when he had spoken, to tell what he had said, yet while he was speaking, it always seemed directly to the point."[6] A curious legacy, that.

"Eloquence," said Benjamin Rush, "is the first accomplishment in a republic, and often sets the whole machine of government in motion."[7] This chapter traces the unique blend of transcendence and pragmatism characterizing U.S. political rhetoric since the founding. This blend is now so familiar, so natural sounding, that its contrivances are invisible. For example, immediately after World War II, the term *freedom* had financial trappings; it meant refrigerators, open elections, job mobility, and consumer choice. Only twenty years later, though, says the historian Daniel Rodgers, freedom meant something entirely different as "Americans found themselves in an era of rights-making more vigorous than ever before in their history."[8] Transcendence and pragmatism take turns, but neither is ever completely forgotten.

The English constitution, says Walter Bagehot, needed "two parts, one 'to excite and preserve the reverence of the population' and the other 'to employ that homage to the work of government.'"[9] In the United States, those twin functions have resulted in a rhetoric that tells people what is happening, what it means, who they are, and who they will become. All people in all nations want answers to those questions, but Americans, I argue here, especially want them because of their pluralism. Perhaps that is why Prince William of the United Kingdom had so much trouble with "that bloody woman," his sister-in-law, Meghan Markle. Schooled as she was in her nation's rhetoric, Ms. Markle complained about her in-laws' classism and racism and did so on national television. A quieter conversation could have been had in a secluded castle somewhere, but because Markle was from Los Angeles, she shared her thoughts with Oprah. Patrick Henry would have liked Meghan's style.

THE SOUND OF POLITICS

When Donald Trump arrived on the political scene, almost everything about him was surprising. His background as an untrustworthy construction mogul, his profligate ways with women, his lethargic brand of secularism, his indeterminate political values, and his taste for televised extravaganzas—all these made for a one-of-a-kind politician. But some things were less surprising: he was functionally

illiterate, with no ability to read through even a dumbed-down brief-
ing; he skipped the Kennedy Center Honors (celebrating artists and
writers) three years in a row; he had no understanding of American
history, once noting that Frederick Douglass "is getting recognized
more and more" and that Susan B. Anthony was a person female historians might want to get to know; he once displayed a Bible (upside
down) in Lafayette Square for a photo op and usually mangled his
biblical quotations; the celebrities he brought to the White House
were mostly business executives (e.g., Robert Craft, Rupert Murdoch,
Jamie Dimon, and Peter Thiel) or discredited media personalities
like Matt Drudge, Sean Hannity, and Sarah Palin.[10]

Joe Biden was less surprising. An old hand in Washington, Biden
came to the presidency knowing everyone. Sometimes he knew too
much. When ballyhooing his infrastructure deal in the summer
of 2021, for example, Biden was too cute by far, slyly warning his
Republican partners they would be expected to bow to his wishes
on other legislation (he later backtracked). Biden normally had good
relations with the press although he sometimes got ill-tempered,
as when he confronted CNN's Kaitlan Collins about the propriety
of a Putin-related question (Biden later apologized), and he subsequently mixed it up again with Peter Doocy of Fox News. Otherwise,
Biden went to church regularly, courted the predictable social activists, invited A-list Hollywood personalities to the White House, and
cozied up to the literati by having a twenty-two-year-old poet dazzle
the crowd at his inauguration.[11] Joe Biden understood the intricate
matrix of American politics.

These examples expose the many players operating on the
political scene in the United States. Politicians talk a good deal,
but so does everyone else: reporters, social activists, the clergy,
lobbyists, corporate CEOs, academics, entertainers, and the people
themselves. To see what makes political discourse distinctive, it is
helpful to imagine these actors in dialogue with one another, as we
see in figure 4.1, which positions a variety of discourse types along
the Pragmatic and Transcendent axes (as calculated by DICTION for
some fifty thousand passages).[12]

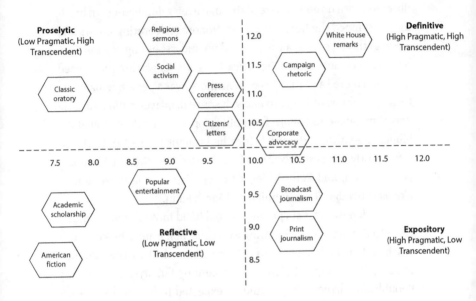

FIGURE 4.1 Rhetorical clusters along the pragmatic/transcendent axes

Contemporary politics (as represented by White House remarks and campaign rhetoric) is distinctively positioned here in two ways: (1) it is mainly based in the upper right-hand quadrant, and (2) it stands quite apart from its competitors. This is not to say that all political speeches fall neatly into this semantic space. Eloquence, after all, results from adapting the pragmatic and the transcendent to the audience addressed, the topic under consideration, and the medium of exchange. Still, politicians generally stay grounded while also showing respect for the verities. The result is the distinctive sound of American (establishment) politics.

Without this distinctiveness, political humor would die aborning. As Will Rogers reminds us, the pragmatic is often a determinative force: "There is no more independence in politics than there is in jail." But the transcendent also makes its demands: "There are many men of principle in both parties in America, but there is no party of principle" (Alexis de Tocqueville). And because meeting both sets of needs is often so difficult, virtually anyone can become a comedian: "Politicians are the same all over. They promise to build a bridge even where there is no river" (Nikita Khrushchev). "A politician is an animal which can sit on a fence and yet keep both ears to the ground" (H. L. Mencken). "Political language is designed to make lies sound truthful and murder respectable, and to give an appearance of solidity to pure wind" (George Orwell).

The sound of politics can be seen in sharpest relief by examining the relationships politicians have with their rivals:

- *Hostility* (politics vs. the press). As we see in figure 4.1, both politicians and the press (print as well as broadcast) "report" the facts of the day, thereby exposing two problematics: (1) Which facts are really facts? (2) Which facts are relevant to the case at hand? Often, reporters accuse politicians of treating hopes as facts (e.g., "the American people are with me on this legislation") or of harping on extraneous statements (e.g., "the Republican Party has always championed freedom of speech"). In contrast, politicians accuse the press of betraying core American values (e.g., "press cynicisms are driving people out of the voting booth") or of concentrating on old matters the people no longer care about (e.g., former extramarital affairs as "gotcha journalism"). The animosity between politicians and the press is fundamental, with root epistemologies at stake: What can be known? Who can know it? Both politicians and the press are scientists of a sort—politicians linking facts to axiology and reporters refusing to do so lest their values (objectivity, fairness, etc.) become a distraction from the real issues of the day.

- *Resentment* (politics vs. religion). As we see in figure 4.1, both politicians and preachers (when sermonizing) specialize in transcendent language, a conversation that sometimes becomes testy. As I have argued in *The Political Pulpit*, the United States has been vexed by political/religious tensions from the beginning, so politicians turn to "civic piety" to regulate things.[13] As a result, a kind of rhetorical contract between church and state privileges ritualistic exchanges over legislative debates, singing one another's praises as often as possible, and maneuvering around difficult issues (abortion, gay liberation, blue laws, prayer in the schools, parental rights, religious displays in public places, etc.). These tensions never abate entirely because true believers still seek political redress and because politicians cannot resist stoking religious tensions for their strategic advantage. Both parties would disavow the contract if they could, but they can't, a difficult situation for all.[14]

• *Deference* (traditional vs. contemporary oratory). Donald Trump liked Andrew Jackson, hanging a portrait of the former president in his office, making a pilgrimage to Jackson's tomb in Nashville, and insisting that he remain on the twenty-dollar bill. Trump especially liked Jackson's style. "He was a very tough person," said Mr. Trump, "but he had a big heart."[15] But Trump and Jackson do not sound the same. Said Jackson when being inaugurated: "A firm reliance on the goodness of that Power whose providence mercifully protected our national infancy, and has since upheld our liberties in various vicissitudes, encourages me to offer up my ardent supplications that He will continue to make our beloved country the object of His divine care and gracious benediction."[16] We have grown apart from such language. Jackson is too sure of himself here, inventing things that cannot be seen, relying on indirection, speaking beyond his moment in time, and reaching too far afield for effect. This is alien language for us. Americans are now an empirical people and that gives politics a certain ballast. The downside, of course, is that ballast weighs things down, making today's discourse less capable of imagined flight.

• *Concern* (politics vs. social activism). Politics and social activism do not mix well, locked as they are in a struggle for public influence. Activists petition Congress but typically do so from afar—out in the hinterlands where the people live. Activists are sometimes unkempt, trashing the sidewalks of Portland to make Black Lives Matter or decamping to tents in lower Manhattan so Wall Street matters less. Rhetorically, social activism sounds more like preaching than politics, with the former having given birth to many of its leaders (e.g., Martin Luther King Jr., Malcolm X, William Barber). Zionists, Catholic Workers, and pro-lifers have blended religious and secular themes, and that has been true for both the Right (e.g., the Moral Majority) and the Left (e.g., the Sanctuary Movement). Some social activists have transitioned from social activism to establishment politics, including two current U.S. senators—Ralph Warnock (D-Georgia) and James Lankford (R-Oklahoma). Generally, though, politicians and activists look at each other warily, maintaining their distance.

• *Bemusement* (politicians vs. novelists). Figure 4.1 finds literature (novels, short stories, etc.) at a great remove from conventional politics. Politics snuggles in the pragmatic-transcendent space; literature rejects both options. While politicians tell stories to make a point, novelists let their stories find their own marks. While novelists use facts to build a storyline, they more often feature their characters' musings or the narrator's interpretations of events. Novels take us to strange places; politics tries to make us feel comfortable. Novels foreswear hasty conclusions; politics embraces them. In Denis Donoghue's terms, novels practice an eloquence "of least means," reveling in "the shock of understatement, where one's excitement arises from the surprise of finding something said so barely yet so definitively."[17] Politics rejects all of this—shock, understatement, surprise, bareness. Order and predictability are its game. Thus, when Bill Clinton decided to write a political novel, he sought the help of James Patterson, a professional writer. As bright as he was, Clinton knew he would have a hard time becoming suddenly bilingual.[18]

• *Irritation* (politics vs. others). Figure 4.1 finds popular entertainment (soap operas, TV narratives, late-night comedy) occupying a space all to itself. It is said that Donald Trump often got upset with *Saturday Night Live* and, some believe, once tried to sic the Justice Department on it. Mostly, though, entertainment shows tend to their own knitting, using inventiveness to decenter things, providing a respite from political drama. Citizens' letters to the editor are another matter entirely, positioned as they are at the crossroads of the pragmatic and the transcendent. In prior research, I have found such letters to be both judgmental and paternalistic, often archly cynical as well. While some letter writers pontificate, they mostly concentrate on local problems, the problems politicians often dismiss.[19] "Corporate advocacy" consists of CEO speeches, annual reports, and public-relations documents. This grouping hovers near the midpoint in figure 4.1, taking care both to avoid value-based matters and to keep unnecessary factual disclosures to a minimum. If corporations have a politics, they normally have a buttoned-up politics lest they get in trouble with the governor of Florida, as the Disney Corporation famously did over the matter of gay rights.

The data reported in figure 4.1 show why American politics sounds the way it does. Politics competes with religion but also backs away from it, steering clear of an unwinnable ideological struggle. Politicians are naturally jealous of journalists' ability to decide which current events to cover and to mask their presuppositions when doing so. Politicians find social activists, entertainers, and citizen-patriots nettlesome and try not to engage them or, if they must, to do so respectfully and briefly. Politicians and novelists are rarely found in one another's company. Given their sharply different rhetorical inclinations, that is probably fortunate for both parties. If politicians can be said to have allies, they can be found in corporate America, a place where the bottom line determines most decisions. All of these voices—alone and collectively—constitute the public sphere in American life. Mainstream politics is what it is, I argue, because it cannot be these other things.

My studies show that the pragmatic-transcendent formula has not changed substantially during the past seventy years. Republicans tend to use both transcendent and pragmatic appeals more often than Democrats, suggesting a more hard-core style of governance. That same effect is found for incumbency, with sitting presidents using both styles more often than challengers, a kind of establishmentarian effect. The pragmatic style is also used more faithfully by winners of presidential elections than by losers, although both employ the transcendent style equivalently.[20] Generally speaking, then, the pragmatic-transcendent model helps explain general electoral trends, but what about individual politicians? Who is pragmatic? Who is transcendent? When and why? It is to these matters that I now turn.

MANAGING TRANSCENDENCE

It may sound risible to use the term *transcendence* with anything as ordinary as American politics. Politics, the art of deciding who should get tax breaks and who should wear COVID masks, seems light-years away from anything truly transcendent. We humans are condemned to the present, after all, moment by bloody moment, and we live or die based on our capacities for consumption. Yet in the Gettysburg Address, notes Gary Wills, "there are no particulars mentioned by Lincoln—no names of men or sites or units . . . Slavery is not mentioned, any more than Gettysburg is. The discussion is driven back and forth, beyond the historical particulars, to great ideals that are made to grapple naked in the airy battle of the mind."[21]

Lincoln knew that we cannot move beyond our immediate circumstances but must try. His strains of transcendence were rooted in the evangelism of the eighteenth century, when preachers like George Whitfield and Gilbert Tennant "championed spontaneity, inwardness, and authenticity against the rigidity of the text-based establishment. They attacked ministers who preached from manuscripts for being dead to true spirituality."[22] This linkage between thought and emotion, between God and mammon, became increasingly familiar in American politics as the years unfolded.

Then came the nineteenth century and, with it, a transmogrified evangelicalism. According to Richard Weaver, oratory of the "broadly ruminative kind" became popular as speakers took on the burdens of "corporate humanity."[23] Such a rhetoric specialized in "large and unexamined phrases," says Weaver, calling up "generalized associations" that presumed a "universal enlightened consensus."[24] Orators of this sort, says Weaver, "talked like a big man," secure in their understanding of ultimate truth.[25] Suddenly, says Kenneth Cmiel, it seemed that "those who ruled were eloquent; those who didn't were not."[26]

The irony remains. The American people, who started out as a nation of tinkers, who then invented the automobile, and who now love all things digital, continued to find new transcendent truths. "Making the world safe for democracy" and "confronting the disease of totalitarianism" became watchwords as the twentieth century unfolded. *Democracy, liberty,* and *freedom,* what Robert Ivie calls "customarily feminized terms," suddenly required "protection from brute forces threatening to overwhelm and subdue them."[27] Somewhat later, Marjorie Taylor Greene appeared, accusing House Speaker Nancy Pelosi of being "guilty of treason," declaring Representative Ilhan Omar worthy of being sent back to the Middle East, and declaring COVID restrictions equivalent to the travails of the Holocaust. Marjorie Taylor Greene: transcendence plus a kick in the pants.

The rhetoric of transcendence is often more elegant than that of Greene and has been depended upon to hold together a nation whose size and diversity boggle the mind. The source of its power lies in four rhetorical functions.

BREADTH

The world is too small without rhetoric. Hubert Humphrey proved that by being "catapulted into the lofty stratosphere of national prominence" by his eight-minute speech at the Democratic convention of 1948.[28] "Humphrey sought incremental reform with an expansive rhetoric," says John Murphy, linking fear of communism to the nation's practices of racial segregation, practices that would cost it the unity it needed to stave off the Soviet menace.[29] Because of Humphrey, civil rights became the center of attention in 1948. "We are being challenged by the world of slavery," Humphrey declared," and "for us to play our part effectively, we must be in a morally sound position."[30] Humphrey sounded like "an old-fashioned carny pitchman," says Ralph Brauer, but that seems an unfair characterization.[31] "Issues," after all, do not simply exist in hyperspace. They must be made to exist. They must also be made grand by being linked to values already having gravitas for an audience.

There is art in all of this. What is one to do, for example, when required, as the activist Emma Goldman was required in 1917, to defend anarchists in the United States? One uses hyperbole and overstatement, attacking religious institutions for being repressive, an economic system for fostering unfair penal practices, and a political system for clinging to cramped patriotism and dangerous militarism.[32] By painting on an overly large canvas, Goldman's rhetoric of distraction had some utility. True eloquence may not have resulted, but political energy surely did.

The labor activist Caesar Chavez adopted a humbler and more interior tone when celebrating the end of his fast of protest—and the beginning of the workers' rights movement—on March 10, 1968. "To be a man is to suffer for others," Chavez declared. "God help us to be men!" "We are poor [and] our allies are few," he observed, "but we have something the rich do not own. We have our own bodies and spirits and the justice of our cause as our weapons."[33] Chavez connects his personal travails here with the larger movement. His religious beliefs also helped: "breaking bread," "a call to sacrifice," "only by giving our lives do we find life."[34] By detailing his personal suffering, Chavez made his protest more than a political stunt. By inviting listeners into his world, he sent them onward and outward.

VISION

Transcendent rhetorics often trade on old beliefs that suddenly seem new. Few speakers were better at that than Ronald Reagan, particularly when delivering his "evil empire" speech on March 8, 1983, to the National Association of Evangelicals in Orlando. In the speech, Reagan reverted to an older, more muscular rhetoric that had not been heard since World War II. Reagan spoke like an Old Testament prophet, says Thomas Goodnight, creating "an ahistorical, dream-like vision of American and world destiny."[35] Secular liberals were responsible for moral decay, said Reagan, giving his address a triumphal sensibility. Although Reagan stated in the speech his desire for peace and the abolition of nuclear weapons, that was not what the press heard. While Reagan needed to "get the attention of the Soviets," he also needed to "convince them that his policies did not threaten war."[36] Alas, his rhetoric ran away with him, causing Henry Steele Commager to call it "the worst presidential speech in American history."[37]

Perhaps. But it is also possible that Reagan's rhetoric did something salvific—putting the Soviet Union on notice that aggression would be met with aggression while simultaneously convincing the American people to have his back. Consider, for example, Reagan's "I believe" statements:

- "I believe in intercessionary prayer."
- "I believe we shall rise to the challenge."
- "I believe that communism is another sad, bizarre chapter in human history."
- "I believe [that] the source of our strength . . . is not material, but spiritual."[38]

There are no grand truths, here but there is a delightful clarity. Reagan's speech was "simplistic" and "sectarian," said the columnist Anthony Lewis, but those were precisely its rhetorical strengths. According to Hillary Carey, Reagan's speech hearkens back to the Middle Ages, a time when "it was assumed that a Christian ruler would seek to bring peace and good order and it was inconceivable that secular and religious power could be exercised independently."[39] This was an outrageous reversion on Reagan's part, but it may have contributed to the end of the Soviet Union eight years later. Visions clearly delivered sometimes have unexpected consequences.

To understand people's responses to Ronald Reagan, says William Lewis, "it is necessary to see and understand Reagan-in-the story, not Reagan-the-policy-maker."[40] The further up the ladder of abstraction Reagan climbed, the more people liked it. Perched on his shoulder as they were, people saw the future as less dim and, because of his enthusiasms, more attractive as well. If Reagan's "story is not true," says Lewis, "it must be true-to-life; if it did not actually happen, it must be evident that it could have happened or that, given the way things are, it should have happened."[41] Reagan's gift lay in his ability to instantiate "rhetorical probability" into his narratives and, thereby, to see the truth even during murky times.

INTENSITY

Ronald Reagan helped advance Barry Goldwater's political campaign when he keynoted the Republican Party's national convention in October 1964. While they had ideological similarities, Reagan and Goldwater were hardly the same man. Reagan's use of transcendent appeals was rooted in a certain political canniness, but Goldwater's instincts ran deeper. Differences between Democrats and Republicans, Goldwater once opined, are not "the result of mere political differences or mere political mistakes." They are, instead, "the result of a fundamentally and absolutely wrong view of man—his nature and his destiny. . . . This nation was founded upon the rejection of that notion and upon the acceptance of God as the author of freedom."[42]

Even sixty years later, it is hard to hear Goldwater's words. One senses no partiality here, no clever maneuvering. One even senses that Goldwater is holding back a bit: "You think that's outrageous? Well how about this . . . ?" Folded into Goldwater's vison is a Calvinist rejection of self-indulgence alongside a man from the Western plains.[43] Millenarianism and militarism blended well for Goldwater. There is no self-glorification in his remarks, no playing to the crowd. In all of the memoirs of the 1964 presidential race, one never finds a "second-thought Goldwater." Even when plummeting to electoral disaster, Goldwater only plummeted harder.

Barry Goldwater and William Jennings Bryan would not have gotten along, but they shared some rhetorical instincts. Bryan embraced the economic and evangelical language of turn-of-the-century populism, says Kristy Maddux, and his icons consisted of

Nebraskan farmers, not Arizona ranchers.[44] While Goldwater came to rhetoric out of necessity, Bryan came to it out of passion. People would never have said this of Goldwater, but they said it of Bryan: "[He] is what they call a popular speaker. He may even be called an orator. But he is not a thinker. He is a shallow and superficial man; a ready and voluble talker who entertains his audience, but never says anything."[45] Yes, but Bryan was also a man of the people, and he had a sense of obligation that made his populism irresistible to many: "Justice is strictly due between neighbor nations as between neighbor citizens," said Bryan, [and] a highwayman is as much a robber when he plunders in a gang as when single; and the nation that makes an unjust war is only a great gang. Many may dare to do in crowds what they would not dare to do as individuals, but the moral character of an act is not determined by the number of those who join it. Force can defend a right, but force has never yet created a right."[46] So said H. L. Mencken's "fundamentalist pope."

COMMUNITY

Given the fractiousness of American politics in the 2020s, it may be hard to think of transcendent rhetoric as a way of pulling people together. But two politicians—Gerald Ford and Ted Kennedy— showed it was possible, although they showed it in different ways. Consider, for example, the challenge facing Ford when taking the oath of office on August 9, 1974: a president deposed, a nation torn apart, and a relatively obscure politician suddenly becoming the chief executive. Ford had none of the usual things that come with being president, says Mary Stuckey, having been denied the "transcendent prompts" on the most important day of his life: no inaugural address, no parade, no evening ball, no body of the ex-president lying in state, no established ceremony to mark the occasion. Given that "the electorate was suspicious of power, suspicious of presidents, and suspicious of politics," says Stuckey, it was difficult "to present any sort of vision. Ford, however, did not even try."[47] Yes, but there is more to transcendence than vision.

When declaring that "our long national nightmare is over," President Ford initiated a healing. The Nixon family has experienced an American tragedy, he said, "in which we all have played a part." "Ugly passions would again be aroused and our people would again be polarized," said Ford, if the Nixon situation continued. "Every deep and compassionate person" is troubled by what has happened," said Ford, and "my primary concern must always be the greatest good of all the people in the United States."[48]

For those of a litigious mindset, this is weak tea—nobody in the gallows, no firing squad at 7 a.m. "But polities are based on human relationships," Ford seemed to be saying, and those relationships must be reestablished for the nation to continue as a nation. Transcendence, he seemed to say, lies in what we can become together, now more than ever before. Well said, said many.

Of the one hundred speeches in the Lucas-Medhurst corpus, the speech given by Ted Kennedy in October 1983 ranked eighth highest on transcendence. And well it should, given the challenges he faced when addressing the student body (and a steely Jerry Falwell) at Liberty University in October 1983. Kennedy, lion of the Senate and heir to the left-leaning Kennedy clan, confronted an enormous ideological chasm between himself and his listeners. Unlike Ford, however, he did not reach out to his audience personally. Instead, he spoke as an intellectual, as one excited by ideas. "Dr. Falwell was hissed and heckled at Harvard," Kennedy reminded the crowd, "but the loudest applause from the Harvard audience came in defense of Dr. Falwell's right to speak."[49] So let it be with us today, Kennedy concluded. To his credit and to theirs, his audience responded in like fashion.

There are, in short, many roads to transcendence—personal and intellectual, philosophical and psychological. Those roads are needed because the American people have always been a nation of believers, and that has been both its bane and its boon. "To find the sources of political power in a society," says Bryan Garsten, "it is always helpful to notice what ambitious people want. In democracies they want to be heard."[50] Transcendence implies that some notions are better than others. That can be dangerous when the available ideas are exotic or when people act on them prematurely. Sometimes, though, transcendence highlights hidden beliefs to which all subscribe and gives people a chance to catch their breath. In a complex democracy, there is much to be said for this option.

MANAGING PRAGMATISM

It is impossible to write a book about political eloquence without thinking of Donald Trump. He was surely not an eloquent fellow, and that raises both political questions (What did people see in the man?) and rhetorical questions (Why did they enjoy listening to him?). Donald Trump was a gift that kept on giving, especially when speaking about transcendent matters:

- On scripture: "As much as I love *The Art of the Deal*, it's not even close. We take the Bible all the way."
- On Holy Communion: "My little wine and my little cracker."
- On his religious supporters: "I've been talking to these people for years; I've let them stay at my hotels."
- On a female evangelist: "A beautiful person both inside and out. . . . She's blonde and cute and perky and endlessly optimistic."
- On the need for forgiveness: "I think if I do something wrong, I think, I just try and make it right. I don't bring God into that picture."[51]

It is hard not to cringe when listening to Donald Trump. Trump was an empiricist to the core of his being. John Locke and David Hume would have voted for him. Trump knew only what he could touch or tabulate; nothing else existed, except in the minds of suckers. And yet Donald Trump became the forty-fifth president of the United States. Why? How?

The historian Carolyn Eastman says that during colonial times, 75 percent of the books available to the colonists had British imprints, so the colonists needed some other way to "learn to be American."[52] With few institutions to guide them, with no long traditions to inform them, the colonists relied on commerce and the lecture circuit to tell them who they were. And who were they? A practical people above all else. So they listened to the Fanny Wrights of the day, social reformers with a "loud voice" and "untasteful attire" who would mingle "with men in stormy debate," frequently "standing up with bare-faced imprudence to lecture a public assembly."[53]

The colloquial style featuring tangible descriptions and frequent repetitions, says Marissa Gemma and her colleagues, is "the linguistic correlate of the democratic ideology that shaped the nation during the 19th century."[54] As time moved on, Americans came to revile "late classical English," searching for a way "to speak United States."[55] Abraham Lincoln was the most American of these new Americans. Even the magisterial Emancipation Proclamation, says Robert Ferguson, was "the work of a legal mind" that used "condensed prose" and a "calculated professional distance" to keep needless emotions at bay.[56] The Gettysburg Address too, says Ferguson, used measured tones, short sentences, and simple words to manufacture brilliance.

The United States' most enlightened visitor, Alexis de Tocqueville, once observed that Americans are "sober, poised, and reserved, and they all wear the same clothes."[57] "Sophistication is a fighting word in American culture," says the literary scholar Ross Posnock, "a phrase that discomfits, raises eyebrows."[58] The new American style, says Kenneth Tynan, must "preserve a certain naivete, a hayseed element, even a touch of the child, and the primitive, if it is to retain its juice and energy."[59] Suddenly, Donald Trump makes sense—it's all about the juice and the energy.

MATERIALISM

Although he would have resisted academic labels, Lyndon Johnson was a walking, talking materialist. Said he to the students at the University of Michigan when announcing his Great Society program on May 22, 1964: "Your imagination and your initiative and your indignation will determine whether we build a society where progress is the servant of our needs, or a society where old values and new visions are buried under unbridled growth. For in your time we have the opportunity to move not only toward the rich society and the powerful society, but upward to the Great Society. The Great Society rests on abundance and liberty for all."[60]

For many Americans, this is a seamless paragraph, but its seamlessness is what makes it so American. Consider, for example, how fluidly Johnson moves across the antinomies: initiative and indignation, needs and visions, servitude and wealth, resting and movement, abundance and determination, life and death. For each abstraction Johnson finds an instantiation; for each somewhere he finds a something. As Michael Weiler notes, it was unnecessary in Johnson's mind "to debate the relative importance of social equality and general prosperity"; as David Zarefsky says, opportunities in the abstract were not meaningful to Johnson.[61] Principles are fine only if they produce a great society.

Lyndon Johnson and Donald Trump were both modernists, although modernists of a different sort. Both embraced "a state of consciousness that elevates science, mastery over nature, mass production, mass consumption, and social engineering."[62] Russell Conwell, who turned a popular speech ("Acres of Diamonds") into a career, a theology, and a university in the early 1900s, paved the way for Johnson and Trump. Conwell was the original can-do fellow, delivering his speech to approximately thirteen million Americans during his career, and his message was simple: "A poor person is a lazy person. A poor person is a weak person. A poor person is not doing God's work." There is something faintly Trumpian here—a harshness, a feeling of inerrancy—but Conwell was no fake populist. His famous speech proceeded anecdote by anecdote, and as he moved about the country, he met his anecdotes in person and spread their fame further.

Russell Conwell was not a deep thinker, and his rhetorical formula was primitive. But it still resonates: twelve-step programs, online testimonials, house flipping, Tupperware parties, lotto millionaires, GoFundMe campaigns, cryptocurrencies, Chip and Joanna

Gaines. "I say again," Conwell reminded his listeners, "that the opportunity to get rich, to attain great wealth, is here in Philadelphia now, within the reach of almost every man and woman who hears me speak. . . . I have come to tell you what in God's sight I believe to be the truth."[63] Conwell's truths were palpable ones, and he would have no patience with today's Senate ideologues willing to sacrifice progress to some faint ideology. If America is not about business, he would ask, what is it about? If values cannot become actualized, what are they worth? Leadership, he would argue, is about making things happen.

IMMEDIACY

Americans have always been an impatient people. Rhetoric is part of that story. The evangelicalism that gave the nation its start—repent now; go sow the seeds; judgment awaits, but it will not wait long—can now be seen in today's twenty-second commercials bombarding the viewer on national television. In the United States, hectoring is everybody's business, causing things to change constantly: individual religions wax and wane; politicians' popularity comes and goes; today's fashions die a quick death tomorrow; everyone loves the new quarterback until they do not.

Malcolm X knew something about immediacy. Compared to Martin Luther King Jr., he was lightning in a bottle, a restless, abrasive preacher willing to wait for nothing. In his "Ballot or the Bullet" speech given in 1964, Malcolm wanted only progress: "If we bring up religion, we'll have differences; we'll have arguments; and we'll never be able to get together." He was a black nationalist, but mostly that meant "we should own and operate and control the economy of our community." He had a clear understanding of prejudice but had no truck with empty theorizing: "We need a self-help program, a do-it-yourself philosophy, a do-it-right-now philosophy, an it's-already-too-late philosophy." He was well versed in the sociology of the working class, but mostly he was impatient: "You're in a position to determine who will go to the White House, and who will stay

in the doghouse. You're the one who has that power." He understood the power of a sit-in, but he hated its connotations: "An old
woman can sit. An old man can sit. A chump can sit. A coward can
sit. Anything can sit. Well, you and I been sitting long enough, and
it's time today for us to start doing some standing."[64]

According to the rhetorical scholar Robert Terrill, Malcolm X
did not just want to change the politics of his day. He wanted to
broaden "the palate of identities and actions from which his audience might choose."[65] His was an in-the-moment quest, a near-revo-
lutionary quest. His dualistic strategy—the ballot or the bullet—was
an attempt to remove the lethargy baked into the African American
community by two centuries of involuntary servitude. The conclusion of his speech demanded "waking up"; it warned against "wast-
ing your time" or engaging in "dilly-dallying" or "pussyfooting." For
Malcolm X, time was destiny—his destiny, his people's destiny.

POPULISM

In the early twenty-first century, the concept of populism exploded
with meaning in the United States and around the world. Cultural
populists (Scottish nationalists, for example) wanted either their
identity back or an end to unchecked immigration (the VOX party
in Spain, for example). Ideological populists (Venezuelan's Hugo
Chavez, for example) operated like autocrats while others called
themselves embodiments of the people incarnate (Hungary's Viktor
Orbán, for example). Economic populists (Argentina's Néstor Kirchner or Bolivia's Evo Morales) were a bit more conventional, arguing
for greater distributive justice.

Throughout the world, the tropes of populism are well known:
citizens must become autonomous, socially and economically; the
leader is the people's savior; government—along with industry—
are the people's oppressors; the upper class is a threat, immigrants
a more dire threat. All this seems clear enough, but rhetoric com-
plicates the picture. Although claiming the populist tag, the United
States' Donald Trump and France's Marine Le Pen are mostly about

keeping power where it has always been kept: in the hands of the moneyed class. Rhetoric aside, it is often hard to tell which populists are Left, which Right, and which are just about themselves.

Former vice president Spiro Agnew (whom some describe as "Trump before Trump") played the populist card in his now famous speech about the evils of televised news in November 1969.[66] In his remarks, Agnew warned how "a raised eyebrow, an inflection of the voice, a caustic remark dropped in the middle of a broadcast" could call into question "the veracity of a public official or the wisdom of a government policy." Reporters were, he said, part of a "fraternity" operating in a "privileged sanctuary" from which they launched "partisan attacks" even while being protected by "a monopoly sanctioned and licensed by government."[67] In our current era of "fake news," Agnew's attack sounds both familiar and outdated, but it was jarring when first uttered. Agnew seemed to know what people were already thinking, and his examples drew on everyday life. The ninety thousand letters, telegrams, and phone calls that flooded Washington within five days of his remarks distinguished Agnew as "the only vice-president to create his own constituency."[68] By emphasizing "orderliness, personal responsibility, the sanctity of hard work, the nuclear family, and the law," says Peter Levy, Agnew helped launch the Republican Party's then glacial, now accelerating claim over the working-class vote, a vote the Democrats had owned for a century or more.[69]

Things were both different and the same forty years earlier when Huey Long of Louisiana held sway. Far more colorful than Agnew, far more genuine as well, Long served up an eclectic "amalgam of ideas from populism, technocracy, and the Bible," and he served it up hot and delicious to the poorest of the poor.[70] "As if sitting in the living room with the kinfolk, Long would read to his [radio] audiences from the newspapers, relating shocking and heart-wrenching stories about victims of the Depression."[71] Although he had an agile intellect and understood the macroeconomic forces at work, Long reveled in the pragmatic. When he was given to theorizing, he would invoke "an angry and demanding God, a God who punished

America with the Great Depression and 'commanded' that the nation's wealth be redistributed."[72]

Unlike his contemporaries in the South, Long found a way of detaching himself from segregationist choplogic, and he did so personally: "Now, Gen. Hugh Johnson says I am indeed a very smart demagogue, a wise and dangerous menace. But I am one of those who didn't have the opportunity to secure a college education or training. . . . Had I enjoyed the learning and college training which my plan would provide for others, I might not have fallen into the path of the dangerous menace and demagogue that he has now found me to be." Unlike Donald Trump, who used personal examples to make himself look better, Huey Long used personal examples to make a point better.

Long's primary focus of attention was on the people he represented: "I said then, as I have said since, that it was inhuman to have food rotting, cotton and wool going to waste, houses empty, and at the same time to have millions of our people starving, naked, and homeless because they could not buy the things which other men had and for which they had no use whatever." That was Long's plebian take on the affairs of the day. Here is his patrician take: "What has become of the remainder of those things placed on the table by the Lord for the use of us all? They are in the hands of the Morgans, the Rockefellers, the Mellons, the Baruches, the Bakers, the Astors, and the Vanderbilts—600 families at the most either possessing or controlling the entire 90 percent of all that is in America."[73]

Lyndon Johnson, Russell Conwell, Huey Long, and Malcolm X were artists of pragmatism. They used transcendent appeals too, as must any American politician, but they specialized in the day-to-day. John Stuart Mill once observed that poetry and rhetoric "are both alive in the expression or uttering forth of feeling." But rhetoric is heard, says Mill, while poetry is overheard. "The peculiarity of poetry," Mill concludes, lies "in the poet's utter unconsciousness of a listener."[74] Johnson, Conwell, Long, and Malcolm X never lost sight of their listeners. They used rhetoric to deliver the goods because they knew that goods were always at stake. Americans all.

BALANCING THINGS

Some people are born to eloquence, and some are not. Hillary Clinton was not. Although possessed of a fabulous intelligence and a canny political mind, she could not charm the birds out of their nests. When confronting an audience, her first instinct was to overwhelm them with facts, and her second instinct was to do so again. While her husband could cry on cue, Hillary Clinton never grasped the soft side of rhetoric. As the columnist Paul Greenberg has said, "she seems to have no feel at all for the poetry of politics."[75]

Barbara Jordan was another story entirely. "She was the Mahalia Jackson of political rhetoric," says Greenberg, with "an eye for the practical and an unswerving dedication to liberty. . . . Never to have heard Jordan speak was to miss one of the great American experiences—educational and spiritual."[76] Barbara Jordan understood the pragmatic and the transcendent. She had both a lawyerly and a preacher's instinct, the former by dint of her formal training, the latter by dint of her cultural upbringing. To listen to Barbara Jordan was to be pinned to one's chair, not wanting to move.

Although the argument of this book is that an ear for the pragmatic and an eye on the transcendent are both required for eloquence, they frequently do not come together, making eloquence a rare thing. When debating the Trump impeachment, for example, Democrats and Republicans often adopted different postures. "I have seen the Senate at its best," said Patrick Leahy (D-Vermont), "rise to the occasion to be the conscience of the nation. If there ever were a time for the Senate to serve as the conscience of the nation, it is now."[77] *Mais non*, said John Cornyn (R-Texas). No doubt the Senate can "do something more productive, like confirming more judges, lowering drug prices and passing a highway/infrastructure bill."[78]

Depending on your politics, it is easy to decry both statements, easy to applaud them as well. Most Americans on most days can imagine having both cheaper drugs and a sense of morality, but not every day. That makes politics unwieldy and rhetoric an approximate thing. Combining the pragmatic and the transcendent takes artistry, and it takes three other things as well.

CREATIVITY

Eloquence is often a surprise when it happens. As well regarded as he was, for example, few thought that John Kennedy would create a scene for the ages when he went to Berlin on June 26, 1963, and declared himself, and ourselves, citizens of that recovering city:

> Freedom is indivisible, and when one man is enslaved, all are not free. When all are free, then we can look forward to that day when this city will be joined as one and this country and this great Continent of Europe in a peaceful and hopeful globe. When that day finally comes, as it will, the people of West Berlin can take sober satisfaction in the fact that they were in the front lines for almost two decades. All free men, wherever they may live, are citizens of Berlin. And, therefore, as a free man, I take pride in the words— "Ich bin ein Berliner."[79]

Kennedy weaves together several incommensurabilities here: freedom and slavery, sobriety and hope, East and West Berlin, all of Germany and all of Europe, the nation and the citizen, the citizen and all who wish to breathe free. His speech was short but still pulled together a tortured history and a hopeful future. His is not an airy speech, not really philosophical either, yet it transports people to a gladder place. As one scholar of international relations has said, Kennedy's speech shows that "the intersection of the human and nonhuman, the material and immaterial, the representational and nonrepresentational, can give rise to forms of language that exceeds lived or conceived geopolitical agendas in unexpected ways."[80]

Germany was also the site of another imaginative speech, this time delivered by Ronald Reagan at the Brandenburg Gate in June 1987. In his speech, Reagan's moral and political boundaries were more sharply defined than Kennedy's, but his remarks were also quite grounded. For Reagan, the Berlin Wall was more than a symbol.[81] It was also a wall, a wall attesting to communism's "technological

backwardness," "declining standards of health," and "too little food."
When imploring Michael Gorbachev to "tear down this wall," Reagan
saw it being supplanted by "free markets," "dramatic advances in
computers," and the "miracle of economic growth." And he imagined
more for Germany as well—better airports, more cultural exchanges,
exciting sports competitions—before concluding with a calculated
abruptness: "The totalitarian world produces backwardness because
it does such violence to the spirit, thwarting the human impulse to
create, to enjoy, to worship. The totalitarian world finds even symbols of love and of worship an affront."[82]

Ronald Reagan was masterful at combining the pragmatic with
the transcendent, but Martin Luther King Jr. did it best, as seen in
his "I Have a Dream" speech. What Reagan did in a contractual way
and Kennedy did in an emotional way, King did via "voice merging,"
presenting himself as a "reluctant," almost "burdened" prophet
lighting a new path for a troubled nation.[83] King's use of "oral poetry
of the black tradition was itself a form of political protest."[84] King's
"training in systematic theology had left him with an appetite for
transcendent ideas, says Howard Sitkoff, but his real genius lay in
finding moral purpose in the quotidian—in the hands of a clock, on a
table for eating, in a check from the bank.[85]

Edwin Black notes that King's pragmatic talk often fell awkwardly
on the ear. His "heat" imagery was ingenious, says Black, but it sat
alongside entirely trite metaphors (the "sunlit path," for example).
But does it matter? asks Black. "No, of course not," he responds. "Show
me a man who can hear that speech and not be stirred to the depths,
and I'll show you a man who has no depths to stir."[86] King's greatest
strength lay in transforming disparate insults—widespread poverty,
broken neighborhoods, police brutality, imprisoned protestors—into
possible impossibilities—stones of hope, symphonies of brotherhood,
rings of freedom—and to frame a narrative out of these transforma-
tions. King's speech is an entire school of social sciences. It has within
it economics, history, sociology, psychology, and geography, and yet it
is a poem. There has never been anything like it since.

PRUDENCE

Prudence is the art of doing what is needed when it is needed. Most politicians, though, want to get everything done yesterday. Lyndon Johnson was no exception, but his greatest speech— "We Shall Overcome," delivered to a joint session of Congress on March 15, 1965—was a lesson in restraint. For a man of the South, Johnson did unprecedented things in his remarks, producing what Martin Luther King Jr. himself called "the most moving, eloquent, unequivocal and passionate plea for human rights ever made by a president of this nation."[87] But what Johnson did *not* do is even more interesting: He did not lay out specific pieces of legislation for quick passage; he did not engage in rank partisanship; he did not make wild accusations in an attempt to instill guilt in his listeners; and he did not throw his white friends from the South onto a burning pyre of recrimination. But he did do this:

> My first job after college was as a teacher in Cotulla, Texas, in a small Mexican-American school. Few of them could speak English, and I couldn't speak much Spanish. My students were poor and they often came to class without breakfast, hungry. And they knew, even in their youth, the pain of prejudice. They never seemed to know why people disliked them. But they knew it was so, because I saw it in their eyes. I often walked home late in the afternoon, after the classes were finished, wishing there was more that I could do. But all I knew was to teach them the little that I knew, hoping that it might help them against the hardships that lay ahead. And somehow you never forget what poverty and hatred can do when you see its scars on the hopeful face of a young child.[88]

An old axiom in international diplomacy is that when two sworn enemies are at loggerheads and cannot find common ground, it is time to talk about children—the creatures that all nations value equally. Lyndon Johnson understood this and other lessons better than most. Although he could threaten to withhold funding for a dam project in a nanosecond, Johnson went transcendent during his "Overcome" speech. For example, he transformed the Selma riots into a mythic event, says Garth Pauley, and made Black protests the story of America itself.[89] He also went theological, says Steve Goldzwiz, turning "Good Friday events" into "Easter Sunday celebrations."[90] Johnson in this speech went further out on the civil rights limb than had any of his predecessors, putting his young administration in political jeopardy. Undaunted, he ended his speech on a transcendent note: "God will not favor everything that we do. It is rather our duty to divine His will. But I cannot help believing that He truly understands and that He really favors the undertaking that we begin here tonight."

Jesse Jackson's prudence is not often featured in his biographies, but prudent he was, as seen when giving a primetime address at the Democratic National Convention in 1984. Jackson had ample reason to be grumpy on that occasion, having won 384 delegates during the Democratic primaries but coming in third to Walter Mondale and Gary Hart. Anyone who had ever lost a race for class vice president in the sixth grade could identify with Jackson on that evening. Many expected him to be petulant as a result, but instead he was gracious. Others expected him to seek retribution, but instead he sought unity. His language was measured, to be sure: "I believe they [Mondale and Hart] will both continue to try to serve us faithfully." And he certainly did not efface his accomplishments during the campaign: "If in my high moments, I have done some good, offered some service, shed some light, healed some wounds, rekindled some hope or stirred someone from apathy and indifference, or in any way along the way helped somebody, then this campaign has not been in vain."[91]

Jackson was a preacher but also a pragmatist. He lived in the world, but more important, he lived on the streets. "Twenty years ago," said Jackson, "tears welled up in our eyes as the bodies of Schwerner, Goodman and Chaney were dredged from the depths of a river in Mississippi. Twenty years later, our communities, black and Jewish, are in anguish, anger and pain." Jackson urged moving forward vigorously into the future, but he also called the roll from the past: "We lost Malcolm, Martin, Medgar, Bobby, John and Viola. The team that got us here must be expanded, not abandoned." Jackson endorsed a new Rainbow Coalition, but he also named names: workers being abused by the Campbell Soup Company, farmers suffering because of Reagan administration policies, babies dying in Detroit at an unacceptable rate, few toxic waste dumps being cleaned up by the Republicans in charge.

This sort of issue listing is standard in a convention speech, but what was not standard was how Jackson threw caution to the winds and became a preacher once again, bringing the transcendent into a direct interface with the pragmatic:

> Young America, dream. Choose the human race over the nuclear race. Bury the weapons and don't burn the people. Dream, dream of a new value system. Teachers, who teach for life, and not just for a living, teach because they can't help it. Dream of lawyers more concerned about justice than a judgeship. Dream of doctors more concerned about public health than personal wealth. Dream of preachers and priests who will prophecy and not just profiteer. Preach and dream. Our time has come. Our time has come. Suffering breeds character. Character breeds faith. And in the end, faith will not disappoint.[92]

BOLDNESS

Politics—and rhetoric—requires making choices, and in neither case has a clear playbook yet been written. So politicians stumble from moment to moment, inventing what they can along the way. Eugene Debs, the great labor agitator of the early twentieth century, was one such grand stumbler, as he revealed in 1908: "We Socialists propose that society in its collective capacity shall produce, not for profit, but in abundance to satisfy all human wants; that every man shall have the inalienable right to work, and receive the full equivalent of what he produces; that every man may stand fearlessly erect in the pride and majesty of his own manhood; that every man and every woman shall be economically free."[93]

"Debs was a political failure in his own time," say Ronald Lee and James Andrews: "the Pullman strike failed, industrial unionism failed, the Socialist party failed."[94] Yet Debs persevered, couching his program "in the words of revolutionary socialism" while also addressing "practical issues of labor agitation."[95] It took considerable moxie to stand firm for socialism during such a conservative moment in American history. Ironically, says the historian Nick Salvatore, Debs somehow found a way of staying "within the patriotic and religious culture" of the United States, acknowledging "the reality of class in America" but also the contravening "power of the dominant [capitalist] ideology."[96]

Debs always combined the pragmatic and the transcendent in his campaigns, but his problem was twofold: while Americans saw the problems he saw—massive unemployment, the terrors of industrialization—the problems frightened them more than they motivated them. Too, while Debs heralded American values (Judeo-Christian charity, justice for all), socialism seemed too extreme a remedy. Eighty years later, Mario Cuomo confronted similar challenges when addressing issues of public morality at Notre Dame University in September 1984. His speech is masterful throughout: unsettlingly thoughtful, elegantly worded, emotionally disclosive. For a devout person like Cuomo to discuss abortion (and his own internal torments) at the nation's preeminent Catholic university took considerable courage.

When addressing the frustrations of church-state relations, Cuomo did not shrink from the challenge, frankly admitting that "there is no Church teaching that mandates the best political course for making our belief everyone's rule, for spreading this part of our Catholicism. There is neither an encyclical nor a catechism that spells out a political strategy for achieving legislative goals." Above all, said Cuomo, in his pragmatic-transcendent way, "whether abortion is outlawed or not, our work has barely begun: the work of creating a society where the right to life doesn't end at the moment of birth; where an infant isn't helped into a world that doesn't care if it's fed properly, housed decently, educated adequately; where the blind or retarded child isn't condemned to exist rather than empowered to live."[97]

Some critics argue that Cuomo's address fell short—that he failed to "translate abstract virtue into a code of concrete justice,"[98] was too "quietist" in his approach to public policy,[99] or became all things to all people in his remarks.[100] Few, however, challenged Cuomo's (or Eugene Debs's) boldness, but that has not been true for others. Former congressperson Shirley Chisholm proved many years ago that intersectionality can be dicey: too much pragmatism can undo coalitions; too much transcendence can result in confusion. Tammy L. Brown has noted, for example, that Chisholm strategically emphasized "her femaleness among women supporters, her black-ness before African-American audiences and . . . the humanity of all Americans [when] in the company of a culturally diverse crowd," thereby, in many people's eyes, failing to deal with issues head-on.[101]

The dilemmas Chisholm faced are complex. It is good to be pragmatic, to lay one's cards on the table, but which cards and how many? It is good to be transcendent, to find principles around which all can rally, but how to phrase those principles without being sycophantic or needlessly provocative? It is good to be bold, to stand with one's words, but there is also the matter of timing: Say it now or wait a bit? Wait too long and miss the rhetorical opportunity?

Sometimes, insufficient boldness can be seen only in hindsight:

- Woodrow Wilson on the League of Nations: "Wilson could have chastised Congress and its 'truth squad' . . . He could have specifically challenged the legislators to do the 'work of the Lord on earth.' He could have put his foes at risk for their 'slothful' ways, prophesying that they would lose their 'immortal souls' and damn everyone else in the process."[102]

- Dwight Eisenhower on the military-industrial complex: "Nowhere in his writings or speeches do we find anything like explicit criteria for making [policy decisions]. Hence, we are left without a standard for evaluation and, what is more important for our purposes here, without a means of deciding conclusively where Eisenhower might stand today in the debate over the MIC."[103]

- Robert Kennedy on the death of Martin Luther King Jr.: "Robert Kennedy's speaking in this situation, however eloquent, ultimately served the purposes of the status quo. I do not mean to imply that Kennedy lacked concern for social progress. He justified that progress, however, through an appeal to the past and to the cause of 'cultural revitalization.' . . . He [did] not propose policy alternatives or engage in social criticism outside of that ideal."[104]

When speaking about great matters like these, it is often hard to know what to say, even harder to know how to say it. The speeches delivered by Wilson, Eisenhower, and Kennedy were masterful in many ways. Each addressed matters of great import—for the nation and for the world at large. But none went as far as they might have gone, philosophically or practically. Naturally, these were but three speeches among the many they gave; there would be other days when bolder work could be done. Rhetorical decisions can be hard to make, even for the best of us.

ADJUSTING WISELY

In identifying the pragmatic and the transcendent as the natural home of political rhetoric, I do not mean to imply that all politicians behave identically on all occasions. My argument is simply that—compared to other modes of discourse—American politics is commonly framed in practical and philosophical terms. But individual speakers sometimes resist that formulary. Instead, they do what works, or what they hope will work.

Figure 4.2, for example, features politicians under pressure. Most of them cluster near the midpoint of the pragmatic-transcendent graph, sometimes to their credit but not always. Jimmy Carter, for example, seemed unsure of his purpose on July 15, 1979, when speaking to a nationwide audience about the energy crisis. "Pilloried in most quarters, the address became a synecdoche for the entire Carter presidency, an administration given to too much thought and

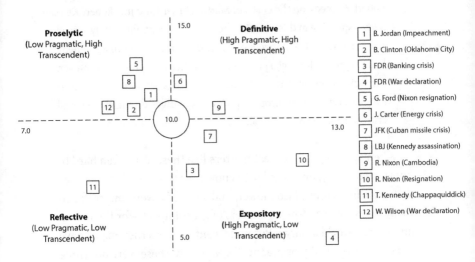

FIGURE 4.2 Differing rhetorical approaches to crisis management

too little action."[105] Carter spoke of a sense of dissatisfaction beset-
ting the American people and he condemned their way of life as
"materialistic and self-indulgent."[106]

Sixty-five million Americans watched his speech, a speech filled
with *introspection* ("I've worked hard to put my campaign promises into law and, I have to admit, with just mixed success"), *moral
preachment* ("Human identity is no longer defined by what one
does, but by what one owns"), and *elliptical policy proposals* ("we
will increase aid to needy Americans to cope with rising energy
prices.").[107] Carter's remarks were somewhat practical, somewhat
philosophical, but not very good at either. The "speech bumped-up
Carter's approval ratings for a few days," says Ronald Lee, but "his
political misfortunes continued."[108] Carter's speech was situated
in the "correct" quadrant in figure 4.2, but it was not comfortably
situated there, being neither bold nor functional. It was too little,
too late, too odd.

Franklin Roosevelt's war message after the attack on Pearl
Harbor was brilliantly different, one of the most eloquent speeches

ever delivered by a U.S. chief executive. Roosevelt's radio address contains no preachment, just specifics delivered in rapid-fire succession. "A mind that wished to wander," said Herman Stelzner, is restrained from doing so by Roosevelt's details: "Japanese air squadrons," "American ships," "armed attack," "Hawaiian Islands," "people of the United States."[109] Roosevelt produced a breathless account as if describing a boxing match—punch, punch, punch, punch. When he did reflect more broadly, Roosevelt was brief: "With confidence in our armed forces, with the unbounding determination of our people, we will gain the inevitable triumph—so help us God."[110]

Woodrow Wilson's address declaring war on April 2, 1917, was quite different. In contrast to Roosevelt's minimalism, Wilson "theorized" the forthcoming battle to give it moral meaning. According to Herbert Carson, Wilson sounded like "a pontiff" on that occasion, combining "the ritual of war with the deliberation of the lecture platform."[111] Wilson's rhetoric was Manichean, says Jason Flanagan, with Germany and its allies seeking "an age of oppression" versus the United States' "age of liberty and freedom."[112] The result was a speech of "uninhibited idealism" and "utter detachment from the passions and claims of the warring parties," claimed Robert Tucker.[113] For these reasons, it is far easier for us moderns to listen to Roosevelt than to Wilson. The former is brisk and to the point while the latter is tendentious and self-satisfied. Said Wilson: "It will all be the easier for us to conduct ourselves as belligerents in a high spirit of right and fairness because we act without animus."[114]

Joining Wilson's address in the "proselytic" quadrant of figure 4.2 are speeches one might expect to be preachy—Barbara Jordan and Jerry Ford wrestling with the Nixon impeachment, Lyndon Johnson reacting to the Kennedy assassination, and Bill Clinton anguishing over the bombing in Oklahoma City in 1995. In stark contrast is a speech by Ted Kennedy (found alone in the lower-left quadrant) in which he confronted the death by drowning of Mary Jo Kopechne after his car veered off the road on Chappaquiddick Island in

July 1996. What facts, what values, can be discussed in such a circumstance? Is there anything a politician can say?

The short answer is no. The longer answer is yes. Kennedy spent much of his time reflecting on his own reflections: "I remember thinking as the cold water rushed in around my head that I was for certain drowning . . . but somehow I struggled to the surface alive." Those were the facts as Kennedy recalled them. These were the incongruities: "My conduct and conversations during the next several hours, to the extent that I can remember them, make no sense to me at all." And these were his sentiments: "No words on my part can possibly express the terrible pain and suffering I feel over this tragic incident."

Kennedy operates here as a third party presenting a first party's thoughts. He is uncertain if his political career will continue ("This will be a difficult decision to make"), and he is aware—as a third party might be aware—that some will say him nay ("I understand full well why some might think it right for me to resign"). Kennedy stands back in his speech, and he even stands back from himself ("I do not seek to escape responsibility for my actions").[115] Kennedy's speech had long-term effects, effectively authorizing reporters to look into politicians' private lives as a matter of course.[116] While some Americans said at the time that Kennedy had suffered enough and should be excused from further humiliation, they have rarely been as generous to politicians since that time.

As we have seen here, while creativity, prudence, and boldness can help make policies relevant and values compelling, inventiveness is also needed. But why listen to political rhetoric in the first place? The psychologist Martin Seligman and his colleagues give us a hint. Human beings, they say, are the only known creatures who spend 30 to 50 percent of their time contemplating the distant future (with the exception of a few primates who store tools for future use).[117] Trapped as we are in the present and concerned as we are with potential threats—increased civil strife, more global warming, higher housing costs—we instinctively look for ways of escaping our predicaments. In this model, politics becomes a kind of augury, a way of discovering what will happen so we can stave it off. Rhetoric is the augur's tool.

CONCLUSION

The legal scholar Robert Tsai says that "in the mind of every citizen lives an image of the Republic" and this image lets the state reproduce itself over time.[118] But what keeps these images vibrant, functional? I have argued here that two contrary forces do so: practical interventions and shared belief systems. Sometimes these old reliables make politicians sound programmed ("it's all politics!") or disingenuous ("they're all liars!"). Today, for example, the Left hates the state because it has not yet accomplished the future; the Right hates the state because it no longer resembles the past. Both hate the state because it has accomplished too much or not enough. What Tsai calls the nation's "governing vocabulary" is constantly being undermined by facts on the ground and beliefs in the air.

As we have seen here, the old transcendent rhetoric of Washington and Lincoln, Jonathan Edwards and Sojourner Truth, has been replaced by more analytical language. Politicians are still preachers, but not like before. Politicians are still activists, but only when it suits them. American politicians have never been poets (Yeats says that "out of the quarrel with others we make rhetoric; out of the quarrel with ourselves we make poetry"), and they are surely not entertainers (unless they are Donald Trump).[119] Sometimes, though, they sound like business executives (especially if they are Donald Trump). Above all else, politicians are not to be confused with the press, although they love-hate them with great ferocity.

It is true that politicians often produce the "grating noises" surrounding us, noises "bereft of the essential moral and ethical refinements" a decent people deserve.[120] And yes, today's political speeches are often composed of "dry, detailed lists of promised programs sandwiched between warmed-over boilerplate."[121] But this is also true: people often like these programs (simpler voting, better child care, smoother highways), and the "warmed-over boilerplate" is better known as their political heritage (e.g., freedom of speech, the right to bear arms, public education). Politicians often fail us, and their rhetoric often fails them. But sometimes their rhetoric has a cultural resonance to it, a just-right blend of pragmatism and transcendence that calms the nation's soul. Democracy brightens when that happens.

5

PERSONAL INVESTMENT

Standing in Gettysburg, Pennsylvania, on June 1, 1865, President Abraham Lincoln famously said "we are met on a great battlefield of that [civil] war. We have come to dedicate a portion of that field, as a final resting place for those who here gave their lives that that nation might live. It is altogether fitting and proper that we should do this. But, in a larger sense, we cannot dedicate—we cannot consecrate—we cannot hallow this ground. The brave men, living and dead, who struggled here, have consecrated it, far above our poor power to add or detract. The world will little note, nor long remember what we say here, but it can never forget what they did here."[1]

Standing 120 miles to the east and separated by 158 years in time, President Joe Biden said this in New Castle, Delaware, on May 30, 2021:

Me and my family, we've tried to participate in this event every year because it's an important tradition in the Delaware community. Even last year, in those early dark days of the pandemic, Jill and I didn't want to let Memorial Day pass like every other day. And there was no event here, but we came to lay a wreath at the plaza. It was the first time we did any sort of event since the lockdown had begun in March because we were determined—determined—to honor the fallen, to pay tribute to the women and men who braved every danger, who made the ultimate sacrifice for their country. . . . We must remember the debt we owe those who have paid it, and the families left behind. My heart is torn in half by the grief.[2]

Two presidents commemorating the fallen, two presidents admitting their inadequacies but prevailing nonetheless. Death challenged both mightily; death challenged them equally. But there are differences too. Lincoln's *we*, for example, includes the nation itself; Biden's *we* consists of him and his wife. Lincoln refers to a hallowed ground while Biden references a local plaza. Lincoln mentions a final resting place, Biden an ongoing pandemic. Lincoln catches us up in a grand mission focused on human liberty and national sustenance, while Biden features specifics—a lockdown, a wreath, a holiday, a local tradition. Biden spoke 1,432 words, after which his audience repaired to their respective Memorial Day activities. Lincoln spoke only 265 words, yet they have resounded in the nation's memory. Joe Biden did his job honorably. Abraham Lincoln did his magnificently.

This chapter focuses on one other difference between Lincoln and Biden. The former never refers to himself—not once—in his brief remarks while the latter did so forty-one times in his admittedly longer speech. Biden's self-references were linked to his friendships (General Francis Vavala of the National Guard), to his departed son, Beau, to his prior service as vice president, to meetings he had had with the Chinese premier and the Russian president, to his international travels, and to his duties as commander in chief. More important, though, is what Biden tells us about his interior self, insights that Americans have come to expect from their chief executives. Lincoln gave us nothing this personal, even though he too had lost a son prior to serving as president. Joe Biden, in contrast, opens himself up on a range of topics:

- His personal tragedy: "Hunter lost his dad and I lost my son."
- The sadness of others: "My heart is torn in half by the grief."
- His emotional self: "I know the black hole that it leaves in the middle of your chest."
- Human incapacities: "I know nothing I can say to ease the pain."
- The available bounties: "I know the pride you feel in your loved one."

Personal investment—a sentiment that says "I stand by my remarks and will be open with you"—is a modern indulgence and very much an American indulgence. It contains two related but equal parts: (1) *self-attachment*, whereby speakers link themselves (sometimes irrevocably, sometimes not) to a particular belief system, policy position, or set of actions, and (2) *self-disclosure*, by which speakers reference their own experiences to add existential authority to their remarks. Such personal talk would have seemed untoward, even déclassé, in Lincoln's time, especially if uttered at the gravesites of fallen soldiers. Today, however, solemnity devoid of a personal touch seems a cheat, a denial of what people hold most precious—the other people in their lives.

Brilliant though it is, Lincoln's Gettysburg Address falls short of this modern mandate. Lincoln offers us breadth of thought ("the world will little note, nor long remember, what we say here, but it will never forget what they did here"), but he seals us off from his own experiences, from anything distinctively Lincolnesque. "I am reaching out to all Americans, to their deepest emotions," Lincoln might counter in his own defense; "I choose not to traffic in the ephemeral or the quotidian, and I certainly do not intend to open my spleen in the presence of others." "You need to relax," Joe Biden might counter, "for life moves quickly, and a politics that fails to touch people's feelings is no politics at all." "We live in a world of machines," Biden might observe, "and, as a result, people crave all the flesh and all the blood they can get."

In these ways and more, Sojourner Truth, one of Lincoln's contemporaries, was considerably ahead of her time. A confirmed abolitionist, an unapologetic feminist, a legal activist, and a popular lecturer, Truth's "Ain't I a Woman?" speech made her almost as famous (and as infamous) as Lincoln himself. Unlike Lincoln, though, Truth threw herself into her remarks, making herself uniquely hearable. Although the provenance of her famous speech is still questionable, her rhetorical style makes her quintessentially American:

> That man over there says that women need to be helped into carriages, and lifted over ditches, and to have the best place everywhere. Nobody ever helps me into carriages, or over mud-puddles, or gives me any best place! And ain't I a woman? Look at me! Look at my arm! I have ploughed and planted, and gathered into barns, and no man could head me! And ain't I a woman? I could work as much and eat as much as a man—when I could get it—and bear the lash as well! And ain't I a woman? I have borne thirteen children, and seen most all sold off to slavery, and when I cried out with my mother's grief, none but Jesus heard me! And ain't I a woman?[3]

"Sojourner Truth gave American audiences a way to perceive the human voice as a primary means of personal agency," says Joyce Middleton, and, as a result, she gave the despised others of her day a way of "participating in American democratic political culture."[4] In the argot of her times, Sojourner Truth was a rapscallion and a scallywag, confronting racial and gender stereotypes directly and self-referentially. As we will see in this chapter, making politics personal in these ways can be problematic, but, with apologies to Abraham Lincoln, it is hard to imagine a modern eloquence without such qualities.

OLD ELOQUENCE, NEW ELOQUENCE

In many ways, Patrick Henry was a man out of his time. True, he was governor of Virginia for three terms, represented his constituents at the First Continental Congress, proposed a Stamp Act Revolution, and was appointed secretary of state by President George Washington (an offer he eventually declined). In these ways and more, Henry was part of the nation's young establishment, but he was also irascible, sure of his opinions, and constantly ready to share them. Unlike Thomas Jefferson, says the cultural historian Jay Fliegelman, Henry spoke in a manner that "was unmediated by the writerly mind," reflecting a "pure, untexual" manner; Henry's speech "might disgust in a drawing room," but it gave him "access to the hearts of a popular assembly."[5] While Thomas Jefferson "enumerated" his arguments, Fliegelman claims, Henry flew in the face of everything old and staid and European to connect to a common sensibility. Jefferson, the most brilliant writer among the founders, paid Henry his greatest compliment when he said that Henry "spoke as Homer wrote."[6]

Patrick Henry's brand of oratory was new in the American colonies, but he was not alone. Others of his comrades produced public readings of the Declaration of Independence in villages and hamlets, turning that brave instrument into an active, propulsive event, creating the popular subjectivity needed to transform airy thoughts into an anticipatory, functioning polity. Doing so required Henry's unique style, a style rife with internal conflict: sincerity versus hypocrisy, logic versus rhetoric, stoicism versus sentimentality, words versus sounds, exteriority versus interiority, and, most crucially, self-effacement versus self-assertion.[7] Here, in Henry's words, are the results:

It is in vain, sir, to extenuate the matter. Gentlemen may cry, "Peace! Peace!"—but there is no peace. The war is actually begun! The next gale that sweeps from the north will bring to our ears the clash of resounding arms! Our brethren are already in the field! Why stand we here idle? What is it that gentlemen wish? What would they have? Is life so dear, or peace so sweet, as to be purchased at the price of chains and slavery? Forbid it, Almighty God! I know not what course others may take; but as for me, give me liberty, or give me death![8]

Augustine would not have approved. The great leader, said Augustine, "disregards personal glory and recognizes God, not reason or the soul, as the source of virtue," encouraging the statesperson "to cultivate a sense of himself as a sinner who resolves to extend the pardon he discovers in God to others."[9] Voltaire, too, would have been aghast. "Enthusiasm," he said, was a "contagious disease" that appeals to the lower classes and that too often "breeds fanaticism, factions, and sects" among the populace.[10] Descartes would have disapproved as well, claiming that while "logic communicates ideas," eloquence "only communicates the deep convictions of the speaker" and hence leads only to vainglory.[11]

All of this may be true, Patrick Henry might observe, but a politics of humility won't cut the mustard. Henry understood that the phenomenology of speech and the phenomenology of writing are entirely different. "A book on a table is waiting to be read," says Denis Donoghue, yet "until I take it up and begin to read it, it is external and objective." "But as soon as I start to read it, it becomes an interior object, part of my 'innermost self.' "[12] Human speech exacerbates all of these tendencies. By adding a *person*, by adding *sound*, by adding the *immediacy* of human interaction, it becomes hard to walk away when listening to someone else—because we are happy, because we are angry, because we are just curious. And with someone like Patrick Henry, walking away was impossible.

Table 5.1 lays out the facts of personal investment, with Sojourner Truth and a retiring George Washington setting the pace and with some of the greatest speeches (Lincoln's "house divided," W. E. B. Dubois's "talented tenth") appearing strangely removed. My studies show that the twentieth-century speakers in the Lucas-Medhurst corpus averaged 40 percent more self-references than the classic orators, while speakers in the Campaign Mapping data set exceeded that total by another 35 percent.[13] "Going to the people" during today's campaigns, that is, means wedding person and persona, making the great speeches of the past seem diffident by comparison. The classic orations spoke for all people but for no one in particular, causing audiences to cower before the ideals being

TABLE 5.1 SELF-REFERENCES FOR CLASSIC ORATORY

SPEAKER/SPEECH	SELF-REFERENCES PER PASSAGE
George Washington, Second inaugural	33.33
Sojourner Truth, Ain't I a woman	30.17
George Washington, First inaugural	20.14
Jefferson Davis, Resignation from Senate	19.16
Walt Whitman, Memory of Thomas Paine	14.62
Charles E. Coughlin, Roosevelt or ruin	12.35
Thomas Jefferson, First inaugural	11.34
Patrick Henry, Liberty or death	11.19
George Washington, Farewell to nation	9.77
John C. Calhoun, Slavery as a good	9.39
John Adams, Inaugural	8.40
Abraham Lincoln, First inaugural	8.35
Booker T. Washington, Democracy and education	8.13
John Hancock, Boston massacre	8.13
Jefferson Davis, Inaugural address	6.73
Samuel Adams, American independence	6.09
William Jennings Bryan, Cross of gold	4.26
William Lloyd Garrison, Death of John Brown	4.05
Marcus Garvey, Separate Black nation	3.50
Susan B. Anthony, Women right to vote	3.00
Jonathan Edwards, Sinners in hands of an angry God	2.88
Jane Adams, Why women should vote	2.24
Albert J. Beveridge, Philippine question	2.17
W. E. B. Dubois, Talented tenth	1.80
Elizabeth Cady Stanton, Destructive male	1.60
Abraham Lincoln, House divided	1.14
Frederick Douglass, Free speech	1.00
Abraham Lincoln, Second inaugural	1.00
Elizabeth Cady Stanton, Sentiments and resolutions	0.98
Abraham Lincoln, Gettysburg address	0.00
Mean	**6.24**

championed—courage, liberty, fairness—and the imponderables being mentioned—God, war, death. Who dares stand in the presence of someone like Frederick Douglass?

> No right was deemed by the fathers of the Government more sacred than the right of speech. It was in their eyes, as in the eyes of all thoughtful men, the great moral renovator of society and government. Daniel Webster called it a homebred right, a fireside privilege. Liberty is meaningless where the right to utter one's thoughts and opinions has ceased to exist. That, of all rights, is the dread of tyrants. It is the right which they first of all strike down. They know its power. Thrones, dominions, principalities, and powers, founded in injustice and wrong, are sure to tremble, if men are allowed to reason of righteousness, temperance, and of a judgment to come in their presence. Slavery cannot tolerate free speech. Five years of its exercise would banish the auction block and break every chain in the South. They will have none of it there, for they have the power. But shall it be so here?[14]

Douglass dictates to us here instead of requesting our succor. The facts he alleges are deemed sufficient to stand on their own; they need no embellishment, no details. Douglass towers over us as well. He reveals no personal motivations, no indication of how these matters have affected his life or that of his family. He tells no personal stories, shares no anecdotes. His words travel well across time but Douglass the man, Douglass the great liberator, stays hidden. His is great oratory, but it is not our oratory.

What, then, is ours? Intimacy, or at least the appearance of it. As we see in figure 5.1, politics has gotten considerably more personal over the years.[15] These trends are glacial but persistent. The underlying reasons are many: because personal talk provides self-therapy (Richard Nixon comes to mind) or a celebration of the self (Donald Trump comes to mind); because self-references add boldness to an argument (Jesse Jackson comes to mind); because personal anecdotes introduce an unknown speaker to a national

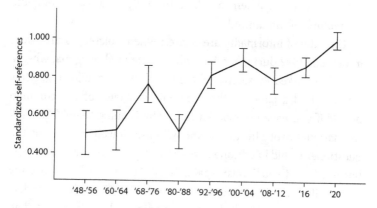

FIGURE 5.1 Self-references in speeches during presidential campaigns

N = 7,825 passages

audience (Ann Richards and Sarah Palin come to mind); because
personal touches endear politicians to their would-be followers
(Ronald Reagan and Bill Clinton come to mind).[16]

As a result, self-references are modernity's bias. Henry David
Thoreau prepared us for this, asking, "What is any man's discourse
to me if I am not sensible of something in it as steady and cheery
as the creak of crickets?" "I take it for granted when I am invited
to lecture," Thoreau continues, "that there is a desire to hear what
I think on some subject . . . and I resolve, accordingly, that I will
give them a strong dose of myself."[17] Thoreau's legacy continues.
There is now something of a curvilinear relationship between self-
references and intimacy. We expect our friends and family members to be open to us, to share their deepest feelings. In this sense,
self-references are a sign of closeness, of trust. But the opposite is
true as well: Those who stand a great distance from us—strangers,
celebrities, authority figures—also intrigue us. We cannot get enough
of them, not because we know them but because we never will.
Relative to them, our reach always exceeds our grasp, so every
tidbit on Facebook or Twitter whets our appetite for more. When
these distant individuals appear before us on television, we study

their every move. When they hide from us, we work to complete the picture left unpainted.

The rules of informality are clearest when violated, as they were in October 1992 during a town hall in Richmond, Virginia, when a questioner asked President George H. W. Bush the following: "How can you find a cure for the economic problems of the common people if you have no experience in what's ailing them?" "I think the national debt affects everybody," Bush bravely began, but the questioner would have none of that: "You, you," he continued, "how has it affected you?" Bush again: "Well, I'm sure it has. I love my grandchildren . . ." Another interruption: "How?" Bush responded, flailing: "I want to think that they're going to be able to afford an education. I think that that's an important part of being a parent."[18]

Bush came to the Richmond debate fortified with fourteen grandchildren, yet none were mentioned, nor were his emotions, nor were his experiences. "Help me with the question and I'll try to answer it," he pleaded, but no help was forthcoming. So Bush proceeded to talk about debt repayment, the impact of recession, the need to stimulate exports, and the demand for better education systems. When he did use self-references, he did so obliquely ("I mean, you've got to care") but then quickly returned to the universal: "Everybody cares if people aren't doing well."

The scholar Henry Day notes that eloquence often occurs when a speaker abandons himself "to the outpouring of thought and feeling with seeming forgetfulness of the minds he is addressing."[19] Kenneth Burke agrees, arguing that "the artist shows his respect for his subject not by laying a wreath at its feet, but by the fullness of his preoccupation with it."[20] On both accounts, Bush failed, hovering above the question rather than pouncing on it—with abandon, with an outpouring of the self. Catherine Langford notes that Bush's real problem was that he constantly borrowed the visions of others, sealing himself off from the issues being discussed.[21]

Sincerity, says Simon Luebke, means that a speaker really believes in something while integrity means that he or she conforms to universally held belief systems.[22] Authenticity, however, differs from both sincerity and integrity. Authenticity is all about the *ownership* of one's thoughts, about "being there" when the roll is called, about performing the attitudes expressed. George H. W. Bush never really understood these distinctions. Bill Clinton, in contrast, sometimes stumbled over this matter of sincerity and Richard Nixon over the matter of integrity, but both left little doubt which team they played for and why.

Personalizing politics is not without its annoyances and, sometimes, its catastrophes. Consider, for example, another presidential debate, that between Donald Trump and Joe Biden in late September 2020, a debate described as "a boxing match" in which Trump jumped "on the ropes, refusing to come down, the referee trying to coax him off, and Joe Biden standing in the middle of the ring with his gloves on and a confused look on his face."[23] Other commentators went elsewhere for their metaphors, looking to the rugby field ("a scrum that hardly represented a contest of ideas"), to urban blight ("hot mess inside a dumpster fire"), to the jejune ("food fights at summer camp"), and to a vulgar sort of theatrical performance ("shit show").[24]

There was plenty of personal investment in the debate for all concerned, with Trump doing a lot of threatening ("If I see tens of thousands of ballots being manipulated, I can't go along with that") and Biden retreating inside himself ("My son, like a lot of people you know at home, he had a drug problem. He's overtaken it. He's fixed it. He's worked on it. And I'm proud of him."). While most observers were disgusted by the proceedings, the *Washington Post*'s Eve Fairbanks was more sanguine. "The candidates actually argued with each other," she observed, instead of engaging "a Kabuki of consecutive, scripted mini-stump speeches." "What's called 'decorum,'" Fairbanks argued, "is, in reality, a rigid, artificially serene format that all but guarantees the candidates show no passion, 'play by the rules,' and don't spar with each other."[25] Here, Fairbanks demonstrates why personal investment has become so central to modern political discourse. Like it or not, voters want to know what they are getting and who is delivering it. They want to know their leaders' personal quirks, their nighttime demons, their inamorata, and their hat sizes. Abraham Lincoln would have been appalled.

THE EXISTENTIAL SELF

All of this self-talk can seem merely strategic, but the philosopher Hannah Arendt argues that the self has always been central to leadership. We only become fully human, says Arendt, when we testify to one another, when we become each other's witnesseses.[26] Ideas can only flourish when we leave the privacy of our own lives and enter the court of public deliberation. Historically, says Arendt, "a man who lived only a private life, who like the slave was not permitted to enter the public realm, or like the barbarian had chosen not to establish such a realm, was not fully human."[27] The word *hero*, she notes, originally did not refer to feats of gallantry but was simply Homer's assignation for those who had participated in the Trojan enterprise, who had shown "a willingness to speak and act," to "begin a story of [their] own."[28]

Arendt tells us what politicians really are: witnesses, deliberators, storytellers, people who live their lives in public and who comment on their lives while living them (think *Meet the Press*, think congressional podcasts). Politicians spend much of their time talking about their motives and prized relationships, but Hannah Arendt has little use for such talk. Political truth can only be found in the *performance* of our beliefs, she says, in *doing* things for one another. "Love, in distinction from friendship," says Arendt, "is killed, or rather extinguished, the moment it is displayed in public."[29] But what politician can resist such displays? What politician can let their motives lie hidden? What politician can let their relationships, their thumping hearts, go unmentioned?

Very few, it turns out, especially in modern times. Table 5.2 lists the twenty-five speakers in the Lucas-Medhurst data set who used the greatest number of self-references. Several themes emerge. Politicians reach inside themselves when *their very selves have been*

TABLE 5.2 MOST SELF-REFERENCES IN TWENTIETH-CENTURY SPEECHES

SPEAKER/SPEECH	SELF-REFERENCES PER PASSAGE
Joseph Welch, No sense of decency	41.02
Anita Hill, Clarence Thomas hearing	38.50
Elizabeth Glaser, DNC address	34.46
Gerald Ford, Taking the oath	33.93
Ted Kennedy, Chappaquiddick	32.57
Richard Nixon, Checkers	29.27
Mary Fisher, A Whisper of AIDS	28.99
John F. Kennedy, Houston Ministerial Assn.	28.24
Gerald Ford, Pardoning Nixon	26.50
Clarence Darrow, Plea for mercy	26.19
Richard Nixon, Resignation address	24.72
Martin Luther King, Been to Mountaintop	24.22
Adlai Stevenson, 1952 DNC acceptance	22.21
Lou Gehrig, Farewell	18.32
Russell Conwell, Acres of Diamonds	17.45
Douglas MacArthur, Thayer Award address	16.87
Eugene Debs, Statement to the Court	15.89
Newton Minow, TV and public interest	15.55
Richard Nixon, Silent majority	14.98
Eugene Debs, The issue	14.96
Hubert Humphrey, 1948 DNC speech	14.11
Ann Richards, DNC keynote	13.47
Elizabeth Gurley Flynn, Smith Act trial	13.06
Geraldine Ferraro, VP acceptance address	12.93
Malcolm X, Confronting white oppression	12.19

questioned (Anita Hill on Clarence Thomas, Ted Kennedy on Chappaquiddick, Richard Nixon on campaign funds and, later, on his removal from office, John Kennedy on his Catholicism, Douglas MacArthur on his reputation); *when a public issue has touched them personally* (Mary Fisher and Elizabeth Glaser on AIDS, Lou Gehrig on ALS, Malcolm X on white oppression, Joseph Welch on communist hunting); *when they have entered the public sphere as comparative unknowns* (Adlai Stevenson, Hubert Humphrey, Gerald Ford, Ann Richards, Gerry Ferraro); and *when they or their clients have been dragged into court* (Eugene Debs, Clarence Darrow, Elizabeth Gurley Flynn). All these cases present an existential crisis of one sort or another. All demand a personal reckoning.

Unsurprisingly, there is a strong statistical relationship between the use of self-references and the discussion of transcendent issues.[30] In the cases cited above, some principle or philosophy or life-and-death circumstance has arisen, so the speakers reach inside and great drama results. The media lavishly cover such speeches, and that was especially true in the later part of the twentieth century. Perhaps more than any other politician, Richard Nixon ignited this explosion. In his speeches, says critic Edwin Black, "Nixon invented a public man" but then went further, stepping back as "he admired his handiwork."[31] Nixon "sought repeatedly to address us directly on the subject of what we should think of him," and, because of that, "his self-indulgence was boundless."[32]

Richard Nixon was indeed complex, but Anita Hill was a quiet professor of law at the University of Oklahoma when President George H. W. Bush proposed Clarence Thomas as a member of the Supreme Court. That nomination proved explosive, in part because of Thomas's ultraconservatism but mostly because of the charges of sexual harassment launched at him by Hill and others. Senate hearings on the Thomas nomination riveted the nation because of its indelicacies: "a high-tech lynching for uppity blacks," "pubic hair on a Coke can," a pornographic film star known as "Long Dong Silver," references to the hyperbolic movie *The Exorcist*, and allegations about Hill's mental stability.

Hill's remarks, on the other hand, were subdued. Although she referred to herself and her experiences constantly during the Senate hearings, she did so in a measured, almost mechanical, way, in sharp contrast to the surrounding pyrotechnics:

- "On one occasion he called me at home and we had an inconsequential conversation."
- "I believed then, as now, that having a social relationship with a person who was supervising my work would be ill-advised."
- "He commented on what I was wearing in terms of whether it made me more or less sexually attractive."
- "In January of 1983, I began looking for another job. I was handicapped because I feared that, if he found out, he might make it difficult for me to find other employment."
- "When I informed him that I was leaving in July, I recall that his response was that now I would no longer have an excuse for not going out with him."[33]

Sorting through Hill's style is not easy. One scholar noted that she "addressed the committee as an impersonal *it* instead of addressing its members as men or senators" while another said that her "character became a façade concealing a profound multiplicity."[34] Hill was forced to become a public-private person, a self you could reach toward but not touch. Despite ranking second out of one hundred speakers on self-references, Hill left the hearing as a known unknown. She was governed during her testimony by the logic of power, says the rhetorical scholar Vanessa Beasley, "dominated by an unknown future employer within an unknowable institution."[35] Her sense of duty made her "present" during the hearings, but her stoicism made her emotionally absent. As a result, Hill's speech had a rare kind of authenticity to it, a speech that violated TV-enforced norms for self-disclosure—be revelatory, be chatty, cry a bit—but that drew her audience in even as it walled them out. There were existential costs in doing so, but Hill's dignity and courage were impressive and remain so to this day.

THE ENTREPRENEURIAL SELF

In addition to its existential complexity, personal investment has a functional component. I find that politicians use considerably more self-references when running for the presidency than when speaking from the Oval Office. That seems obvious, but one must ask "Why?"[36] Why does the presidential self shrink after inauguration day and expand so embarrassingly on the stump? Because governance is about analytics and campaigning about relationships? Because governance is serious and campaigning a farce? If so, why do we want it that way? "It is good to be back in Topkea. I was last here in 2003 when my wife and I took a bus tour . . ." Is this what we want as a nation? Is this the best we can do?

My studies show that Republican campaigners use considerably more self-references than do Democrats. As we see in figure 5.2, that trend began in the Reagan era and has continued to the present day, although Democrats have ratcheted things up in recent years

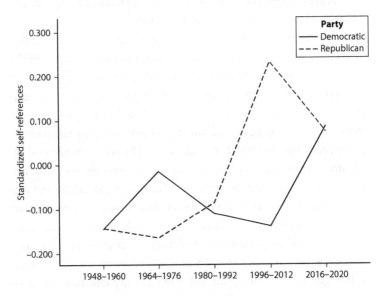

FIGURE 5.2 Self-references over time during campaigns by political party

thanks to Hillary Clinton and Joe Biden and, really, thanks to Donald Trump (who made everything personal). Trump's self-aggrandizing is part of this picture, but so too are his vicious personal attacks: Carly Fiorina ("Look at that face"), Rosie O'Donnell ("very unattractive person inside and out"), Mark Cuban ("dopey"), Joe Biden ("fake president"), and Hillary Clinton ("pathological liar"). Donald Trump turned all rhetoric into a weapon featuring his nighttime musings, his transitory loyalties, his lust for money, and his taste for the jugular.

But Trump may be part of a larger trend. Table 5.3 compares the number of self-references used during campaign speeches with those used in speeches delivered from the Oval Office. The tendency is not quite linear, but recent presidents seem to have forsaken the campaigning-versus-governing distinctions. Donald Trump was obvious in these ways, blowing his accomplishments out of proportion wherever and whenever he spoke. Barack Obama, in contrast, was more traditional: tell them who you are on the campaign trail, tell them what you have done in the Oval Office. Ronald Reagan, on the other hand, made his presidency more personal, turning his natural warmth and aw-shucks demeanor into White House staples, an approach also employed by George W. Bush, Joe Biden, and, with differential effectiveness, by Jimmy Carter. In sum, table 5.3 provides a bit more evidence of what scholars have called the "permanent campaign" in the United States, whereby a sitting chief executive is never not running for reelection.

Presidents also reach more deeply into themselves on special occasions or when the issues at hand are especially troubling. So, for example, Jimmy Carter increased his self-references by 40 percent when addressing the national energy crisis in 1979, although he did so in a rambling, introspective way, inspiring one commentator to liken him to a "presidential Robert Pirsig" (i.e., a Zen philosopher).[37] Ronald Reagan increased his self-references as well when declaring the Soviet Union an "evil empire" in 1983, although he, too, took an odd approach to personalization. The scholar Thomas Goodnight described Reagan's speech as "festooned with stories, jokes,

TABLE 5.3 PRESIDENTIAL FORMALITY LEVELS: CAMPAIGNING VERSUS GOVERNANCE

| | | SELF-REFERENCES | | |
STYLE	SPEAKER	CAMPAIGNING (N = 3,833)	GOVERNANCE (N = 1,412)	CG DIFFERENTIAL
Formal	Kennedy	12.327	4.248	8.079
	Truman	10.929	3.403	7.526
	Eisenhower	10.576	3.524	7.052
	Bush41	15.658	9.348	6.310
	Obama	12.270	6.017	6.253
Colloquial	Ford	16.637	11.239	5.398
	Johnson	10.929	6.065	4.864
	Clinton	12.173	8.620	3.553
	Nixon	11.815	8.442	3.373
	Carter	13.356	10.643	2.713
	Biden *	15.158	12.451	2.707
Solicitous	Bush43	11.482	10.756	0.726
	Reagan	8.855	8.906	−0.051
	Trump	12.933	14.030	−1.097
	Overall	**12.303**	**8.095**	**4.208**

* 2021 ONLY

biblical quotation, and personal revelations which together create an ahistorical, dream-like vision of American and world history."[38]

It was Lyndon Johnson, however, who explored his personal depths most profoundly when endorsing the Voting Rights Act of 1965. Johnson was not a natural public speaker, declared Garth Pauley, so he was "unable to transfer his considerable interpersonal communication skills to the public forum."[39] In March 1965, some doubted LBJ's commitment to civil rights because of his upbringing in the South. To address those concerns, Johnson spoke to a joint session of Congress, attaching himself to everything that warranted an attachment: *existential involvement* ("My first job after college was as a teacher in Cotulla, Texas, in a small Mexican-American school"); *conflicting attitudes* ("I know how difficult it is to reshape the attitudes and the structure of our society"); *genuine oppression* ("I recognize that outside this chamber is the outraged conscience of a nation"); *policy commitments* ("I intend to protect all those rights as long as I am permitted to serve in this office"); *bipartisan openness* ("I came down here to ask you to share this task with me and to share it with the people that we both work for"); and *future possibilities* ("I want to be the president who helped the poor to find their own way and who protected the right of every citizen to vote in every election").[40] This was one of Johnson's greatest speeches, bringing his quintessential self to the fore.

It is hard to know if John Kennedy had a quintessential self. He was a complex man—superbly educated, a subtle thinker, a knowledgeable historian, and a rhetorical artist. Nominally a Roman Catholic, the Harvard-educated Kennedy was not given to matters theological. "Jack is such a poor Catholic," his wife Jackie once complained; "I have never seen him pray aloud," declared his close friend and speechwriter, Ted Sorensen.[41] "If vagueness was thus a theological virtue," one scholar noted, "then John Kennedy certainly had done his divinity homework well."[42]

Kennedy's race for the presidency in 1960 brought these matters to a head. He soon found himself facing the Greater Houston Ministerial Association in September 1960. Although Al Smith, also a Catholic, had run for the highest office in the land in 1928, no Catholic had ever served as chief executive prior to Kennedy, and only one has been elected since that time—Joe Biden in 2020. For many Americans in 1960, Kennedy's Catholicism was considered a "strange and threatening dogma enforced by blindly devoted practitioners of mysterious ritual, with headquarters in a foreign country."[43] Kennedy understood these biases, so he crafted a speech in which he embraced his Catholicism without it being suffocating and embraced his Americanism without it seeming shameless.[44]

Kennedy's speech had the eighth highest number of self-references in the Lucas-Medhurst data set, and it may have won him the 1960 election. During his address, Kennedy directly faced his detractors with a series of "I believe" statements:

- ". . . in an America where the separation of church and state is absolute."
- ". . . in an America that is officially neither Catholic, Protestant nor Jewish."
- ". . . in an America where religious intolerance will someday end."
- ". . . in a president whose views on religion are his own private affair."[45]

Kennedy also mentioned that he had fought in the South Pacific, that his brother had died for the nation, and that he had recently visited the Alamo. But we hear very little of the personal John Kennedy, nor do we hear about his religious experiences. We do, however, hear a clear and detailed summary of what he thought about international Catholicism and where he drew the line between his religion and the duties of the presidency. Throughout the speech, Kennedy's commitment to secularism and pluralism took center stage, thereby creating one of the most personal-impersonal speeches on record.

During the Army-McCarthy hearings in 1954, attorney Joseph Welch took an entirely different approach. Welch studiously avoided the theoretical, cutting through Senator Joe McCarthy's anticommunist, homophobic bafflegab by showing how McCarthy's rhetoric had dehumanized Welch's young client, Fred Fisher. Welch's speech (the highest on self-references in the Lucas-Medhurst corpus) stuck to the known facts, telling the congressional committee who Fred Fisher was and how he lived his life. He then concluded as follows:

I beg your pardon. Let us not assassinate this lad further, Senator. You've done enough. Have you no sense of decency, sir, at long last? Have you left no sense of decency? I'll say it hurts! Senator, I think it hurts you, too, sir. Mr. McCarthy, I will not discuss this further with you. You have sat within six feet of me and could ask—could have asked me about Fred Fisher. You have seen fit to bring it out, and if there is a God in heaven, it will do neither you nor your cause any good. I will not discuss it further. I will not ask Mr. Cohn any more witnesses. You, Mr. Chairman, may, if you will, call the next witness.[46]

Especially in the world of politics, where pontifications so often rule the day, Joe Welch reminds us that politics is a people's science. The critic James Darsey says that Joe McCarthy fashioned "a dark world where things were not always what they seemed to be, a world where evil forces worked behind a veil of secrecy."[47] In contrast to McCarthy's phantasms, says Darsey, Welch was clear, plodding, and obdurate, remaining his own rumpled self so he could touch the souls of others. Welch *inhabited* his remarks, remaining "uncontroversial and ordinary," a devastating counterforce to McCarthy's arrogant dogmatism.[48] Joe Welch: score one for humanity.

THE PROPHETIC SELF

Thus far, we have seen how personal investment draws on speakers' inner reserves and how it can advance their policy agendas. Perhaps the most dramatic use of self-references occurs when a speaker becomes the embodiment of a given cause. This is the voice of the prophet: "Great things lie ahead. I shall lead you." All eras produce prophets, but the twentieth century proved unusually fertile because of the issues at stake—pacifism, anticommunism, civil rights, women's rights, gay rights, environmentalism, Christian evangelism, anti-Semitism, a new internationalism.

Some of the most moving speeches in the Lucas-Medhurst corpus are prophetic in nature. Here, the speakers fully invest themselves in their remarks (as we see in table 5.2), and the results can be dramatic.

Commentaries on their speeches often focus on the political tensions and rhetorical energy thereby produced.

- Eugene Debs on civil liberties (1918): His speeches "bear the marks of the self-taught. Debs' speeches are, in their best moments, vivid, fervent, and touching, at their worst, they are sentimental, gushing, and maudlin . . . a rhetoric unabashed at its own pathos."[49]
- Huey Long on a new populism (1934): "The conflict between the 'people' and the enemy initiates the populist crisis; the corrupted system accelerates it. Good is losing the battle to evil."[50]
- Hubert Humphrey on human rights (1948): Had Humphrey's motion lost, "Truman could have disavowed Humphrey and destroyed his career. That outcome hung in the air as the delegates began to vote."[51]
- Malcolm X on racial injustice (1963): He "did his thinking orally. . . . Malcolm's rhetoric, then, is consummatory rather than instrumental; it fulfills its revolutionary purpose through performance."[52]
- Martin Luther King on his mortality (1968): "The epic hero is someone who has come close to death and who has a special relationship to the divine. [King] asserted his own importance by putting himself in a hypothetical conversation with God."[53]
- Ann Richards on women's roles (1988): "Richards' self-disclosure and self-deprecation celebrate the strength and self-awareness gained through mature introspection. The contents of [her] narrative are experiences peculiar to women."[54]
- Jesse Jackson on civil rights (1988): "Jackson often seemed "out of control and that he would encourage others to lose control. . . . In oral traditions, knowledge is not grounded in statistics or facts; there is no knowledge divorced from human activity or the human life world."[55]

As we see in these remarks, the prophetic voice is never whole, never seamless. Instead, it is experimental, often bearing the unique stamp of its author: Huey Long is demagogic, Hubert Humphrey earnest, Malcolm X hyperbolic, Ann Richards ironic. Prophets are often given to narratives—the long term in the case of Eugene Debs, what happened last week for Jesse Jackson. Prophets are also attracted to dialectic: life and death, the righteous versus the unclean, mystical revelation versus the prevailing facts. The prophet is often a person of superior strength (because they have suffered, because they have triumphed), and the audience is poor and benighted, afraid of change but still attracted to it.[56] Transformation is a constant theme for the prophet who, like Moses of old, knows not when change will occur but that it is nonetheless guaranteed. The prophet sees an upside-down world where the poor are wise and the rich foolish, where men have power and women have righteousness. Above all, the prophet has *lived experiences* that have helped them find the way.

Elizabeth Glaser, a remarkable woman who lost a child to AIDS because of an in utero transfusion and who launched a national movement as a result, brought together all these motifs when speaking to the 1992 Democratic National Convention. "Exactly four years ago my daughter died of AIDS," Glaser began. "She did not survive the Reagan Administration. I am here because my son and I may not survive four more years of leaders who say they care but do nothing. I am in a race with the clock." Here the prophet sets the scene and authorizes what is to come. She quickly moves away from her personal circumstances to more global concerns but always with a personal touch: "I have learned my lesson the hard way, and I know that America has lost her path and is at risk of losing her soul. America wake up: We are all in a struggle between life and death."

The prophet often recounts a time of travail: "When you cry for help and no one listens, you start to lose your hope. I began to lose faith in America. I felt my country was letting me down—and it was. This is not the America I was raised to be proud of." The darkness then deepens: "When I tell most people about HIV, in hopes that they will help and care, I see the look in their eyes: 'It's not my problem,' they're thinking." Solutions are needed, the prophet declares, but the solutions must not be counterfeit: "I go to Washington to the National Institutes of Health and say, 'Show me what you're doing on HIV.' They hate it when I come because I try to tell them how to do it better. But that's why I love being a taxpayer, because it's my money and they must feel accountable."

Prophets always have a bottom line, so Glaser returns to the personal tragedy that called her forth: "My daughter lived seven years, and in her last year, when she couldn't walk or talk, her wisdom shone through. She taught me to love, when all I wanted to do was hate. She taught me to help others, when all I wanted to do was help myself. She taught me to be brave, when all I felt was fear. My daughter and I loved each other with simplicity. America, we can do the same."[57]

Prophets like Elizabeth Glaser are remarkable, seizing upon personal tragedies to advance the human community. Personal investment becomes a stimulus, forcing the prophet out of their privacy to take on the world at large. When doing so, they often come up against long odds. If things were clearer, prophecies would not be needed. But the best of the prophets persist, knowing that the odds are against them, and, in some small way, they are delighted by the challenges. As James Darsey has said, a prophet like Eugene Debs is "marginal in the way that a horse fly is marginal to a horse; his influence was in his sting."[58]

THE SOVEREIGN VOICE

Self-attachment and self-disclosure are not the only ways of demonstrating personal investment. In fact, some would argue that too much self-talk can raise suspicions about a speaker's motives ("Why is she opening up to me?") or their personality ("Are there no limits to his ego?"). Indeed, the electronic media have encouraged politicians to be self-revelatory, thereby creating oversize expectations for them ("How could such a good 'friend' behave so poorly?"). The more we get to know public figures from their appearances on late-night TV, the easier it is to become disappointed with them. The list is a long one: Woody Allen, Bill Clinton, Kanye West, Rudy Giuliani, Sarah Palin, Bill O'Reilly, and, so often and so cringingly, Donald John Trump.

Hyperpersonalization is thus a mixed blessing, but most politicians find it a risk worth taking. Table 5.4 presents the alternative: invest yourself in the issues at hand and impress people with your seriousness of purpose. Fifteen of the twenty-five speakers in table 5.4 are from the first half of the twentieth century, when formality was the norm. Many of the rest spoke either during commemorative moments (when personal reflections would have been untoward) or during wartime. Others spoke during annunciatory moments when supporting some new entitlement. Overall, the speeches in this grouping seem less destined for a given locale and are instead meant for the ages (many, in fact, have become cultural touchstones). "This is not about me," such speakers declare, "but it is most assuredly about us."

Crystal Eastman, an early-twentieth-century feminist, adopted precisely this posture, creating a legacy that is "oddly ambiguous."[59] Indeed, says Amy Aronson, Eastman was "marginal within the institutional narratives of the very movement organizations she helped to found," and "some histories omit her almost entirely. Over time, she has become a strangely elided figure—commemorated, paradoxically, as one of the most neglected feminist leaders in American history."[60] Eastman spoke into the teeth of the dominant perspective, says Aronson, and was "perpetually transgressive," becoming known as "an iconoclast or gadfly within every organization she knew."[61]

My studies show that Eastman spoke in an oracular way (few self-references). She stood apart from her own experiences, speaking as a third party might speak: "Woman does not live by bread alone. What she needs first of all is a free soul." At times Eastman sounds like a sociologist ("[Woman] counts herself as a loyal soldier in the working-class army that is marching to overthrow that system"), and at times she sounds like a soothsayer: "We must institute a revolution in the early training and education of both boys and girls. It must be womanly as well as manly to earn your own living, to stand on your own feet." At yet other times, she sounds like a beat

TABLE 5.4 FEWEST SELF-REFERENCES IN TWENTIETH-CENTURY SPEECHES

SPEAKER/SPEECH	SELF-REFERENCES PER PASSAGE
FDR, Arsenal of Democracy	4.22
Hillary Clinton, Women's Rights Human Rights	4.20
Lyndon Baines Johnson, The Great Society	3.97
Woodrow Wilson, War message	3.88
Woodrow Wilson, First inaugural	3.82
Ronald Reagan, Time for Choosing	3.57
John F. Kennedy, American University commencement	3.54
John F. Kennedy, Inaugural address	3.43
Ronald Reagan, Fortieth anniversary of D-Day	3.43
Eleanor Roosevelt, The Struggle for Human Rights	3.33
Margaret Sanger, Children era	3.25
Mario Cuomo, DNC keynote	3.23
FDR, Pearl Harbor	3.00
FDR, Four Freedoms	2.43
FDR, Commonwealth Club	2.31
Ted Kennedy, Robert Kennedy eulogy	2.22
William Jennings Bryan, Imperialism	2.11
Teddy Roosevelt, Man with a Muckrake	1.71
Cesar Chavez, Mexican-Americans and church	1.50
Crystal Eastman, Female suffrage	1.50
Carrie Chatman Catt, The crisis	1.35
John Lewis, Rights of labor	1.21
Shirley Chisholm, Equal Rights Amendment	1.07
Woodrow Wilson, Fourteen Points	0.33
Carrie Chatman Catt, U.S. Congress address	0.00

reporter who, after surveying the terrain carefully, has seized upon a summary for the Sunday paper: "The average man has a carefully cultivated ignorance about household matters—from what to do with the crumbs to the grocer's telephone number—a sort of cheerful inefficiency which protects him better than the reputation for having a violent temper."[62]

Along these same lines, it is interesting how often Franklin Roosevelt appears in table 5.4 since we associate him with his "fireside chats," which, presumably, were highly informal. But even on the radio, Roosevelt was patrician, mixing the pragmatic with the colloquial but eschewing "rhetorical terms of endearment."[63] According to the political scientist Elvin Lim, Roosevelt's remarks hearkened "back to the platform style of the early twentieth century."[64] He was simultaneously conversational and declamatory, reaching people as a traditional father might reach a traditional child.

- "We well know that we cannot escape danger, or the fear of danger, by crawling into bed and pulling the covers over our heads."
- "Evil forces which have crushed and undermined and corrupted so many others are already within our own gates."
- "No man can tame a tiger into a kitten by stroking it. There can be no appeasement with ruthlessness."
- "Is it a negotiated peace if a gang of outlaws surrounds your community and on threat of extermination makes you pay tribute to save your own skins?"[65]

Yet another governor of New York, Mario Cuomo, took a page out of Roosevelt's book. He was "priestly" like Roosevelt as well as "lawyerly," two professions not known for their intimacy.[66] Even worse, says David Henry, Cuomo was "professorial," frequently intertwining "allusions to literature, philosophical texts, and religious tracts with the facts of the given case."[67] "Quotations from John Donne, the Bible, or John Dos Passos were common in his public speeches," says Henry, in part because Cuomo had an old-school sensibility and in part because he had a writerly sensibility as well.[68]

His magnificent speech at the 1984 Democratic National Convention put all of these qualities on display; as many commentators have noted, Cuomo soared above his audience, asking them to reach higher than do most convention speakers.

Not surprisingly, Cuomo almost never mentioned himself during the first 90 percent of his speech. Instead, he used the first-person plural to exhort his audience to elect Fritz Mondale president. His remarks were pointed and luxuriant, a rare treat for those tired of standard convention speechmaking. Not surprisingly, though, it was the conclusion of Cuomo's speech that became famous. He ended with a narrative (convention speakers often do), but Cuomo's narrative was uncharacteristically personal. Said he:

> [Here is] a story, ladies and gentlemen, that I didn't read in a book or learn in a classroom. I saw it and lived it, like many of you. I watched a small man with thick calluses on both his hands work 15 and 16 hours a day. I saw him once literally bleed from the bottoms of his feet, a man who came here uneducated, alone, unable to speak the language, who taught me all I needed to know about faith and hard work by the simple eloquence of his example. I learned about our kind of democracy from my father. And I learned about our obligation to each other from him and my mother. They asked only for a chance to work and to make the world better for their children and they asked to be protected in those moments when they would not be able to protect themselves. This nation and this nation's government did that for them. . . . And ladies and gentlemen, on January 20, 1985 it will happen again, only on a much, much grander scale.[69]

Mario Cuomo tells us two things here. One is that a speaker can signal personal investment by being well versed in a subject matter, by knowing the facts in depth, by being passionately committed to the arguments being made, and by showing love for the people being addressed. But Cuomo teaches us another lesson as well: that beginning in the mid-twentieth century, personal investment has been most reliably signaled by speakers sharing what is inside them. There is existential risk in doing so, but audiences are often strangely forgiving in such instances, so sharp is their appetite for human engagement in an increasingly anonymous world. For these reasons, a rhetoric of self has become the rhetoric of the day, an outcome that is open to many, conflicting opinions.

CONCLUSION

Richard Nixon was addicted to personal investment. Wherever he looked, wherever he turned, he found himself. During his campaign fund scandal in 1952, when he hovered near political death, Nixon declared himself wrongly accused but smart enough to have married a woman with a good cloth coat and a faithful dog named Checkers. Then came a run for the presidency in his own right in 1960, when he was pitted against a man of "superior arete manifest to all," and that had consigned him, Nixon, to being a man of "concealed arete" whose zeal was "plodding and pedestrian" by contrast.[70] Next came defeat and then resurrection (in 1968). "Patiently and industriously, be brought himself back to political health" by the early 1970s; along the way, he picked up a Silent Majority who also were despised and who, like Nixon, intended to prevail.[71] It was hard being Richard Nixon, and therein lay his joy.

The story continues. Again there were monsters afoot; again there were un-Americans disguised as Americans. But Nixon felt good about his decision to expand the war in Cambodia in 1970 despite its cost. "I would rather be a one-term president," he declared, "and do what I believe was right than to be a two-term president at the cost of seeing America become a second-rate power."[72] War was not war for Nixon; it was a test of wills. Nixon differentiated himself from everyone in his speech on Cambodia—from former presidents, from campus protestors, from moral inferiors who took the easy way out. Nixon was president, but more importantly, the presidency was him.[73]

Nixon's resignation speech produced more of the same. He left office as he had entered it—with complete identification between his job and his inner being ("I have always tried to do what is best for the nation," "I have never been a quitter").[74] Richard Nixon was not an eloquent speaker, but he was a compelling piece of human psychology. More than most politicians, he seemed perfectly comfortable exploring his inner self in public. At times that did him some good, as when it extricated him from political oblivion in 1952, but more often it got in the way—as it had for other presidents— when he could not distinguish between what was in the country's best interest and what made him feel better about himself. Without question, we need our presidents to be invested in their jobs and to explain as fully as possible why they make the decisions they make. But when doing so, they must also keep in mind the pragmatic things that need doing and the transcendent values that should inform their decision making. Personal investment is a fine thing, but it is never enough on its own.

6

POETIC IMAGINATION

Poetry and *politics* should never be used in the same sentence. Poetry, with all its incandescent beauty, is a world apart—two worlds apart—from day-to-day politics. The politician mucks about in pedestrian things while the poet, according to Wallace Stevens, is "the priest of the invisible" and, according to E. B. White, one who "unzips the veil from beauty but does not remove it." "Poetry is ordinary language raised to the Nth power," says Paul Engle. "Poetry is boned with ideas," he continues, "nerved and blooded with emotions, all held together by the delicate, tough skin of words."[1]

Politics is none of those things. The very word *politics* calls up a host of sins—graft, manipulation, double-dealing, expediency—and worse things too—agitation, revolution, bedlam, war. Politics attracts leaders who cannot live a quiet life and who instead promise one thing today, another thing tomorrow, and deliver on neither next week. Look at a politician's bank account and you will find only ready cash. Long-term fiduciaries like Honesty, Trust, Dependability, and Responsibility are nowhere to be found. On its best days, politics is a trauma. Or so it would seem.[2]

Yet poetry and politics are star-crossed lovers who cannot live apart. "If more politicians knew poetry and more poets knew politics," John Fitzgerald Kennedy once said, "I am convinced the world would be a little better place in which to live."[3] Some politicians have heeded Kennedy's call by producing poetry of their own: Jimmy Carter, William Cohen, Vaclav Havel, Winston Churchill, John Milton. Poets, too, have turned to politics: Walt Whitman eulogizing Abraham Lincoln, John Greenleaf Whittier opposing slavery, Robert Duncan critiquing the Vietnam War, Allen Ginsberg attacking middle-class morality, Maya Angelou denouncing racism, and Adrienne Rich decrying patriarchy. All poets, all politicians.

Some have argued that politics is never political until it is "translated" into words. "Culture is an ensemble of texts," anthropologists argue, an ensemble that scholars "strain to read."[4] Until cruelties such as bombings and lynchings are "narrated" for people, argues Michael Silverstein, they cannot galvanize the mind.[5] Similarly, says Robert Brown, it sometimes takes people like Barack Obama to change things through the majesty of their words. "There is much music in presidential campaigns," says Brown, and it is this music, these words and phrases, that reach inside of us.[6] Like Walt Whitman, Obama had "an ear for the poetry of the common, laboring men and women," people unaware of their poetic sensibilities.[7]

Nonsense, say others. Politics deals with what is real, what is needed, and therein lies its majesty. As Max Weber has said, it is the willingness to take on the knottiest problems that redeems politics. Poetry, in contrast, is often thought "pretentious, cryptic, elitist and futile," observes Alex Gallo-Brown. "One needs a master's degree to understand it. It's irrelevant to the larger culture. It makes nothing happen."[8] This last critique—that poetry makes nothing happen—is the cruelest cut of all. Politics may be slow, the argument goes, but things happen when politicians act.

Margaret Chase Smith, formerly a member of the House of Representatives and later a senator from the State of Maine, once said, "I speak as briefly as possible [today] because the issue is too great to be obscured by eloquence."[9] What could the good senator possibly have meant? If brevity is magical, does that make twenty-second commercials works of art? If something is truly important, should it not draw on our very best language skills? Why sideline eloquence when the world is awry?

As it turns out, Senator Smith could not resist the siren song of eloquence. In her most famous speech ("Declaration of Conscience"), a speech given in 1950 that bravely attacked the Communist-hunting Joe McCarthy, a fellow member of the U.S. Senate and a fellow Republican, Smith used twenty-eight distinct metaphors in a fifteen-minute speech, roughly one metaphor for every sixty-five words spoken. In the words of scholar Nathan Crick, Smith performed "the consummate democratic act—that of provoca-tion," the very function that Ralph Waldo Emerson had reserved for eloquence.[10] Smith spoke of her opponent's "bitter words" and "cancerous tentacles" and how he used the "Four Horsemen of Calumny—fear, ignorance, bigotry and smear"—to attack innocent people. She told how fellow politicians had been "mangled" by McCarthy and how the Senate had been turned into a "rendezvous for vilification" via the "tools of totalitarianism."[11] In short, despite her best efforts to foreswear it, Smith turned to eloquence. The issues she cared about left her no other choice.

They never do, and so politicians become poets—at least a bit, at least sometimes. This chapter examines how Smith and the ninety-nine other speakers archived in the Lucas-Medhurst corpus used metaphors to make their cases. Most of these individuals were not "literary people," but they knew that the world was too complicated to depend on literal language alone. The visions they embraced and the passions they felt required something more. They were poets by necessity, not poets by choice, and this chapter explains why.

FUNCTIONS OF METAPHOR

Every use of metaphor is an admission of defeat. We turn to met-aphor when our first drafts are not clear enough, not inspiring enough, not angry enough, not tender enough to say what needs to be said. The eloquent individual, says Emerson, is "inwardly drunk with a certain belief," a belief "that ignites and tears him, and perhaps almost bereaves him of the power of articulation."[12] The image here is of a person stumbling about, needing to say something but unsure how. To choose eloquence is to rescue feelings that would otherwise perish. This happens in three ways.

IMAGINING

Even in the presence of others, we live alone. What another person is feeling, how they are processing the world, can never be known with certitude. In a way, says Cynthia Ozick, "metaphor is the enemy of abstraction," a way of making plain what would otherwise be dim or fuzzy.[13] "We cannot imagine what it is to be someone else," says Ozick, so metaphor becomes a "reciprocal agent," a "universalizing force" that makes it possible "to envision the stranger's heart."[14] By drawing upon the familiar (for example, money) and connecting it to the elusive (for example, fairness), Martin Luther King, Jr. can declare that "the bank of justice is not bankrupt," thereby literalizing the nonliteral for an eminently literal people.[15]

According to Joseph Grady, metaphors make some matters easier to think about (e.g., "human arteries are like water pipes"), thereby becoming a survival tool when, for example, a patient takes blood thinners to "clean out the pipes."[16] Metaphors "break through the noise of chaotic public discourse," says Grady, expanding what we can think about.[17] Perhaps this is what Friedrich Nietzsche meant when declaring that "truth is a mobile army of metaphors" that, after habitual use, become "solid, canonical, and binding to a nation."[18] "Truths are illusions," says Nietzsche, "about which it has been forgotten that they are illusions."[19] So, for example, some Americans see Canadians as "friendly neighbors" while regarding equally proximate Mexicans as "bothersome intruders."

Metaphors are also "adventuresome," says Michael Osborn, giving us new places to travel.[20] So, for example, a nation's history is reimagined from time to time, allowing today's Far Right to discuss "African immigration" in the seventeenth and eighteenth centuries without mentioning the indelicate matter of slavery. An associated danger is imagining new things out of whole cloth. Some metaphors become "lexicalized," says Andrew Goatly, causing their figurative qualities to disappear. So, for example, we forget the ornithological roots of *construction cranes* or, more ominously, the colonizing of *third world* countries by *first world* citizens.[21] Metaphors like these rearrange "the furniture of the mind."[22]

The psychologists Shelly Chaiken and Charles Stangor note that metaphors are "peripheral" way of changing attitudes, as opposed to the "central" route of persuasion traversed by formal arguments.[23] Other social scientists have found that even though metaphors are humble in appearance, they increase both persuasiveness and comprehension when used consistently over time—as, for example, when China is described by Westerners as "the sick man of Asia," "dangerous brainwashers," "ping pong diplomats," or the "butchers of Beijing."[24] If one is deluged with such metaphors, it is hard to imagine other Chinas.

Metaphors also help us imagine the hard-to-imagine. So, for example, a new entity like *Big Data* is framed as a "force of nature" that needs to be controlled (e.g., "a tsunami") or, conversely, a source of nourishment that cannot be resisted (e.g., "the new bacon") or without which the machinery of the world would suddenly grind to a halt (e.g., "the new oil").[25] In an interesting study of four hundred thousand online posts authored by 402 U.S. politicians, researchers found that using metaphorical versus literal framings increased engagement among Facebook users and elicited more emotional reactions as well.[26] All of us, it appears, need help with our imaginations.

DEFINING

People—important people, everyday people—use metaphors to tell others who they are. They do so instinctively, typically unconsciously. "We don't see things as they are," says the anthropologist Danica Škara; "we see things as we are."[27] So, for example, land-based cultures speak of "catfish" even though there is nothing feline about the waters in which they swim. Similarly, "sea lions" are hardly ever seen in an African jungle. The "foot of the mountain" cannot walk toward us and the "eye of the hurricane" cannot return our gaze. By projecting our experiences onto the world, we attest to our own puniness as a species. We are foolish to use metaphors—which is to say, we are human.

Metaphors can be used to define things that resist definition. The human brain, for example, is a wondrous thing, but it has no wiring or silicon chips, so it is hardly a "computer." Too, if the brain has "pathways," they are not like those found in a sylvan glade.[28] To use such metaphors is to admit that we do not know what we are talking about, brains being inordinately complex. But all metaphors have entailments. Labor, for example, sustains human life (planting, reaping, cooking, etc.) but things change when money enters the picture. Then, work can be considered routine ("punching the clock") or punitive ("working for the man"). Labor can also be theological ("corporal works of mercy") or psychological ("working things out"). As George Lakoff and Mark Johnson remind us, "cheap labor" is never cheap because it is always exploitative.[29]

The more often a metaphor is used (and used reflexively), the greater its social influence. Consider, for example, the difference between "machine politics" and "political theater." The former metaphor implies that things happen authoritatively, with the citizen left out of the picture. The latter metaphor is more permissive, with the theatergoer, the citizen, having greater agency.[30] Metaphors, as a result, always have "points of view." Lyndon Johnson, for example, used an equal number of stereotypically female and male metaphors in his informal conversations, thereby projecting his worldview.[31] Johnson was a tough-minded negotiator but he was also a charmer who got his way by building close relationships. Johnson's politicking rarely failed because it never stopped.

Politics reveals itself in interesting ways when we look at the definitional power of metaphors. In a detailed study of interviews conducted with Belgian parliamentarians, for example, Pauline Heyvaert and her colleagues found that *construction* and *battle* metaphors fought for dominance when legislators discussed their jobs, a sign that the bottom line was never out of sight.[32] A more hopeful study of mayoral speeches in the United States found that while female mayors used more *nurturant* metaphors and males more *moral* metaphors, both genders made *industrious* metaphors their second choice, signaling their common commitment to American pragmatism.[33] In another study comparing metaphors used by U.S. and British politicians, Jonathan Charteris-Black found three times more *journey* metaphors, and five times more *creation* images, used in the United States than in the UK.[34] America is still America, that is, where everything that has not yet been invented can still be invented, a country that is still restless, still on the move.

Metaphors keep things in place, says Mary Felstiner, giving us a sense of what is "natural."[35] So, for example, when a polity is described in familial terms—the "brotherhood of man," "founding fathers," "mother country"—the logic of monarchy begins to make sense. If a kingdom is a family, says Felstiner, who could resist having a knowing and benevolent patriarch in charge? Metaphors help us distinguish what is right from what is scandalous.

CHALLENGING

Politics seems innocent when a cheery "sunset provision" is written into a piece of legislation or when one bill becomes a friendly "stalking horse" for another. But things heat up quickly in politics when "poison pill" legislation is passed or when "pork barrel" shenanigans enter the picture. Foreign leaders may be described as "figureheads" overseeing a "puppet government," only to be replaced by one with "star chamber" proclivities. These are not exactly fighting words—they are only metaphors, after all—but they can still land a glancing blow.

Metaphors constantly "cheat" in these ways, arguing that "A is B, but not really."[36] Through such subtleties, says Sally Wyatt, metaphors can "reinforce power structures that serve to exclude groups, organization, or regions."[37] So, for example, something radically new like the internet appears to have been "born innocent," but it can be quickly politicized. The "internet as a superhighway," for example, implies that the state is in charge, while "the internet as a town hall" suggests that citizens are its superintendents. The "internet as a repository" conjures up images of well-mannered librarians running the show, while the "dark internet" is more ominous, with nefarious actors invading our laptops and mobile devices.

The literary scholar Martha Nussbaum claims that the imaginative is always subversive, at least in part. Any novel, says Nussbaum, "tells its readers to notice this and not this, to be active in these ways and not those ways."[38] Like literature generally, metaphors "hold back" their arguments, implying that no argument is being made at all. But metaphors inevitably "narrow" things, making it hard to imagine their alternatives. For example, members of the "Beltway crowd" in Washington, DC typically live inside the beltway, not outside of it, and they rarely behave like members of a mob, dressed to the nines as they are when dining at swanky Georgetown restaurants.

Martha Nussbaum urges us not to "give up on 'fancy' lest we give up on ourselves" and yet it is also true that "fancy" can lead us astray or, worse, create enemies where none are needed.[39] The political scientist Seth Thompson notes, for example, that important legislation was set adrift in the 1990s when the nation's health-care system was described as having "the compassion of the IRS and the efficiency of the Post Office," a metaphor that undermined confidence in three independent branches of government simultaneously.[40] Similarly, Robert Maslem finds that describing capitalism as "predatory" or "bestial" lowers people's faith in politics as a whole.[41] Along these same lines, Andreas Musoff finds that although descriptions of immigrants as "parasites" are routinely decried by the press, such images persist in online blogs.[42]

But do most people really pay attention to metaphors? Does imagery really make a difference? While more work needs to be done on these questions, there is evidence that belligerent metaphors make strong partisans more likely to vote and that highly aggressive people are motivated by metaphors in nonvoting activities as well.[43] The brute fact is that metaphors have been with us since the time of Eden, and that is unlikely to change. The world as we know it will never be large enough, hence metaphor. The thoughts we think will never be precise enough, hence metaphor. The feelings we harbor will never be orderly enough—or consistent enough, or expressible enough—hence metaphor. True, metaphors can encourage people to be clever at the cost of their humanity. But metaphors are central to eloquence and, hence, to making political leaders worthy of our respect. There is much to be said for that.

TYPES OF METAPHOR

This chapter and the one that follows focus exclusively on the hundred speeches anthologized in the Lucas-Medhurst volume. Following the procedures outlined in chapter 3 and limned in chapter 3's text box, I categorized 3,795 metaphors, each of which consisted of two independent axes (e.g., "*taxes* are *hell*"). The speakers in the Lucas-Medhurst corpus produced an identifiable metaphor once every seventy-seven words, a high percentage but explainable by the speeches' notoriety and their historical settings. Quantitatively, Republicans and Democrats used metaphors equally often, as did men and women; speakers used slightly more metaphors in ritualistic versus crisis settings, but the differences were marginal.

There were also no major differences in metaphorical use over time, nor was the speaker's role a determining factor: officeholders (but not all of them) used metaphors heavily, but so too did social activists and political celebrities (although, again, not all of them). William Jennings Bryan used more than a hundred metaphors when decrying imperialism in 1900; Martin Luther King Jr. used roughly the same number when denouncing the Vietnam War sixty-seven years later.

Metaphor, in short, is an equal-opportunity resource. No speaker wishing to have an effect can avoid them entirely, but it is also true that using a metaphor is an idiosyncratic decision. John Kennedy used sixty-two metaphors when speaking to the German people in 1963; Ronald Reagan used only twenty-three metaphors in a similar setting twenty-four years later, even though his speech was four times longer than Kennedy's.

Table 6.1 reports how often the individual metaphorical axes were deployed in the Lucas-Medhurst corpus, with examples. Clearly, some axes were used more than others, but each is hardy, and each has a story to tell. Politics, for example, is ultimately a matter of who will live, who will die, and what happens in between. Politicians intervene in this process by starting wars and ending wars, by increasing health care or reducing it, so *Bodily* metaphors abound. But why all this talk of bodies?

The "body politic" is an ancient phrase. In the twelfth century, the "excellent city resemble[d] the perfect and healthy body," says historian Barbara Rosenwein, "all of whose limbs cooperate to make the life of the animal perfect."[44] For John of Salisbury, the king was the body's head, the priest the soul, the councilors the heart, the eyes and ears the magistrate, the hand the army, and the feet the common people.[45] These are old concepts, silly concepts, yet the talk of bodies persists: dead bodies in Iraq, new bodies in the maternity ward, weary bodies on the nation's farms, endangered bodies on the streets of Chicago, flawless bodies in the Olympics. Alongside each of these bodies stands an aspirational politician.

Caring for the human body is clearly the politician's highest calling, but *Natural* metaphors remind us that the ecosystem constantly intrudes: wildfires in California, tornadoes in New Orleans, floods in Tennessee. We humans struggle with nature, taming it when we can with new erosion practices and colorful solar panels, but nature is also whimsical, so FEMA exists. "The business of America is business," declared Calvin Coolidge, so *Utilitarian* and *Industrious* metaphors also abound, attestations to human ingenuity and, to be fair, human greed. Human labor is a commodity and the built environment a miracle, hence the presence of K-Street lobbyists whenever the nation's legislature is in session.

TABLE 6.1 METAPHORICAL CHOICES IN TWENTIETH-CENTURY SPEECHES

INDIVIDUAL AXIS	N	%	EXAMPLES
Bodily	1,058	13.94%	"Courageous people must stand shoulder to shoulder," "Her son was flesh of her flesh," "I need the hearts and hands of this party," "With thirsty ears I hear the bugles blow," "I've tried to smile through my tears"
Moral	980	12.91%	"Destiny matches reason with principle," "The Nazis justify themselves with pious frauds," "We must turn away from the apostles of bitterness," "I honor the spirit of the Constitution," "Principles are the soul of our party"
Utilitarian	900	11.86%	"They can weigh things more objectively," "Some don't want to rock the boat," "She's become a lamp in the lighthouse," "There are no doors we can't unlock," "There's emotionalism on all sides of the fence"
Diminished	845	11.13%	"Your loss must not paralyze you," "Asia now rejects the shame of subjugation," "We must bear the burden of struggle," "Negroes have been scarred by fear," "The risks will be ashes in our mouths"
Natural	828	10.91%	"They tell you how the cow ate the cabbage," "We know that old dog won't hunt," "I've tried in vain to the sweep back the tide," "We're thrown into a mare's nest," "We must break the silence of the night"

(continued)

TABLE 6.1 *(CONTINUED)*

INDIVIDUAL AXIS	N	%	EXAMPLES
Communal	684	8.97%	"Women have a pleasant partnership with each other," "We must be dedicated to the family of man," "We must marry common sense with compassion," "The people of the world are partners in peace"
Empowered	681	9.01%	"Impeachment is a check on those in power," "Our government has a great majesty," "The nation must recapture its strength," "The answer is a predominance of courage," "The people are the rulers of democracy"
Industrious	605	7.97%	"We must not mortgage our grandchildren's assets," "All of us owe this duty to the Negroes," "Money built your churches," "Unsafe workplaces shouldn't be the price of a job," "The business of our nation goes forward"
Liberating	600	7.91%	"God is the author of our freedom," "There has been a revolution of scientific research," "It is time to write the next chapter," "The genius of man should be unleashed," "We must sing the anthem of freedom"
Conflictual	409	5.39%	"Republicans have fought a war on drugs," "Retaliation is not a winnable fight," "Technology can destroy poverty around the world," "We must wipe out the last traces of bondage," "Soldiers face the bitterness of separation"
Total	**7,590**	**100.0**	

Diminished metaphors appear more frequently than *Empowered* metaphors but not by much—just enough to suggest that the ship of state is constantly unsettled. Politicians traffic in optimism (raucous crowds, gaudy campaign hats), but they are really in the business of hope, a reckoning that a dollar earned today can be lost tomorrow and, as a result, political insurance is needed. One of the great ironies of modern life occurs when politicians attack their own kind. "Politics is a doomed enterprise," the candidate declares, "and only my politics can set matters aright." This is a daft appeal, but there appears to be no other.

Communal and *Liberating* metaphors appear in nearly equal proportions, and that too is a story. Americans seem unable to quench their thirst for freedom. Whether it is the unlicensed AK-47 or the latest all-terrain truck, the lure of the frontier persists. "Getting away from it all," of course, means getting away from one's neighbors, the same folks who ask you to get the latest COVID shot so their kids won't get sick in school. "This is a disease of the unvaccinated," declares the state health director. "Your vaccines are killing my people" comes the response. Politics exists to make communities possible, so constraints are needed—speed limits, lynching laws—as well as their opposites—free speech, foul speech. As a result, many believe that the real problem with America is Americans. Remarkably, the country survives.

The remaining metaphors—*Moral* and *Conflictual*—tell the story of the Great Agon: God and the devil, truth and perdition, Christians and Saracens, heaven and hell. This is heady stuff, but politics is a heady business, so politicians enter the priesthood: twice as many *Moral* as *Conflictual* metaphors. The Lord provides, and Eugene Debs provides as well: "When we have stopped clutching each other's throats, when we have stopped enslaving each other, we will stand together, hands clasped, and be friends. We will be comrades, we will be brothers, and we will begin the march to the grandest civilization the human race has ever known."[46]

The consistency of metaphorical usage—across time, gender, role, party, and setting—tells a cultural story, a way of sounding

American: Yes We Can, Make America Great Again, Build Back Better. There is an emptiness here—a yawning, embarrassing emptiness—but there is pluckiness too. To use a metaphor is to say "I see the world as it is" and "I see the world as it might be." Americans often confuse these assertions, resulting in their own definition of the political project:

> Politics is an enterprise that helps human *bodies* deal with the *natural* world by *empowering* a sometimes-*diminished* people, offering them *community* in a world of *conflict*, *liberating* them from rank *utilitarianism*, and providing *moral* sanction for their *industriousness*.

This is a layered definition, but political rhetoric adds a lightness to it, making it feel natural. The political tropes it generates become a lullaby, a soothing reminder that the nation's fundamental circumstances have not changed, that they cannot change. While this definition may not be uniquely American, it is quintessentially American, opening up the nation to both acclaim and caricature.

The American story takes on greater detail when we examine how the individual components are mingled to make a metaphor a metaphor. That is, when the ten axes described in table 6.1 are combined, forty-five permutations are possible, but eleven constitute more than a third of them. Table 6.2 presents the most common pairings. Even a brief perusal shows the human body implicated in all things—the moral, the communal, the utilitarian, and much else. This is the promise of politics—making the world safe for people even as it liberates and empowers them. We also see that life can be hard, so politicians come to the fore, bringing moral and utilitarian resources to bear on the problems of the day. This all sounds therapeutic, and of course it is. Table 6.2 is filled with palliatives, practical ways of changing people's lives but spiritual and axiological solutions too.

These metaphors show that politics is a prayer: a reflection on what has gone wrong and a request for surcease. People resort to prayer when human remedies prove unworkable, so the *Moral*

TABLE 6.2 MOST COMMON METAPHORICAL PAIRINGS IN TWENTIETH-CENTURY SPEECHES

PAIRED AXES	N	%	EXAMPLES
Bodily-Moral	181	4.77%	"My words gave birth to evil," "Her soul issued a cry of thankfulness," "Only the spirit can save the flesh," "Americans have set our faces against tyranny," "We must not point the finger of judgment," "The Constitution is color-blind"
Natural-Moral	139	3.67%	"Those seeking total power want heaven on earth," "Our movement is now a great Niagara," "Freedom is the fruit of tradition," "They were uprooted by an evil man," "This is the ethic of a wild beast," "He spoke of the sunshine patriot"
Utilitarian-Moral	137	3.62%	"The door of hope should not be closed," "The U.N. Charter is a guiding beacon," "This is a troubling hour of our history," "The cornerstones of religions condemn this," "We could drift on the ship of Reaganomics," "We must tear down racism"
Diminished-Bodily	136	3.60%	"I do not shrink in fear," "Every pulse of his heart was compromised," "Women are bread and butter slaves," "The farmer's limbs are often shackled," "One man's meat is another's poison," "The slum was not born inside of you"
Communal-Bodily	115	3.04%	"We must speak for the common good," "It reflects our whole-hearted support," "The eyes of America are upon you," "Many have taken me by the hand," "We are joined by shared blood," "Cities should serve our hunger for community"
Diminished-Utilitarian	111	2.93%	"Barriers must be broken down," "We must move out of the dark chamber of horrors," "Despotism is a chain of abuses," "Workers are often shown the door," "That mill grounds out the extra poor," "Some children sit at an empty table"

(continued)

TABLE 6.2 *(CONTINUED)*

PAIRED AXES	N	%	EXAMPLES
Diminished-Natural	107	2.81%	"The light we have is imperfect," "Human society is now stationary," "The rich are like a dog in the manger," "There's been an erosion of our conscience," "You can't enjoy the thorns and the thistles," "Negroes live on an island of poverty"
Utilitarian-Bodily	105	2.78%	"We once heard the roar of the cannon," "I wasn't born with a silver spoon in my mouth," "We can't drink from the cup of bitterness," "We must put our shoulders to the wheel," "We need a bureau of the unborn," "Physician heal thyself"
Diminished-Moral	104	2.73%	"Eliminating grief is God's work," "Communism boasts it will bury us," "Progress won't come from stagnant conservatism," "The spirit of faction is dangerous," "Religion in America often divides our loyalties," "The soul of America is at risk"
Empowered-Bodily	101	2.65%	"We must now look with fearless eyes," "The writer has an inexhaustible voice," "Our heroic hearts are strong in will," "The leadership of the U.S. is in good hands," "It's time to do some standing up," "Victory hangs within our grasp"
Liberating-Bodily	97	2.55%	"Steps must be taken to change things," "He can open our hearts," "Moses wrote so clearly a blind man could see it," "We must satisfy our thirst for freedom," "The astronauts had a hunger to explore," "They wield a free hand in decision-making"
Subtotal pairings	**1,333**	**35.1%**	
Total pairings	**3,795**	**100.0%**	

becomes implicated in all things—the *Bodily*, the *Natural*, the *Utilitarian*. Although Eugene Debs can sound a bit antique, one can imagine a "Black Lives Matter" banner hoisted behind him and perhaps a "Me Too" chorus in the vestibule when he spoke:

- "The little children in this [labor] system are robbed of their childhood and in their tender years are seized in the remorseless grasp of Mammon."
- "In very truth, gold is God today and rules with pitiless sway in the affairs of men."
- "Let the people everywhere take heart of hope, for the cross is bending, the midnight is passing, and joy cometh with the morning."
- "While there is a soul in prison, I am not free."[47]

Fifty years later, Bobby Kennedy made the case for freedom to a new generation of South Africans. Reflecting on the new technologies of travel, Kennedy declared that "our new *closeness* is *stripping* away the *false masks*. The *illusion* of differences is the *root* of injustice and of hate and war." "Only *earthbound* man," said Kennedy, "still *clings* to the *dark* and *poisoning superstition* that his world is *bounded* by the nearest *hill*, his universe ends at *river shore*, his common humanity is enclosed in the *tight circle* of those who share his town or his views or the color of his skin."[48]

There is much going on here. Kennedy's metaphors are splintered but brilliantly so, as he links the human senses—the eyes, the hands, the skin, the mouth—to the physical world—the land, the hills, the river, the proximate. Kennedy contrasts South Africa's natural resources—coal, steel, electric power—to its sorry treatment of Black Africans, and he weaves a moral thread throughout his geography lesson. The evils he describes, the topography he mentions, become freighted with meaning: "the road is strewn with many dangers," "a tiny ripple of hope," "only . . . love can climb the hills of the Acropolis," "[raw ambition] is not the road history had marked out for us." Scholars have argued that this was Kennedy's finest speech; if so, that may be because he used material things to take on elusive things—human justice and racial inequality.

Metaphors add color to a person's remarks, but too much color can be confounding, especially in courts of law. Emma Goldman's defense of charges that she had obstructed military draft operations during the lead-up to World War II is a case in point. Perhaps because the case against her was so strong, Goldman threw caution to the winds, accusing the government of having used "a weak and flimsy net for their big catch" and claiming that when "the anglers pulled their heavily laden net ashore, it broke, and all the labor was so much wasted energy." The police, said Goldman, had "the habit of running away or hiding under the bed," turning the case against her into a "farce comedy." The government treated Goldman's office as a "battlefield," as if they were "invading Belgium" to make New York City safe for democracy. Her case was a "tempest in a teapot," Goldman declared, with the district attorney "doctoring" documents, liberty being "watered by the blood of martyrs," people "unscrupulously worshipping at the altar of the Golden Calf," and the "industrial yoke being placed upon the necks of the American people."[49]

The rhetorical scholar Martha Solomon notes that Goldman was habitually given to overstatement, leaving her audience with no "clear path to implementation of the new anarchic order" she championed.[50] One also senses that metaphors became her overseer rather than she theirs. On this score she was not alone. Politics and passion have always been a combustible mixture. Being accused of a federal crime (and of tacitly sponsoring a socialist rebellion) only added to that combustibility. Unlike with Goldman, one always had a sense of where Eugene Debs was headed, even though he too was a political radical and even though he too gave vent to his passions. Idiosyncrasies like these often drive rhetoric, a matter to which we will now turn.

INDIVIDUALITY AND METAPHOR

Metaphors come in all shapes and sizes. Some are colorful, some dull. Some are gorgeous, some frightening. Some metaphors are unique to the individual. The great Louisiana populist, Huey Long, is a case in point. As the rhetorical scholar Joshua Gunn observes, the power of a demagogue like Long "is precisely his ability to deploy and maintain suspicion among his lovers that he may possibly be insincere, that he may have other lovers in play."[51] Long's metaphors often inspired this sort of double feeling.

In his lively speech, "Every Man a King," Long described how some of his constituents had to "start out from scratch" in the hope of getting "a fair shake of the dice." In contrast, more fortunate individuals would "weep and howl for the miseries that had come upon them" even though they basked "in the splendor of sunlight and wealth." There was something systemic about inequality, Long insisted: "The same mill that grinds out the extra rich" was the same mill "that will grind out the extra poor." How to change things? Strip the billionaire's fortunes "down to frying size," said Long, so he can no longer "hide his face to keep from seeing the sunlight."[52] For Long, the root societal tension was between the built environment and the natural environment, between industrial machines and God's green earth. Hence the need for populism.

One of Long's brothers-in-arms, the labor agitator John L. Lewis, ran his metaphors at an even higher pitch. This "blunt, pragmatic fighter," says the scholar Richard Rothman, was "weaned on the treatment of the strike breaker and the blackjack" and hence was well versed in "the savage in-fighting of the vicious labor arena of his day."[53] Not surprisingly, Lewis's metaphors were stark, including "tin hat brigades of goose-stepping vigilantes," public officials "skulking in hallways and closets," and industrialists "driving their knives into labor's defenseless back." These atrocities, said Lewis in 1937, were "annoying to the ears of justice," thereby "adding to the weight of labor's woes."[54] But aren't these mixed metaphors? They are indeed, Lewis might reply, but in a world where some people are unduly privileged and others unduly burdened, only mixed metaphors will do.

Some of the most distinctive uses of metaphor focus on identity rights. The suffragist Carrie Chapman Catt was particularly colorful. Speaking at the turn of the twentieth century, Catt used rhetoric that often seemed barely under control, and that was its brilliance. Catt spoke of "new ideas floating in the air" that needed to be "plucked out of the clouds" and then "seized with vigor." "The woman's hour has struck," she announced, and would soon "give so severe a jolt to organized society that it would vibrate around the world." Catt spoke of institutions being "shocked" by women's empowerment and activists who would "crack the fetters" with which they had been bound. Even the most "adamantine rock gives way under the constant dripping of water," Catt noted; the old, patriarchal foundations would either relent to the "vast volume of water tumbling over its ledge" or be "overgrown with the moss and mold of time."[55] Even today, reading Catt's words leaves one breathless.

In sharp contrast, but equally distinctive, was the speech Mary Fisher gave at the 1992 Republican National Convention when addressing the scourge of AIDS. "Nearly every news story on Fisher's speech," says critic Jennifer McGee, "made note of the fact that, as her speech progressed, the noisy, distracted audience grew still."[56] What silenced them? Fisher's quiet metaphors. She spoke of a "shroud of silence draped over the issue of HIV and AIDS" and of "the lonely gay man sheltering a flickering candle from the cold wind of his family's rejection." She spoke of people killed by ignorance and prejudice and of parents "leaning too long over the bedside of a dying child."[57] She spoke of the good that had gone unheralded, the "prayers of strength" that had been offered, the "stalking disease" confronting the nation, and the "whisper of AIDS" that threatened all. Remarkably, it was Fisher's contemplativeness that made people listen—even at a rowdy political convention.

As these examples show, distinctiveness has many mothers. For Huey Long it was his groundedness, for John Lewis his pugnacity, for Carrie Catt her kinetic spirit, for Mary Fisher her emotional intensity. Like a good bottle of wine, metaphors reflect their terroir, the circumstances attending their birth. We see that in the most controversial speech Martin Luther King Jr. ever gave, a speech at Riverside Church in New York City that was met by "near universal condemnation" as King tried to thread the needle between the goals of the civil rights movement and the nation's involvement in Vietnam.[58]

King's speech is filled with tensions from beginning to end. He had always been fond of *Bodily* and *Natural* metaphors, but this time his metaphors were more anguished. He spoke of conformist thought housed "within one's own bosom," of having a limited "field of moral vision," of "the burnings of my own heart," and of "America's soul being totally poisoned." But King goes further afield as well, addressing the "deadly game" of war, "the wounds of a frail world" fostered by "drugs of hate," and the "smashed hopes at home" resulting from the nation's "vocation of agony" in Vietnam. King's tone is plaintive, and he ends by recalling the "broken cries" he has heard, contributing to "the fierce urgency of now."[59] King explored his own conflicted self here, and the speech is haunting because of that.

Poignancy often results when people's personal experiences clash with larger historical circumstances. Ted Kennedy's address to the 1980 Democratic convention was indeed poignant. Kennedy had tried, and failed, to keep Jimmy Carter from being renominated, and the bruises were still felt (by both Kennedy and Carter) when Kennedy spoke. The resulting speech was both deliberative and therapeutic, says the scholar Steven Depoe, although the Carter campaign called it "vainglorious and opportunistic," a perceived attempt to upset Carter's applecart at the last moment.[60] Nevertheless, Kennedy's speech was interrupted by applause fifty-one times and is remarkably free of rancor. Much of the speech consisted of standard Democratic fare, with Kennedy describing Republicans' frequent "voyages into the past," their "scrap heap of inattention and indifference" to the poor, and the "parade of scapegoats" they constantly summon forth.

But it was Kennedy's conclusion that people remember. In it, he insisted that Democrats not be "shadowed by fear" or succumb to the "counsel of retreat." The tears began to flow when Kennedy reflected on his campaign experiences:

> In closing, let me say a few words to all those that I have met and to all those who have supported me at this convention and across the country. There were hard hours on our journey, and often we sailed

against the wind. But always we kept our rudder true, and there were so many of you who stayed the course and shared our hope. You gave your help; but even more, you gave your hearts. And because of you, this has been a happy campaign. You welcomed Joan, me, and our family into your homes and neighborhoods, your churches, your campuses, your union halls. And when I think back of all the miles and all the months and all the memories, I think of you. And I recall the poet's words, and I say: "What golden friends I had."[61]

The journey Kennedy describes here was, of course, a business trip, a nine-month long attempt to ascend to the highest office in the land by replacing a sitting president from his own party, but it feels like something more, something personal. His *Natural* metaphors feel right for an avid sailor from the shores of Cape Cod, but they also feel right for bringing Democrats aboard—all of them—as they set sail for the fall campaign. There is a simplicity to Kennedy's remarks and a wistfulness too, a sailor who has given his all but whose campaign finally ran aground. His remarks are easy to understand, easy to feel. His metaphors remind us who he was, what made him special.

DECIDING ON METAPHOR

Everyone, consciously or unconsciously, uses metaphors. Some use a great many, some just a few. Figure 6.1 shows how often they were used in the Lucas-Medhurst corpus. Except for a few outliers (notably, Martin Luther King Jr.'s "I Have a Dream" speech), the metaphor density scores are normally distributed.[62] But why use metaphors at all? Because of how we've been raised? Because of habit? Because some of us have an ear for lyricism? Because they suit our personalities?

We tend to think of metaphors as the grand tools of grand persons, but sometimes metaphors reveal our limitations. To the best of our knowledge, for example, the Big Bang made no noise

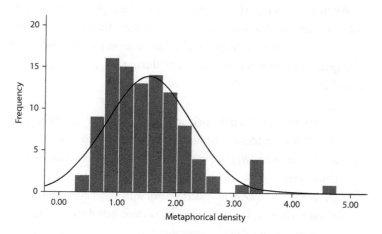

FIGURE 6.1 Distribution of metaphorical density scores by speech

SOURCE: LUCAS-MEDHURST CORPUS, N = 100

(as we think of noise), but the metaphor lets us talk about celestial matters that could not otherwise be discussed. Bob Dylan used to sing that "chaos is a friend of mine," but of course this wasn't true; every Dylan fan knows that Louie Kemp was his BFF. Dylan probably meant that things sometimes get so confusing that we cannot shake them loose. The world sometimes fails us, and metaphor offers a respite.

Some people are drawn to metaphor for complex reasons. One such person was Adlai Stevenson. By Donald Trump standards, a person like Stevenson is unimaginable. A former governor of Illinois, ambassador to the United Nations, and twice the Democratic Party's nominee for president of the United States, Stevenson had "a deep psychopathic fear of [his] own greatness."[63] When Stevenson campaigned, says the rhetorical scholar John Murphy, he often "made the case against himself," presuming that "only those who disdain power are worthy to hold power."[64] As a result, says Murphy, Stevenson's "long sentences, his complex arguments, and his broad vocabulary" signaled his "distance from the ordinary American."[65]

We find the essential Stevenson, says political psychologist Jonathan Cowden, in the speeches he stewed over, sometimes keeping his campaign plane circling the sky "as Adlai edited on and on."[66] The results, though, were striking, as during his 1952 nomination acceptance speech:

- *On the presidency*: "Its potential for good and evil now and in the years of our lives, smother exultation and converts vanity to prayer."
- *On the recent past*: [We] will raise the hearts and hopes of mankind for that distant day when no one rattles a saber, and no one drags a chain."
- *On Republicans*: "[We must reject] a party with a split personality [and] a leader whom we all respect but who has been called upon to minister to a hopeless case of political schizophrenia."
- *On the twentieth century*: "This portal to the golden age mocks the pretensions of individual acumen and ingenuity, for it is a citadel guarded by thick walls of ignorance."
- *On his supporters*: "Help me to do the job in these years of darkness, of doubt, and of crisis which stretch beyond the horizon of tonight's happy vision."[67]

Adlai Stevenson was a wordy fellow. That was his peril, and that was his glory. He was a ruminator, always worried, always questioning. His statements were filled with sights and sounds, but the action occurred outside of himself, with Stevenson—the silent witness—observing from a distance. Even when he was trying to inspire his audience, some alien force was also present (vanity, illness, pretension, darkness, doubt). It was as if Stevenson felt ill-equipped to lead the charge. His metaphors provided his excuse.

The world was no simpler twelve years later, but by this time Ronald Reagan was at the ready. Reagan's speech endorsing Barry Goldwater at the 1964 Republican convention (his debut on the national stage) produced the third highest proportion of metaphors in the Lucas-Medhurst corpus. There was something primitive about Reagan's remarks, something oral, not written.[68] Agency was also present. Unlike Stevenson, Reagan refused to get lost in his own muddle.

The enemy awaited: an "ant heap of totalitarianism," "the schemes of do-gooders," "freedom slipping from our grasp," "fear taking a stand," and you, "while feeding the crocodile, hoping he'll eat you last."

There was no retreat in Reagan, only propulsion. His used metaphors of *motion* ("flying as high as his strength and ability will take him") and *restoration* (of our history, of our freedoms, of individual choice). He and his audience had a "rendezvous with destiny" because, collectively, they were "the last best hope of man on earth." Only the "architects of accommodation" could undermine Americans, and Ronald Reagan had no intention of letting that happen.[69]

Reagan had a gift for metaphor, which is to say, he had a good eye and a good ear. One of the clearest examples was his speech at Pointe du Hoc, France, on the fortieth anniversary of D-Day. Metaphors perform many functions, but their real strength is to help cushion the passage of time. The past, after all, is filled with pain that must be acknowledged. But the past is also past, and the future is not yet here. We pretend that this is not true, that we know what lies ahead, but the future is never ours to command, so we talk among ourselves to gain purchase on what lies ahead.

Confronted by these circumstances, what could Reagan do? He could draw on all the senses, recalling the "terrible shadow" of the war, the "faces of the cliffs" to be climbed, the "roar of the cannon," the "vivid air signed with the honor" of heroes who were "pinned down" as they "hit Juno Beach." Here we find Reagan the dramatist, of which there was none better. We can also find Reagan the ideologue, brandishing the "shield for freedom," remembering the "bitter lessons" of tyranny, calling for the need to "seize the beachhead" of peace with the Soviet Union.[70] Most memorably though, he tells us about "the boys of Pointe du Hoc," the then seventy- and eighty-year-olds seated before him, allowing Reagan to make "the realities of war visually present" as he spoke.[71]

Metaphors, in short, give speakers another chance at life. What has been lost can be resurrected, and forgotten lessons can be learned anew. When roads are closed, metaphors open them up. When time seems short, metaphors add months, years, to our calendars. All of this, of course, depends on the willing suspension of disbelief by the audience involved, and that, in turn, depends on the rhetorical skills of the speaker. Adlai Stevenson on occasion, and Ronald Reagan almost always, rose to the challenge.

In contrast, some speakers resist metaphor. For different reasons, Harry Truman, Stokely Carmichael, and Hillary Clinton used very little imagery in their most heralded speeches, ranking, respectively, eighty-fifth, eightieth, and ninety-fifth among the hundred speakers in the Lucas-Medhurst corpus. For Truman, resisting metaphor was probably a matter of taste. A plainspoken Midwesterner, Truman was, according to the historian Dennis Merrill, a modernist to the core who prized "science, mastery over nature, mass production, mass consumption, and social engineering," especially when compared to the pontifications of rivals like Herbert Hoover.[72] When laying out the Truman Doctrine in March 1947, a doctrine that recommitted the nation to its international responsibilities but foreswore military adventuring, Truman tried to undercut the harsh rhetoric of the American right. The result was a speech that was blunt in style,[73] more local than international in scope,[74] and idealistic but still protectionist.[75] Truman spoke of "stable" economics, "liquidated" commitments, investments to be "safeguarded," and international agreements being "undermined." These are stolid images, the kind of poetry an engineer might fashion.[76] That was perfectly fine with Harry S Truman.

Stokely Carmichael was something else entirely. "He was an actor-showman with a gift for histrionics," says the rhetorical scholar Charles Stewart, but more a philosopher than a poet.[77] Carmichael's basic purpose was to ground his audiences in the lived reality of the urban poor and to translate that experience for white Americans. If he used a metaphor, it was likely to be crude rather than poetic. In his famed address at UC Berkeley in 1966, for example, Carmichael decried phony academics ("intellectual masturbation"), Democratic politics ("the drug of integration"), soldiers who had donned the uniform ("black mercenaries"), and the spoils of internationalism ("blood money"). Mostly, though, Carmichael abandoned imagery to take direct, political shots at nearly everyone: Southern racists, religious missionaries, Lyndon Johnson, the Pepsi Generation, and even the Peace Corps. Carmichael needed no metaphors. He was a hip, brash twenty-five-year-old with a gift for the quip, and he told it like it was:

> I maintain that every civil rights bill in this country was passed for white people, not for black people. . . . I knew that I could vote and that that wasn't a privilege; it was my right. Every time I tried, I was shot, killed or jailed, beaten or economically deprived. So somebody had to write a bill for white people to tell them, "When a black man comes to vote, don't bother him." That bill, again, was for white people, not for black people; so that when you talk about open occupancy, I know I can live anyplace I want to live. It is white people across this country who are incapable of allowing me to live where I want to live. You need a civil rights bill, not me. I know I can live where I want to live.[78]

Hillary Clinton gave a fine speech in Beijing on women's rights in 1995, and she too eschewed metaphor, perhaps because of personality factors (she was more a technocrat than a bard) and because she was speaking about women's rights in an autocratic society.[79] Her resulting speech was called "ambiguous" by some,[80] unemotional by others,[81] and she produced no colorful sound bites. The few metaphors she used were either trite ("common ground," "pressing problems") or banal ("eve of a new millennium," "a message that echoes forth").[82] Mostly, though, she spoke in the first person, first as an American (for women "raising children on the minimum wage, women who can't afford health care") and then as a citizen of the world (for "women who are denied the chance to go to school or see a doctor or own property"). Rather than sailing metaphors aloft, Clinton stayed grounded, producing an honest, American spareness.

Metaphors contribute to eloquence, but not always. They can be unhelpful in situations demanding clarity (as in diplomatic exchanges or during a charged press conference), when precision is required (in scientific treatises or in courts of law), or when ideology would be distracting (in congressional hearings or when speaking to a diverse audience). Calculating the exact cost of using a metaphor is not easy.

EFFECTS OF METAPHOR

Effective use of metaphors is more art than science. Some circumstances call forth powerful images, and others do not. Bureaucracies, for example, inspire more banality than originality, as a speech by Dwight Eisenhower shows us. For a career military man, Eisenhower was a surprisingly good writer—clear, informal, succinct—but his metaphors had no lift to them, perhaps because, as his aides reported, he labored over his drafts excessively.[83] The farewell address he delivered on January 17, 1961, critiquing the military-industrial complex, is a case in point. Ike's speech warned that individual freedoms and group loyalties were equally important but that moving too far in either direction could be dangerous.[84]

Eisenhower used a good number of *motion* metaphors in his talk ("our chartered course toward permanent peace," "the road we wish to travel," "the long lane of history"), but none was memorable and none said precisely where the nation should be headed. His speech was also rife with *balance* metaphors (between public and private responsibilities, between domestic and international challenges, between good and bad judgment), but no vivid examples accompanied his toing and froing. He warned against being "captured" by the nation's elites and of "mortgaging" our grandchildren's futures, but these were trite images devoid of real-world consequences. With a few beguiling exceptions—as when he decried the "insolvent phantom of tomorrow" or when he praised the "proud confederation of mutual trust"—Eisenhower's prose was lifeless.[85]

Richard Nixon's address on November 3, 1969, in which he identified the "silent majority" of Americans supporting his Vietnam policies, was one of his most important speeches. In it, he put his presidency on the line personally, essentially arguing "buy me, buy my war."[86] When making his case, Nixon linked himself to revered presidents (e.g., Woodrow Wilson) but also complained about the mess left by his predecessor, Lyndon Johnson.[87] Nixon's speech was filled with facts, figures, and logistics, but he never reached his audience's inner core. Images like "great stakes" and "breaking the deadlock" were so worn out as to be dismissed upon mention. Other images ("bitter hatred," "reign of terror") had more emotional valence, but they too had been used many times before. Other images like "negotiating front," "exploring avenues," and "wheel of destiny" were little more than Washington-speak.

Nixon's imagery failed literarily, but, more important, it failed existentially. His adoption of off-the-shelf metaphors suggests he was tired—tired of the Democrats in Congress, tired of the hippie protestors on the Washington Mall, tired of the smarmy intellectuals interviewed on the evening news. Nixon made his case, but it was largely a meta-strategic case that failed to address the boots on the ground—the soldiers taking the fight to the North Vietnamese. By the time Nixon spoke, 31,000 young Americans had been killed in Vietnam and 540,000 remained in the country. They deserved better, Nixon said, than to be linked to a "frozen timetable," a "critical juncture," or a "redeemed pledge."[88] Unfortunately, his largely managerial speech did neither them nor himself much honor.

In contrast, what gives metaphors their spark? I see four qualities:

• *Thematic unity*: Vice President Spiro Agnew's attack on the mass media (given ten days after Richard Nixon's Vietnam speech) was arresting in many ways. Agnew "did not speak like a cautious politician issuing inoffensive paeans to motherhood and apple pie," says the journalism scholar Norman Lewis, "but instead saw himself as an intrepid representative for patriotic, law-abiding Americans."[89] Some of Agnew's metaphors were punchy—"horrors of war," "multitude of tongues," "consumers as crusaders"—but it was Agnew's factional metaphors that really hit home. Instead of painting a mural, Agnew produced a cameo featuring the TV establishment: "small band of commentators," "roundtable of critics," "enclosed fraternity," a "privileged sanctuary" that "basked in their own provincialism."[90] Any adult recalling the bullies in the junior-high lunchroom could connect to Agnew's remarks.

• *Emotional accessibility*: Ann Richards, former governor of Texas and a keynoter at the 1988 Democratic National Convention, never met a stranger. Her speech on that occasion was based on "human experience rather than abstract reasoning," say the critics Bonnie Dow and Mari Boor-Tonn,[91] and her trademark humor was disruptive of gender norms, social roles, and traditional power positions.[92] Her speech brought rural Texas culture, along with a pronounced feminist sensibility, to the national spotlight. Humor was her hole card. Richards remembered being "cut down to size" in her youth but also how those "who put on airs" got their comeuppance. She described how the "Baptist pallet" drew family members together on Sunday evenings to discuss how "the cow ate the cabbage" and how her rival, George H. W. Bush, had been born with a "silver foot in his mouth." She also pointed out that Republican politics was "an old dog that won't hunt" in modern times.[93] If you couldn't catch Ann Richard's drift, you just weren't listening.

• *Strong dialectic*: The civil rights leader and minister for the Nation of Islam, Malcolm X, was a galvanizing speaker. He "revealed" rather than "argued," says the rhetorical scholar Robert Terrill, and "he did his thinking orally," quickly jumping from broadside to broadside to fulfill his "revolutionary purpose."[94] Malcolm saw clashes everywhere: Black versus white, Islam versus Christianity, domestic versus international, history versus modernity, Southern history versus Northern entitlement. Even if there were more than two sides to a matter theoretically, Malcolm saw only two sides rhetorically. His resulting metaphors crackled with contrasts: "A time to be cool and a time to be hot," "the thorns" of Americanism versus "its thistles." Malcolm's metaphors inevitably found "the Man" responsible for his people's ills: fanning nationalism "to a high flame," using "tricky logic" to keep his people down, and causing African Americans to "parrot what the man says."[95] There were always two sides to Malcom's coin; both were often counterfeit.

- *Lilting observations*: It was probably unfair of Professors Lucas and Medhurst to include novelist William Faulkner on their list of the hundred greatest speakers. What politician, after all, could compete with the fellow who wrote *The Sound and the Fury*? But Faulkner's speech accepting the Nobel Prize in December 1950 was a "classic statement of humanist affirmation" and "more widely known than anything else Faulkner wrote."[96] Faulkner's is a wandering address, with a "hodge-podge of literary allusions," but also with some strikingly personal observations.[97] Faulkner meditates on the poet's role in a nuclear age. His metaphors pile atop one another as he imagines "the agony and sweat of the human spirit," "the problems of the human heart," and "the ding dong of doom." The poet "labors under a curse," says Faulkner, often achieving "victories without hope" when being presented with "the last red and dying evening." But is there hope? There is, says Faulkner, and the poet must "help man endure by lifting his heart," by becoming "one of the props, the pillars to help him endure and prevail."[98] Here, Faulkner does what poets do best: he opens new doors.

Metaphors tell us so very much. By linking two separate things to make a third, independent thing, metaphors reflect the mind that produced them as well as the people for whom they are intended. Not all metaphors work well, either because they are weary from overuse or because they are simply bizarre. But all of us are trapped by metaphors in one way or another, compelled by their ability to say new things about old matters. Politics, too, needs fresh ways to imagine tomorrow's possibilities. So politics and metaphor are joined at the hip. Really, but not really.

CONCLUSION

Scholars have found that metaphors and other poetic images are more heavily used in formal speeches than in spontaneous remarks.[99] That seems reasonable since formality involves a departure from the routine, creating space to reflect on more enduring truths. People dress differently in formal settings, a sign that they expect something out of the ordinary to happen. Scholars also find more figurative language being used when the press is present.[100] Politicians are always worried that their casual remarks will be recorded for posterity or, worse, for tonight's newscast. Metaphors help during such moments, providing a sense of clarity but leaving room for later emendations.

We need to know more about the effects of metaphor, and scholars are beginning to explore such matters. The linguist Ana Chkhaidza and her colleagues have found, for example, that using *beast* metaphors (versus *virus* metaphors) to describe criminals increases the call for more stringent law enforcement. Similarly, *war* metaphors promote greater concern about climate change than when the problem is portrayed as a *race* against time. More optimistically, when immigration was framed as a *boost* for the economy, it produced less backlash than when described as a *flood* or an *invasion*.[101] Formed as they are out of nothingness, metaphors still create options. As Nathan Crick observes, imaginative writing "uses the language of heaven to represent the possibilities of the earth."[102]

The connection between politics and poetry is strange for many reasons. Politics—the world of nuclear weaponry and COVID-19, of racial discrimination and sexual harassment—abhors the immaterial. Politics has no time for it, no patience for it. Yet the immaterial surrounds us: when people are afraid, when they are without hope, when they feel nobody cares. During such moments, they want things—more money, additional legal franchise, fewer potholes—and politicians address these matters. But money is always limited, asphalt too, so politicians talk their talk, buying time while they reimagine the endgame. Citizens recognize these tactics as tactics, and yet they listen, giving politics another day.

7

ELOQUENCE ASSESSED

H ad he been available, Ralph Waldo Emerson would have been a fine research assistant for this book's project. Emerson, America's premier essayist in the nineteenth century, was also an avid lecturer, a part-time philosopher, and an occasional poet who considered Henry David Thoreau his closest comrade but who also befriended William Wordsworth, Samuel Taylor Coleridge, Thomas Carlyle, Oliver Wendell Holmes, and other leading lights of his era. But it is Emerson's collection of essays, *Society and Solitude*, that particularly recommends him. Here, Emerson ruminates on many things—art, civilization, farming, books, courage, domestic life, success, and old age. Each essay offers piercing observations along with a sly, often winsome, take on life. Ordinary wonders never escape Emerson's attention—a ship at sea converting salt water to fresh water, a child greeting the first snowfall of the year with predictable joy, and how a passion for sudden success can quickly become "rude and puerile."[1]

On matters rhetorical, Emerson had much to say. Wry though he often was, Emerson still had high standards for eloquence, noting that some people have a "small-pot-soon-hot" style of talk that lets their enthusiasms run away with them.[2] Eloquence, Emerson sternly noted, alters "the convictions and habits of years" and therefore requires multiple, distinct talents.[3] Once a listener has encountered eloquence, Emerson noted, "he cannot hide from himself that something has been shown to him . . . which he did not wish to see; and, as he cannot dispose of it, it disposes of him."[4]

Emerson's essay on eloquence in *Society and Solitude* is winding and anecdotal, and he shows no need to measure rhetoric as I have measured it here. I like to think, however, that he would have agreed with my overall conceptual model:

- *On pragmatics*: The eloquent speaker "is a graduate of the plough, and the stub-hoe and the bushwhacker; he knows all the secrets of swamp and snowbank and has nothing to learn of labor or poverty or the rough of farming."[5]
- *On transcendence*: "The highest platform of eloquence is the moral sentiment. . . . It conveys a hint of our eternity when [the listener] feels himself addressed on grounds which will remain when everything else is taken, and which have no trace of time or place or party."[6]
- *On selfhood*: If a speaker "should attempt to instruct the people into that which they already know, he would fail; but by making them wise in that which he knows, he has the advantage of the assembly every moment."[7]
- *On imagery*: "Put the argument into a concrete shape, into an image—some hard phrase, round and solid as a ball, which they see and handle and carry home with them—and the cause is half-won."[8]

Emerson was an Americanist; he knew only the oratory he knew. His model of eloquence, like mine, reflected his life experiences. Although he openly admired Demosthenes, Pericles, Luther, Burke, and Chatham, he repeatedly returned to his utilitarian roots when discussing eloquence, declaring that it "must be grounded in the plainest narrative. Afterwards, it may warm itself until it exhales symbols of every kind and color, speaks only through the most poetic forms; but, first and last, it must still be at bottom a biblical statement of fact."[9] For Emerson, and for me, eloquence is an assemblage, a blending of diverse elements that, when combined, open up listeners to something new and compelling.

In this chapter, I describe what happens when these elements come together. Take, for example, Elizabeth Glaser's brilliant speech at the 1992 Democratic National Convention. Glaser's remarks are stunningly personal, a speech delivered in prime time to a nation of people she did not know. Nonetheless, Glaser wasted no time introducing herself:

> I'm Elizabeth Glaser. Eleven years ago, while giving birth to my first child, I hemorrhaged and was transfused with seven pints of blood. Four years later, I found out that I had been infected with the AIDS virus and had unknowingly passed it to my daughter, Ariel, through my breast milk, and my son, Jake, in utero. Twenty years ago I wanted to be at the Democratic Convention because it was a way to participate in my country. Today, I am here because it's a matter of life and death. Exactly four years ago my daughter died of AIDS. She did not survive the Reagan Administration. I am here because my son and I may not survive four more years of leaders who say they care but do nothing. I am in a race with the clock. This is not about being a Republican or an Independent or a Democrat. It's about the future—for each and every one of us.[10]

Here, Glaser was using her own life to make her argument. She did more than that as well. As we see in figure 7.1, Glaser made her personal investment unmistakable (via a series of "I believe" structures), interweaving them with the three other components of eloquence. Of the hundred great speakers in the Lucas-Medhurst corpus, Glaser ranked number 3 on self-references, number 5 on transcendence, number 32 on pragmatism, and number 24 on metaphorical usage. By standardizing these four scores before combing them, I generated an Eloquence Index for Glaser and the other speakers in the Lucas-Medhurst corpus (she ranked number 4 on Eloquence overall).

In this chapter, I will use the Eloquence Index to distinguish between what a speech does and how it sounds; to separate political

I believe in America, but not with a *leadership of selfishness* and greed—where the wealthy get health care and insurance and the poor don't. Do you know how much **my AIDS care** costs? Over 40,000 dollars a year. Someone without insurance can't afford this. Even the drugs that **I hope will keep me alive** are *out of reach* for others. Is their life any less valuable? Of course not. This is not the America **I was raised** to be proud of—where rich people get care and drugs that poor people can't . . . **I believe** in an America where our *leaders talk straight*. When anyone tells President Bush that the *battle against AIDS* is seriously underfunded, he *juggles* the *numbers* to mislead the public into thinking we're spending twice as much as we really are. While they *play games with numbers*, people are dying.

Pragmatic Appeal

I believe in America, but an America where there is *a light in every home*. A *thousand points of light* just wasn't enough: **My** *house has been dark* for too long. Once every generation, history brings us to an *important crossroads*. Sometimes in life, there is that moment when it's possible to make a change for the better. This is one of those moments. **For me**, this is not politics. This is a *crisis of caring*.

Transcendent Appeal

FIGURE 7.1 Combining the components of eloquence

SOURCE: ELIZABETH GLASER AT THE 1992 DNC CONVENTION

efficacy from rhetorical efficacy (a distinction often overlooked by scholars); to explain why journalists pay more attention to some speeches than to others; and, most important, to shed light on four discernible effects of eloquent speech. Without doubt, it is risky to use quantitative methods to explain something as complex as human language. If doing so can open a door or two, however, the risk seems worth it. This chapter offers my defense of that proposition.

THE LUCAS-MEDHURST STUDY

Just when the twentieth century was becoming a memory, Professors Stephen Lucas of the University of Wisconsin–Madison, and Martin Medhurst of Baylor University did something interesting:

they asked scholars throughout the United States to examine the last hundred years of public discourse and to list the most important speeches produced during that time period. Roughly following procedures employed by the Modern Library when assessing great novels and pieces of nonfiction, in September 1999 Lucas and Medhurst sent questionnaires to 282 communication scholars throughout the United States, asking them, first, to list the twenty-five best speeches of the twentieth century; then, to rate (using a 5-point Likert scale) each of those speeches on "impact" and "artistry"; and, finally, to rank-order the top five speeches on their list.

A total of 137 individuals completed the questionnaire, for a respectable 49.6 percent response rate. Of those respondents, 62.8 percent were men and 37.2 percent women, and 83.5 percent were Caucasian/white. The respondents hailed from forty of the fifty states, and 90 percent were between thirty and sixty-nine years of age. All the respondents were employed at four-year colleges or universities; collectively, they had authored or edited some 430 books and in excess of 2,800 journal articles or book chapters.[11] Generally speaking, the respondents represented the rhetoric and communication field as it was constituted in 1999, a field that has become considerably more diverse since then. Once the survey data were analyzed, a list of the top hundred speeches was issued, and it received considerable press coverage. Subsequently, Oxford University Press published *Words of a Century: The Top 100 American Speeches, 1900-1999*, a volume containing all the speech texts along with wonderfully helpful commentaries prepared by Professors Lucas and Medhurst.

"No adequate history of the United States in the twentieth century can be written," the editors declared, "without regard to the abiding power of the spoken word."[12] The list they produced attests to that proposition, but it also attests to the academy's long-standing (sometimes conflicting) orientation toward liberal, establishmentarian voices. Of the speakers selected for inclusion, 20.7 percent were sitting presidents, 5.2 percent were vice presidents, 18.9 percent were cabinet officers or congressional leaders, 5.2 percent were state or local politicians, and, importantly, 29.3 percent were social activists or labor leaders. The remaining 20.7 percent of the speeches were delivered by attorneys, religious leaders, authors or artists, military officers, and celebrities.

In terms of partisanship, 67.2 percent of the speakers selected were either Democratic politicians or progressive activists, 20.7 percent were Republican officeholders or social conservatives, and the remaining 12.1 percent had no announced political orientation. The conservative speakers not chosen for inclusion were nonetheless impressive, among them deft writers like William F. Buckley, George Will, and Charles Krauthammer; influential politicians such as Arthur Vandenberg, Everett Dirksen, Clare Boothe Luce, Newt Gingrich, and George H. W. Bush; and media-savvy personalities like Billy Graham, Paul Harvey, Fulton Sheen, Jerry Falwell, William Safire, and Bill O'Reilly.

Partisanship aside, it is hard to quibble with those included in *Words of a Century*. Even when viewed in time's rearview mirror, the issues the speakers confronted were daunting: international turmoil resulting from two world wars; vexing domestic issues of poverty, disease, and racial discrimination; the tragedies of Korea and Vietnam; the trials of human rights and the tribulations of gender rights. That so many U.S. leaders issued clarion calls about these matters is—even decades later—profoundly inspiring. *Words of a Century* does not represent all Americans, but it represents some of what is best in Americans.

As impressed as I was with the work of Professors Lucas and Medhurst, something seemed wrong with the survey results. How was it possible, I asked myself, for Joe Welch's brave confrontation with McCarthyism to be ranked 97th out of 100? How could Gerald Ford's gracious oath-taking and pardoning speeches be judged 85th and 94th, respectively? How could Ronald Reagan's moving remarks at the Brandenburg Gate be ranked only 92nd and Lyndon Johnson's heartfelt response to the Kennedy assassination be ranked 96th? But there were more unsettling things as well: Richard Nixon's manipulative "Checkers" speech ranking near the top of the Importance list, at number 6; Douglas MacArthur's self-serving farewell to Congress coming in at number 14; and Robert Kennedy's unremarkable paean to MLK being ranked number 17. How could these things happen? How could the survey respondents have seen the world so differently from me?

I quickly realized that my colleagues were not the problem. They had done exactly what they had been asked to do: use their own, personal criteria to make judgments of rhetorical worthiness. They were told that "impact" could include a speech's short-term or long-term influence on human values, public policies, or national attitudes. "Artistry" was even broader, including how well speakers organized their arguments, how clever were their words and how elegant their gestures, or how responsible a speech was ethically, morally. Broad-based criteria like these—criteria applied individually by 137 different evaluators—necessarily produce considerable "conceptual noise." So, for example, Respondent A may have ranked Martin Luther King's "I Have a Dream" speech number 1 because of his logical case-making while Respondent B may have liked King's metaphors and Respondent C his sonorous voice.

Judged historically, though, the Lucas-Medhurst list makes sense. As one looks at those at the top of the list, one finds revolutionary presidents like John Kennedy and Franklin Roosevelt, compelling social activists like Barbara Jordan and Malcolm X, and authors of far-reaching (and determinative) statements by Douglas MacArthur, Woodrow Wilson, and Theodore Roosevelt. No matter what these individuals might have said, *the fact of their saying it* was undeniably important. Similarly, those at the bottom of the list—people like Margaret Sanger, Shirley Chisholm, Elie Wiesel, and the young John Kerry—no doubt added to the national agenda even though they may not have produced immediate, tangible effects. They may have spoken to their moments in time but not to the moments that lay ahead.

As I thought about these matters, it became clear that I was interested in one thing only—eloquence—while the Lucas-Medhurst project was concerned with many things—history, politics, language, culture, audiences, social change. Lucas and Medhurst were interested in *importance* while I was concerned with how language happens. Then came a second, gnawing, realization: I did not know what eloquence was. Not really, not exactly. I had instincts about it, but I was not literate about it. I certainly could not explain it to a third party.

For example, I was appalled that any survey could have judged Richard Nixon's whining about his dog, his wife, and his bank account (his "Checkers" speech) to be the sixth most impressive speech of modern times. True, that speech preserved Nixon's place on the Republican ticket in 1952, made him a viable presidential candidate in 1960, and an even more powerful force when he ran again for the presidency in 1968. Without Checkers, there would have been no détente with the Soviet Union, no opening toward China. Without Checkers, there would have been no Watergate. So, yes, the Checkers speech was important, even though Mr. Nixon may have been deaf to the music of the English language.

Richard Nixon convinced me that I needed to understand what I did not understand. I had feelings about eloquence, but I did not have clear thoughts about it. I had no model of discourse, no clear way of judging a text. The humanist in me was fascinated by the question of eloquence, but the social scientist in me was appalled by my ignorance. Hence this book.

IMPORTANCE VERSUS ELOQUENCE

Eventually, I was able to document what I knew—that eloquence is the product of *cultural resonance* ("I'm from here: I know what's going on and your values are my values"), *personal investment* ("I stand by my remarks and will be open with you"), and *poetic imagination* ("There are fresh possibilities if we just think a bit differently"). It is, of course, presentist to apply newly developed measures to discourse generated fifty or a hundred years ago. Curiously, though, I found no statistical differences in the Eloquence Index across eras. I also found no differences by gender, no differences by political party, and no differences by genre. Shorter speeches were a bit more eloquent than longer ones (especially very long speeches), but the effect was modest.[13]

Eloquence, in short, is an individual commodity. Some people have it and some do not; some have it on some occasions but not on others. That is, although each of the speakers represented in table 7.1 occasionally scored well on Eloquence, their remarks did not always rank highly. So, for example, John Kennedy's inaugural address ranked number 10 on Eloquence, but his speech at American University (on the possibility of nuclear war) ranked dead last among the one hundred speeches tested. Similarly, FDR's Pearl Harbor speech is supremely eloquent, but his last-minute remarks on economic oligarchism given to the Commonwealth Club in 1932 fared poorly on my measures.

TABLE 7.1 ELOQUENCE SCORES FOR FREQUENTLY INCLUDED SPEAKERS (LUCAS-MEDHURST CORPUS)

SPEAKER	NUMBER OF SPEECHES	MEAN ELOQUENCE INDEX
Martin Luther King Jr.	3	1.20
Lyndon Johnson	4	0.40
Ronald Reagan	6	0.27
John F. Kennedy	6	−0.05
Richard Nixon	4	−0.24
Ted Kennedy	4	−0.48
Franklin D. Roosevelt	6	−0.52
Woodrow Wilson	5	−1.26
Total/mean for selected speeches	38	−0.72
Total/mean for all speeches	100	−0.31

The appendix presents an Eloquence ranking for all the speeches contained in *Words of a Century* and juxtaposes it to the Importance rankings generated in the Lucas-Medhurst study. The table invites controversy, but it presents the facts as I know them. Although Martin Luther King Jr.'s "I Have a Dream" speech ranks number 1 on both measures, there is a low, negative relationship (–.189) between the Importance and Eloquence rankings, suggesting that the two measures tap entirely different things. That is, by knowing a speech's Importance, one has little ability to predict its Eloquence (and vice versa). So, for example, some JFK speeches rate well on both measures—his speech in Berlin, his inaugural address, and his speech to the Houston ministers—but Kennedy's civil rights address in 1963 and his speech on the Cuban missile crisis were judged more Important than Eloquent.

All research methods have their limitations. The Importance score, for example, is the product of many different minds answering the same question, giving it the power of "coincidental observation." On the other hand, we do really not know *why* 137 different scholars made the judgments they made. The Eloquence score, in contrast, is highly reliable, producing the same results time after time, but it is also a quantitative assessment of highly qualitative matters. Can we really understand what words mean when they are taken out of context? Can any measure be trusted that elevates the earnest Geraldine Ferraro over the sainted Eleanor Roosevelt? the workman-like Jimmy Carter over the esteemed Woodrow Wilson? the earthy Ann Richards over the elegant Mario Cuomo?

Why were some speeches deemed more Important than Eloquent? I see four predictors: (1) *annunciatory events*—Barbara Jordan on impeachment, George Marshall on the Marshall Plan; (2) *contro-versial matters*—Ted Kennedy on Chappaquiddick, Emma Goldman on draft resistance; (3) *novel circumstances*—Spiro Agnew on media news, FDR's fireside chat; and (4) *progressive politics*—Malcolm X, Stokely Carmichael, Huey Long, Mario Cuomo. All these speeches were impressive in their own ways, but their moment in history, their encounter with destiny, overrode any stylistic merit they may have had (or not had).

When, in contrast, are some speeches judged more eloquent than important? Again, I see four factors at work: (1) *philosophical statements*—Jimmy Carter on national malaise, Lou Gehrig's fond farewell; (2) *moments of self-risk*: Richard Nixon's dénouement, Anita Hill on the Clarence Thomas nomination; (3) *début events*—Gerald Ford taking the oath of office, Hubert Humphrey putting civil rights on the national agenda; and (4) *moments of high passion*—Ronald Reagan on the anniversary of D-Day, Ted Kennedy at the 1980 DNC convention. It is not as if these speeches were deemed irrelevant when presented; they were not. But in each case, their emotional simplicity cost them the "grandeur" expected of great oratory or, at least, of how great oratory has been judged in times past.

To get some understanding of how the speeches in the Lucas-Medhurst corpus were treated by the nation's press, I used Google's media database to track how much coverage each speech received. From a research angle, the Google repository is not without its problems (in terms of comprehensiveness, consistency, and orderliness), but it helps uncover broad trends. My searches raised as many questions as answers, but statistically the trends were clear: long speeches received more "media hits" than short speeches;[14] female speakers, surprisingly, received more coverage than male speakers;[15] and judicial and ritualistic speeches received considerably more hits than other speech types (e.g., campaign speeches and crisis management remarks).[16]

But here was an especially curious result: a strong, positive correlation (.355) was found between a speech's Eloquence and the media coverage it received. In contrast, there was a modest, but significant, negative relationship (-.200) between how Important a speech was (as judged by survey respondents) and the coverage it received. Given the relatively small sample size, these findings may be artifactual, but they are nonetheless intriguing. At least two explanations are possible: (1) the mass media may have an "ear for eloquence," thereby overreporting products meeting certain rhetorical standards; (2) academics, in contrast, may have an "ear for history," paying more attention to the circumstances surrounding a text than to its rhetorical nuances.

Statistics can get us only so far. The real value of the Eloquence Index is that it invites us to examine discourse more closely, to see how rhetoric operates. Accordingly, the remainder of this chapter will follow the hints provided by the appendix rankings, paying special attention to these Eloquence/Importance inconsistencies. Eloquence looks different when placed under the microscope than when popularly assessed. Eloquence, I argue, is the product of certain specialized configurations of language, but it is also heart and soul and poetry. Eloquence can explain why we react as we do to human speech. We must become its students.

EFFECTS OF ELOQUENCE

Everything that could happen to a person happened to Douglas MacArthur, and his career was distinguished as a result: the youngest major general in American history; awarded the Medal of Honor for his service in the Philippines; commander of the U.S. Army in the Far East; superintendent of West Point; awarded the Distinguished Service Cross and (on seven occasions) the Silver Star; accepted Japan's World War II surrender on September 2, 1945. These things happened because MacArthur made them happen. Other things happened as well: he defied the advice of Dwight Eisenhower about a domestic disturbance in the District of Columbia; he criticized the pacifism of the Roosevelt administration on multiple occasions; he sued two famous journalists (Drew Pearson and Robert S. Allen) for defamation; he openly defied President Harry Truman on Korea and China policy, for which he was relieved of command. Douglas MacArthur never went gently into that good night.

Sometimes MacArthur was eloquent, but not always. In his farewell speech to a joint session of Congress (delivered eight days after he was sacked by Truman), MacArthur detailed his objections to Truman's policies and presented a cogent analysis of international relations before concluding with "Old soldiers never die, they just fade away." MacArthur's speech ranked number 47 on Eloquence, a midrange judgment but one with which others agreed.

- *Richard Rovere (journalist):* "A good deal but not a great deal better than the general run of public prose in the United States today. . . . MacArthur has eloquence of a kind, but it strikes me as a rather coarse eloquence."[17]
- *Dewey Short (member of Congress):* "We saw a great hunk of God in the flesh, and we heard the word of God."[18]
- *Robert Newman (scholar):* "There was nothing in MacArthur of the common touch."[19]
- *William Evjue (editor):* "The climax of Lincoln's greatest speech was a deathless expression of the ideal of democracy. The center of Douglas MacArthur's speech was Douglas MacArthur."[20]
- *Samuel Perry (scholar):* "[MacArthur] constructed the Pacific as his frontier and himself as a frontier hero."[21]

There was another MacArthur, a more chastened MacArthur, who accepted the Thayer Award at West Point one year later and who, this time, spoke of duty, honor, and country. Said he: "Those three hallowed words reverently dictate what you ought to be, what you can be, what you will be. They are your rallying points: to build courage when courage seems to fail; to regain faith when there seems to be little cause for faith; to create hope when hope becomes forlorn." This was a more provisional MacArthur, who acknowledged the cadets' "appetite for adventure" but who also urged them to "stand up in the storm," "to reach into the future," and to drain "deep the chalice of courage." "In the evening of my memory," MacArthur promised, he would remember the "rattle of musketry" and the "scars of war," but, more important, he would hear his soldiers "with thirsty ears" and the "witching melody of faint bugles blowing."[22]

The classicist Christian Kopff called MacArthur's West Point speech "the greatest improvised oration in American literature."[23] The journalist John Gunther admitted that he had "seldom met anybody who gives such a sense of the richness and flexibility of the English language" as MacArthur, who drew "out of it—like Winston Churchill—as out of some inexhaustible reservoir."[24] My measurements show MacArthur's speech to be number 2 on Eloquence, second only to the magisterial Martin Luther King Jr. Unlike in MacArthur's address to Congress, there is a thematic humility in his West Point speech as he opens himself up to his own emotions and to the still developing emotions of the cadets he addressed. Regardless of one's politics, it is hard not to get caught up in MacArthur's speech.

Eloquence, I shall argue, does four things that run-of-the-mill speech does not. Eloquence is in some way *definitive*, giving one the sense that the most important issues to be discussed have been discussed. An eloquent speech is also *righteous*. It goes beyond the prosaic, beyond the transactional, to lay bare the moral issues at stake. An eloquent speaker is also *available*, personally disclosive, while being sympathetic to the audience's own feelings and experiences. Finally, an eloquent speech is *expansive*, opening up a topic in new ways so the future feels less daunting. MacArthur's duty, honor, and country speech had all of these qualities and more, providing us with a road map to the terrain of eloquence.

DEFINITIVE

FDR's speech after the Pearl Harbor attack (#16 on Eloquence) and Ursula Le Guin's 1983 commencement address at Mills College (#15) were definitive but in such different ways. Roosevelt's remarks said all that needed to be said and did so in a spare, almost mechanical way. His address, says Herbert Carson, was devoid of fine distinctions and empty packets of idealism. It was a forthright talk, "reassuring because of its emotional tone" but devoid of convoluted reasoning.[25] The enemy was at hand:

> Last night, Japanese forces attacked Hong Kong. Last night, Japanese forces attacked Guam. Last night, Japanese forces attacked the

Philippine Islands. Last night, the Japanese attacked Wake Island. And this morning, the Japanese attacked Midway Island. Japan has, therefore, undertaken a surprise offensive extending throughout the Pacific area. The facts of yesterday and today speak for themselves.[26]

Roosevelt's remarks were specific, immediate. He referred not to an *air force*, says critic Herman Stelzner, but to *air squadrons*, "a sharper, definable form" that provides an "image of small groups, of well-defined patterns in the total mass, of tightly knit units sweeping in and out over the target."[27] Angry though Roosevelt was, says Stelzner, there was also a formality in his remarks, a signal "that the United States respects the conventions of diplomacy even when confronted by dastardly actions against the accepted conventions."[28] Roosevelt did not muse in his speech; his thinking was done, his language decisive.

Forty years later, in a pristine setting, the science fiction writer Ursula Le Guin declared a different kind of war, a war against patriarchy. Speaking to an all-female student body, Le Guin observed that "there is no more subversive act than the act of writing from a woman's experience of life using a woman's judgment." To ensure that she could not be misunderstood, says the rhetorical scholar Cindy Griffin, Le Guin blurred "the distinction between public and private knowledge,"[29] speaking in everyday terms, women's terms:

So what I hope for you is that you live there not as prisoners, ashamed of being women, consenting captives of a psychopathic social system, but as natives. That you will be at home there, keep house there, be your own mistress, with a room of your own. That you will do your work there, whatever you're good at, art or science or tech or running a company or sweeping under the beds, and when they tell you that it's second-class work because a woman is doing it, I hope you tell them to go to hell and while they're doing it to give you equal pay for equal time. I hope you live without the need to dominate, and without the need to be dominated. I hope you are never victims, but I hope you have no power over other people. And when you fail, and are defeated, and in pain, and in the dark, then I hope you will remember that darkness is your country, where you live, where no wars are fought and no wars are won, but where the future is.[30]

The contrast between Roosevelt and Le Guin could not be starker, yet both said what needed to be said. Roosevelt painted in black and white. Le Guin was more philosophical but also sensitive to coloration: "darkness is your country," "put the mask on," "valley of the shadow." She, like Roosevelt, also spoke of war, but she did so poetically: "words of power," "battle of life," "captives of a psychopathic social system," "a place of exile." Le Guin distinguished between the airy world of men—where wars can be made out of nothing—and the grounded world of women "where human beings grow human souls."

If direct language leads to eloquence, what leads away from it? I see three sets of circumstances: (1) the prolixity of legal proceedings, (2) the agonistic style of international affairs, and (3) the ambiguity dogging social activism. Take, for example, the remarks Barbara Jordan made during the Nixon impeachment proceedings in July 1974. Jordan was never a stylist, but she had a fine mind and easily made herself understood. Law, on the other hand, is the enemy of beauty. Jordan's speech (#72 on Eloquence) is low on pragmatics, low on transcendence, low on self-disclosure, and low on metaphorical usage, far removed from her famed 1976 address at the Democratic National Convention (#30 on Eloquence).

Jordan's sentences were impossibly long—overfilled with qualifications, subordinate clauses, and aimless hypotheticals: "It is wrong, I suggest, it is a misreading of the Constitution, for any member here to assert that for a member to vote for an article of impeachment means that that member must be convinced that the President should be removed from office." Jordan uses eight prepositional phrases here, some nestled inside others. The passive voice, too, is the enemy of clarity, and Jordan used it heavily, adding still more prepositional phrases: "This morning, in a discussion of the evidence, we were told that the evidence which purports to support the allegations of misuse of the CIA by the President is thin."[31]

Jordan's speech was ranked number 13 on Importance by the survey respondents, and it was indeed important. Her language, however, was labyrinthine at best.[32]

By their very nature, international relations are complex, and that can get in the way of eloquence. George Marshall's description of the European Recovery Program in June 1947 (#73 on Eloquence), for example, was a dry, State Department–infected text doomed from the start. For the Marshall Plan to be passed by Congress (thereby providing aid to Turkey and Greece after World War II), it had to stir up the juices of anticommunists. But to be consistent with President Truman's more moderate rhetoric, it had to sound reasonably progressive lest it foment global tensions.[33] The result was an ambivalent speech containing nothing for the ages.

It is hard to imagine John Kennedy being anything but eloquent, but his speech at American University in June 1963 on the danger of nuclear confrontation was not one of his best. The speech provided few specifics, often resorting to truisms: "Our problems are man-made. Therefore, they can be solved by man and man can be as big as he wants." Kennedy offered no bold call for the future but simply said what everyone already knew: "Peace need not be impracticable, and war need not be inevitable." To be fair, Kennedy was confronting the eternal dilemma of international affairs: discuss only what you can control, and remember that you don't control very much. The result was offering with one hand while retrieving with the other: "So let us not be blind to our differences but let us also direct attention to our common interests and the means by which those differences can be resolved."

Although Kennedy speech ranked number 100 on Eloquence, it ranked number 37 on Importance, no doubt because *something* had to be said about growing U.S./Soviet tensions. Kennedy was "trying to transcend the typical rhetoric of the Cold War," said James Kimble, and according to Denise Bostdorff and Shawna Ferris, he was also making "a clear effort to refrain from assigning blame directly to the Soviet government."[34] Given these conflicting stage directions, it is little wonder that Kennedy came up short.

Law and diplomacy have long been stumbling blocks to eloquence. Movement activism can also be tricky. An activist must choose between being clear (thereby buoying up one's supporters and antagonizing one's detractors) and being obscure (hence disappointing one's supporters in an effort to mollify one's opponents). Mario Savio's speech on students' rights delivered at U.C. Berkeley in December 1964 confronted this dilemma. Savio believed that political success was the product of radical ideas plus negotiating skills, says Theodore Windt, but, given that goal, precisely what does one say?[35] Savio's speech (#84 on Eloquence) couldn't find a happy midpoint, resulting in an esoteric discussion of students' rights. Savio focused "less on specific policies and concrete enemies," says Dominic Manthey, "than on the broader requirements of personal fulfillment."[36]

The rhetorical scholar Richard Gregg has noted that, for a variety of reasons, "a person may choose to address himself" when speaking in public.[37] "To know of the existence of one's selfhood," says Gregg, "there must be not only a feeling of being noticed, of being attended to, but a perception of being able to control at least a portion of the situations in which one finds" oneself.[38] That seems to have been Mario Savio's preference as well. When speaking of the "political machine" that was subverting student radicalism, Savio observed:

> There's a time when the operation of the machine becomes so odious, makes you so sick at heart that you can't take part! You can't even passively take part! And you've got to put your bodies upon the gears and upon the wheels, upon the levers, upon all the apparatus— and you've got to make it stop! And you've got to indicate to the people who run it, to the people who own it—that unless you're free the machine will be prevented from working at all!![39]

Without question, Savio's speech "felt right" to many of his Berkeley supporters. But politics, as Max Weber reminds us, "is a strong and slow boring of hard boards." Savio's speech was short on details and short, too, on a set of overarching beliefs that could tie the student movement together. Everyone was riled up, everyone was fed up, when Savio spoke, but it would take more time, more voices, and, sadly, deeper involvement in Vietnam before the student movement could make its case definitively.

RIGHTEOUS

For many Americans, the word *righteous* leaves a bad taste in the mouth. It smacks of something imperious. Even worse, it smacks of something old, of hellfire and damnation. But the sound of righteousness has never really left the American shores. Congressional member Rashida Tlaib has righteousness in her throat, as does Senator Ted Cruz, as do the anti-vaxxers and the climate doomsayers. They all know sinfulness when they see it; they all know the need for repentance.

There exists a kinder and gentler righteousness, however, one that treats our failings as inevitable and that celebrates our capacity to do better. The righteous speaker is the opposite of the technocrat, who looks for externalities—money, machines, work routines—to solve human problems. In contrast, the righteous speaker looks to our moral priorities, our emotional capacities, and our ethical assumptions to set things right.

Barbara Jordan knew the language of righteousness. When delivering her speech to the 1976 Democratic National Convention (#30 on Eloquence), Jordan spoke in the aftermath of Vietnam, Watergate, and decades of institutional racism. She mentioned those exigences in passing but spent most of her time arguing that "the American dream need not forever be deferred." "I, Barbara Jordan, am a keynote speaker," she noted with a sense of incredulity, and isn't that a "grand distinction"? Jordan's speech, she declared, would not be an occasion to bash Republicans and lionize Democrats. Doing so would only point us away from the "spirit of harmony" the nation needed to survive. We must focus instead, Jordan declared, on beliefs "etched in the national conscience" and prepare ourselves "to suffer the discomfort of change." The language Jordan used had a Judeo-Christian ring to it—"the people of America sit in judgment," "people "bound together by common spirit," people who must not "blaspheme our political heritage"—but it was not a jeremiad.[40] It was instead, says Brian Kaylor, a "covenant" speech that substituted mutuality for hierarchy.[41]

Jordan's was not a brilliant speech. It had a lawyerly quality—logical for a former champion debater and career legislator. While she had gravitas, her rhetorical reach was limited. Jesse Jackson was altogether different. Jackson was an activist, a preacher, and a media personality; his emotions were constantly available for inspection. As a result, his keynote at the 1984 DNC convention (#22 on Eloquence) contrasts sharply with Jordan's. Politically, Jackson was a Southern populist who attacked big business and who championed family values. But he also stressed self-help and self-respect, which distinguished him from today's Left.[42] Mostly, though, Jackson was a rhetorical animal. Words were his magic.

And the Bible was his go-to resource. He tapped the Old Testament ("cannot afford to lose our way," "lead us out of the crisis," "bound by shared blood") as well as the New Testament ("we must watch for false prophecy," "a revival of the spirit," "redeem each other and move on"). Jackson also loved metaphors, which frequently ran away with him.

- *Natural things*: "confusion is in the air," "rainbow coalition," "sun setting in life," "fruit we must bear," "my grape turned into a raisin," "struggle with the crosswinds"
- *Mechanical things*: "skyrocketing interest rates," "linchpin of progressive politics," "danger index has risen," "truth is magnetic," "short-circuit voting rights"
- *Spiritual things*: "vote of conscience," "lose our souls," "raise up truth," "suffering breeds character," "character breeds faith," "moral higher ground"
- *Corrective things*: "heal some wounds" "resilient enough to bounce," "smile through your tears," "make room for new wine," "slum is not born in you"

- *Disruptive things*: "hard-fought battles," "gunboat diplomacy," "nuclear standoff," "fractured state," "locked out of Congress"
- *Community things*: "American quilt," "solid foundation," "play the game," "the team that got us here"[43]

Categorizing Jackson's metaphors like this is misleading. In reality, Jesse Jackson was never that tidy. It was often hard to know where he was going in his speeches or where he had been. Each image built upon its predecessor but in an indeterminate way. About halfway through his remarks, for example, Jackson launched into a detailed policy discussion complete with facts and figures and then, just as suddenly, returned to his moral exegesis. One didn't listen to Jackson's speech; one careened through it.[44]

Jackson's speech had no "economy of style," no suturing to make the manuscript whole. Instead, he let the Lord of Spontaneity guide him. To modern ears, the effect was exhilarating. Woodrow Wilson was another matter entirely. President of Princeton University and president of the United States though he was, Wilson consistently ranked poorly on my measures of eloquence. Why?

Rhetorically, Wilson's presidency began poorly and never really recovered. His inaugural addressed ranked number 78 on Eloquence even though Wilson had resolved to speak directly to the people, according to Jedediah Purdy.[45] Remarkably, though, Wilson's experiment contained few self-references. "I am naturally extremely reserved," Wilson once remarked, "and I rarely consult anybody."[46] Wilson was "solitary, aloof, cold, dictatorial," says the rhetorical scholar Robert Oliver; in addition, "the no-less-damning adjective *academic* has been freely applied to him."[47] The professorial Wilson sounded like this:

We have squandered a great part of what we might have used, and have not stopped to conserve the exceeding bounty of nature, without which our genius for enterprise would have been worthless and impotent, scorning to be careful, shamefully prodigal as well as admirably efficient. We have been proud of our industrial achievements, but we have not hitherto stopped thoughtfully enough to count the human cost, the cost of lives snuffed out, of energies overtaxed and broken, the fearful physical and spiritual cost to the men and women and children upon whom the dead weight and burden of it all has fallen pitilessly the years through. The groans and agony of it all had not yet reached our ears, the solemn, moving undertone of our life, coming up out of the mines and factories, and out of every home where the struggle had its intimate and familiar seat.[48]

What we find here is excessive wordiness, with each sentence containing multiple clauses and with broad generalizations crowding out clear, concrete examples. Although Wilson comes across here as ecologically sensitive (and rather prescient in that regard), one finds no miners, no factory workers, and no homemakers whose lives would be disrupted by the technological determinism he decries. With Wilson, people become a backdrop, gray and lifeless. In Jeffrey Tulis's words, he fails to "articulate a picture of the future and impel a populace toward it."[49]

My data show that when pragmatics were called for, Wilson was too transcendent, and when compelling images were needed, Wilson became dull and plodding. Wilson's most precious invention, the League of Nations, especially fell victim to these tendencies. His campaign for the League was, according to Sean Cashman, "a forlorn attempt" mostly because, according to William S. White, he "could not make magic with his words."[50] Wilson had an especially hard time capturing a sense of righteousness, of "bridging the gap between the spiritual and the secular."[51] He began by drawing on the nation's civil religion to give the League its needed moral compass. When that failed, he switched to raw pragmatism, taking on his congressional opponents directly (sometimes by name), thus forsaking the transcendent credits he had amassed.

During his campaign for the League, says Michael Hogan, Wilson drifted toward demagoguery, striking "a defiant prose" and ultimately resorting to "maudlin emotionalism."[52] In effect, says Hogan,

Wilson claimed that "the boys who had died in Europe died for the League of Nations and to reject the League now would not only diminish their sacrifice but also tarnish their memory."[53] Nonetheless, Wilson barnstormed the country, presenting three dozen speeches in less than a month. The two speeches on the League contained in *Words of a Century* are his best, in Des Moines in early September 1919, and his last, in Pueblo, Colorado three weeks later. They rank, respectively, numbers 61 and 56 on Eloquence, a modest return on his investment and one that left him in poor health at the end of his tour.

His Pueblo speech is the most tortured. His political enemies, Wilson declared, were essentially plunging a dagger "into the vitals of the Republic" by attacking the proposed League of Nations. Those who opposed him were "enemies of the Republic" who had "sympathy with foreign nations." The League promised "a great sweep of practical justice" and the elevation of humanity," an outcome ensuring that "the moral forces of the world are mobilized." The League, Wilson believed, would give "the great voiceless multitude" in India political influence for the first time and the people of China would, finally, be afforded "a standing before the jury of the world." There is "no middle course" but to endorse the League, Wilson declared, and then, at the very end of his speech, he got to a place where he should have begun—with the sound of righteousness:

My clients are the children; my clients are the next generation. They do not know what promises and bonds I undertook when I ordered the armies of the United States to the soil of France, but I know, and I intend to redeem my pledges to the children; they shall not be sent upon a similar errand. Again and again, my fellow citizens, mothers who lost their sons in France have come to me and, taking my hand, have shed tears upon it not only, but they added, "God bless you, Mr. President!" Why, my fellow citizens, should they pray God to bless me? I advised the Congress of the United States to create the situation that led to the death of their sons. I ordered their sons overseas. I consented to their sons being put in the most difficult parts of the battle line, where death was certain, as in the impenetrable difficulties of the forest of Argonne. Why should they weep upon my hand and call down the blessings of God upon me? Because they believe that their boys died for something that vastly transcends any of the immediate and palpable objects of the war. They believe, and they rightly believe, that their sons saved the liberty of the world.[54]

Wilson had finally found his argument: abstract geopolitics did not demand a League of Nations; everyday Americans did. Here was a personal Wilson, opening himself up to those who stood before him. Here Wilson tells us what it feels like to be a president—to send soldiers off to war and to receive the returning caskets. This was a rare Wilson, but the best Wilson. Righteousness at last.

AVAILABLE

When people sit face to face across a table having coffee, they become available in a special way. Their physical closeness creates intimacy, as does their eye contact. They speak spontaneously, giving each other permission to discuss whatever comes to mind. Interactions like these are treasured because they are ordinary, private. There are risks in the openness they encourage, but the risks are reciprocal.

Public interactions are different. People are physically removed from one another, so listeners' attention can wander without the speaker knowing it. Television brings things closer, but even then it is all video pixels, not flesh-and-blood people. Sometimes, though, public rhetoric takes a private turn, as when Ted Kennedy eulogized his brother Bobby, or when George W. Bush stood amid the rubble of 9/11. On those occasions, Kennedy and Bush became "present" in a special way. They opened their doors, and we opened ours in return. Such moments sometimes inspire eloquence. Five factors explain why.

- *Humility*: Lou Gehrig, the Iron Horse of the New York Yankees in the 1930s, ranked number 17 on Eloquence. An eloquent athlete? How could that happen? The speech Gehrig gave when retiring from baseball (because he was suffering from ALS) was only 278 words long, yet it became known as "baseball's Gettysburg Address."[55] Gehrig's "personality was ill-suited to public speaking," says the biographer Richard Sandomir, and he "did not need to say much as a Yankee superstar," a sharp contrast to today's Broadway idols.[56] Unlike his teammate, Babe Ruth, who had no filters, Gehrig would rather have "struck out in the ninth with the score tied, two down and the bases loaded," than to walk out on the field and give his speech.[57]

But speak he did, and his goodbye left not a dry eye in the ballpark. "When the New York Giants, a team you would give your right arm to beat, and vice versa, sends you a gift—that's something," Gehrig admitted. "When everybody down to the groundskeepers and those boys in white coats remember you with trophies—that's something," he continued. And "when you have a wonderful mother-in-law who takes sides with you in squabbles with her own daughter—that's something," he admitted. Gehrig's tone—friendly but not fawning, brave but not prideful—seemed straight out of a Thornton Wilder play, an earnest fellow down on his luck who was still thinking of other people. This was not the voice of ballplayer/celebrities like Reggie Jackson, Barry Bonds, or Alex Rodriguez. Gehrig's statement was an understatement.

- *Novelty*: Geraldine Ferraro's acceptance speech for the Democrats' vice presidential nomination in 1984 was ranked number 56 on Importance by the survey respondents but, shockingly, number 3 on Eloquence. Geraldine Ferraro, the self-designated "housewife from Queens," ranked higher than all the male potentates—the Kennedys and Roosevelts, Eisenhower and Wilson—even though she had only recently been plucked from obscurity to become the first woman on a major-party ticket. Because all this was so new, her speech had to be strong but not too strong, says the scholar Denise Bostdorff, lest she overshadow the head of the ticket.[58]

She had to be traditional yet bold, say Karlyn Campbell and Claire Jerry, responsive to the dictates of second-wave feminism.[59] She was an Italian American and a Roman Catholic, says Catherine Dobris, so she had to avoid seeming too "urban" for folks in the heartland.[60]

Ferraro coped with these challenges by inviting the audience into her life. She would speak, Ferraro resolved, "in the inaudible language of the heart." She talked about being the daughter of an immigrant, of her work as a public school teacher and night school law student, and of her recent trip to Fritz Mondale's hometown in Minnesota where, on the Fourth of July, "they hang flags out on Main Street" while in Queens "they fly them over Grand Avenue." She opened up her values for inspection, declaring that women should not make 59 cents for every man's dollar. At times she touched on policy matters—jobs, taxes, voting rights—but mostly she hewed to the values of her neighborhood—where people get their "fair share," where the rules are not "rigged" against people, where college grads don't have a "mountain of debt," and where compromises are "hammered out."[61] Ferraro used ordinary metaphors, making it easy to feel superior to her speech. Therein lies its majesty.

  • *Closure*: Poor Gerald Ford—unexpectedly thrust into the vice presidency and then, two years later, thrust into the presidency. Life happened to Ford, and then he happened back, pardoning the now disgraced Richard Nixon, whom he had succeeded as president. Then he had to explain his decision on national television. His speech ranks number 20 on Eloquence but 94 on Importance, with many scholars panning his rhetoric. By linking himself to Nixon, Mary Stuckey argued, Ford reduced his claim to legitimacy.[62] His speech cost the nation a sense of control, says Robert King, by letting Nixon off too easily.[63] Ford lost moral authority, said James Klumpp and Jeffrey Lukehart, by choosing clemency over punishment.[64]

To provide the nation with a sense of closure, Ford wrapped himself in the cloak of civil religion.[65] "I have asked for your help and your prayers," said Ford, "not only when I became President but many times since." Devoid of clear legal precedents on which to depend, Ford had to bank on his own conscience. "I do believe, with all my heart and mind and spirit, that I, not as President but as a humble servant of God," said Ford, "will receive justice without mercy if I fail to show mercy."[66] Only the most profound cynic could fail to be impressed by Ford's openness, by his admitted feelings of inadequacy. Ford was ontologically incomplete, but he ended things—clearly, definitively. Suddenly, Nixon was gone.

• *Grief*: Death takes our breath away and often our words with it. Words seem inadequate when a loved one is lost, but words are all that is left. Public deaths, sudden deaths, transfer these feelings to a grander scale, as it did when the space shuttle *Challenger* exploded seventy-three seconds after liftoff on January 28, 1986, taking with it seven brave astronauts. President Ronald Reagan was left behind to mourn. His speech (#18 on Eloquence) was "neither the smoothest nor the most internally cohesive of speeches," said one scholar, but it brought back the "frontier myth" that had long defined the American imagination.[67] Steven Mister notes that these sorts of tragedies create epistemological challenges—how could this have happened?—but even more profound philosophical challenges—what does it mean?[68] Finding meaning was Ronald Reagan's job.

With the help of his speechwriter Peggy Noonan, Reagan found his meaning—not in what the dead astronauts had done but in why they had done it. He brought the crew members to life emotionally, not biographically. He spoke of "that special grace, that special spirit" that motivated them and the "hunger to explore" that kept them going. He spoke of the astronauts' families, who felt "the full impact of this tragedy." He spoke of the nation's schoolchildren who had watched the shuttle's takeoff and gotten their first, painful lesson in bravery. Reagan also addressed those who worked at NASA and how their talent and dedication were now overridden by anguish. Reagan populated his speech with people—the families, the children, NASA employees—to explain why the *Challenger* crew did what they did. His speech was filled with the living, not just the dead.

- *Incongruity*: Richard Nixon did not do particularly well on my rhetorical measures, but the one speech that did stand out was his resignation address (#12 on Eloquence). The *Nation*'s columnists disagreed with my assessment, declaring Nixon's remarks "unmatched for moral squalor, irredeemable tackiness, poverty of imagination, and absence of authentic personal feeling."[69] This is too harsh an evaluation, especially since Nixon's speech differed so dramatically from his normal, ego-protective, style. The psychohistorian James Hamilton notes that Nixon's self-esteem had "always been extremely fragile and his sense of personal identity poorly defined and tenuous," causing him to be a classic passive-aggressive.[70] But his resignation speech was different. As Gerald Wilson notes, it had a conciliatory tone and a touch of dignity.[71] Nixon explained what it was like to be Nixon.

"I have felt it was my duty," he began, "to persevere, to make every possible effort to complete the term of office to which you elected me." "I would have preferred to carry through to the finish whatever the personal agony it would have involved," Nixon admitted, but the interests of the nation removed that option. Nixon then offered a series of admissions: he had never been a quitter; he felt great personal sadness; he wanted the nation to heal; his judgments had sometimes been wrong; he felt no bitterness toward his opponents; he was proud to have left the nation in peace; he sought God's blessings on all he left behind. This was a new Nixon, a contrite Nixon. He seems weaker, humbler, more available. He offered no recriminations—odd for one who had lived his life in the arena. This new Nixon, this incongruous Nixon, was a better Nixon. Would that he had shown up earlier in life.

A speech can be compelling, a speech can be depthless, but it can also be unavailable. Elie Wiesel's lecture in the White House on August 11, 1999 (#95 on Eloquence, #93 on Importance) was one such speech. Wiesel began promisingly: "Fifty-four years ago to the day, a young Jewish boy from a small town in the Carpathian Mountains woke up, not far from Goethe's beloved Weimar, in a place of eternal infamy called Buchenwald. He was finally free, but there was no joy in his heart. He thought there never would be again." Wiesel begins in the third person, standing apart from his own story. He then continues, revealing what the young Wiesel witnessed: "Liberated a day earlier by American soldiers, he remembers their rage at what they saw. And even if he lives to be a very old man, he will always be grateful to them for that rage, and also for their compassion."[72]

Perhaps a speech on the Holocaust should be unavailable lest its horrors overwhelm us. "It is so much easier to look away from the victims," Wiesel observes, "so much easier to avoid such rude interruptions to our work, our dreams, our hopes." So Wiesel maintains his distance, turning his speech into a survey of Jewish heritage, human indifference, the Nazi mentality, U.S. immigration policy, and ethnic cleansing in eastern Europe. Wiesel's travelogue is oddly unemotional. He tells no stories of real people, nor does he detail the events he mentions. To do so, perhaps, would have been too raw, too overwhelming, for a White House audience. Wiesel may have decided that full-throated eloquence was not needed on this occasion, that resetting the national agenda was work enough. In the rhetorical scholar Brad Vivian's terms, Wiesel may have chosen to open the door for "witnesses in waiting, witnesses to come" and to leave specific matters for another day.[73]

Elie Wiesel's unavailability was perhaps strategic, but John Kerry's was cultural. Kerry, a former U.S. senator, presidential candidate, secretary of state, and special presidential envoy on climate change, first came to public attention with a brave speech denouncing the war in Vietnam. A Yale graduate and a recipient of three Purple Hearts, Kerry spoke on behalf of the Vietnam Veterans Against the War to the Senate Foreign Relations Committee on April 22, 1971. Only twenty-seven years old at the time, Kerry was a formal fellow who did not laugh easily and who treated gladhanding as suspect (which later made things hard for him on the campaign trail). His speech to the Senate ranked number 85 on Eloquence (100 on Importance).

Former vice president Spiro Agnew said that, even when speaking informally, Kerry sounded as if his remarks had been "ghosted for him by a former Kennedy speechwriter,"[74] while others called

Kerry an "inauthentic opportunist" lacking any "populist appeal."[75] These judgments are unduly punitive. John Kerry is simply a serious guy who comes from a part of the country, New England, where good fences make good neighbors. As a result, Kerry forsook personal investment, focusing instead on the topic at hand. "I am not here as John Kerry," he began. "I'm here as one member of a group of 1,000, which is a small representation of a very much larger group of veterans" opposed to the war. Then Kerry got down to cases—brutal, bloody, horrific cases. Recalling a meeting in Detroit in which veterans had relived their wartime experiences, Kerry left no stone unturned:

> [The veterans] relived the absolute horror of what this country, in a sense, made them do. They told the stories of times that they had personally raped, cut off ears, cut off heads, taped wires from portable telephones to human genitals and turned up the power, cut off limbs, blown up bodies, randomly shot at civilians, razed villages in the fashion reminiscent of Genghis Khan, shot cattle and dogs for fun, poisoned food stocks, and generally ravaged the countryside of South Vietnam in addition to the normal ravage of war and the normal and very particular ravaging which is done by the applied bombing power of this country.[76]

Kerry's is an important speech but "available" only to those with a strong constitution. It is an in-your-face rendition of events, some of which seem chosen for their shock value: "A friend of mine was lying in a bed two beds away and tried to help him, but he couldn't. They rang a bell and there was no one there to service that man, and so he died of convulsions." Kerry takes aim at the Nixon administration, which, in its "blindness and fear," disregarded the veterans' service even though their "scars and stumps of limbs are witness enough" that they served the nation faithfully.

Kerry's metaphors are also consistently stark—"reputations bleaching in the sun," troop losses being "shrugged off," "the cheapness of Asian lives," and "monsters" otherwise known as soldiers.

Kerry buries himself in the details of war, avoiding all transcendent flourishes. This is a young man's speech, an angry man's speech. While Kerry may have helped turn the tide against the war, a still conflicted nation needed something else. A more invitational speech would have better served his purposes.

EXPANSIVE

Each of us lives in a tiny world, and mostly we like it that way. We like knowing the name of the clerk at the dry cleaners, and we like listening to the same radio station each day in the car. We like taking vacations to parts unknown, but we like returning to our slice of hometown even more. Rhetoric interrupts all of this. As Dennis Donoghue notes, "eloquence does not allow anything to be merely itself; it enhances it, or condenses it, but in any case changes it, bringing a larger perspective to bear."[77] Rhetoric "robs us of our freedom," says Matthew Bevis, by disrupting our complacency, forcing us to consider this and not that, more and not less, there and not here.[78] Rhetoric changes our agendas, making them less orderly.

Inaugural addresses are often a time for expansion. That was especially true on March 3, 1933, when Franklin Delano Roosevelt took office (#34 on Eloquence). Roosevelt arrived in the direst of times—a quarter of the population out of work, failed banks and failed businesses, a deep and abiding depression. Roosevelt declared war on the moneychangers, arguing, according to Davis Houck, that the economic system was sound but that some individuals were scandalously corrupt.[79] "Only a foolish optimist can deny the dark realities of the moment," Roosevelt declared, but "nature still offers her bounty and human efforts have multiplied it. Plenty is at our doorstep." "Happiness lies not in the mere possession of money," said Roosevelt. "It lies in the joy of achievement, in the thrill of creative effort."[80]

Roosevelt implied that everything had to be reimagined—the nature of work, the country's stability, the range of human possibilities. People were still poor after Roosevelt's speech, but they began to see themselves differently. Roosevelt gave them a sense of agency, convincing them that they were "capable of being better than their own found condition."[81] Within a week, says Thomas Farrell, "the mood in Washington and in Congress was completely different: confident, enthusiastic, perhaps inspired."[82] "The country needed a story with drama," says Houck, "with heroes and villains, easy explanations and archetypes—all wrapped up in a memorable style."[83]

It is simplistic to imagine that a single speech could cure a nation, but Roosevelt made people feel larger, more capacious. Observers, Roosevelt argued, must become participants: "We must act and we must act quickly." "These, my friends, are the lines of attack." We must put "our national house in order." "This great army of our people" must be mobilized. The people must grow, Roosevelt said, to match the size of their country.

In contrast to Roosevelt's well-crafted miniature, John F. Kennedy (#10 on Eloquence) painted a mural. Roosevelt spoke domestically; Kennedy internationally. Roosevelt emphasized immediate solutions; Kennedy spoke of a New Frontier. Everything about Kennedy's speech was overstated . . . but in a good way. "Let the word go forth," Kennedy said, "from this time and place, to friend and foe alike, that the torch has been passed to a new generation of Americans."[84] Kennedy's language was also kinetic: Challenges would be "split asunder" and "iron tyranny" eviscerated. The "bonds of mass misery" would be broken, and the nation would "stay the hand of mankind's final war."

Kennedy's speech sounded like a Cecil B. DeMille movie. He spoke of trumpets "summoning the people," the "burden of long twilights," the "terrors of science," but also the "revolution of hope." Kennedy filled his canvas with couplets: a "new balance of power" versus "a new world of law"; the "generosity of the state" versus "the hand of God"; the "instruments of war" versus the "instruments of peace."[85] Kennedy expanded the world to include the Soviet Union, of course, but also Europe and South America and, implicitly, Africa and the Middle East.

Kennedy's speech contained Cold War themes, but it never made one feel cornered, set upon. That was less true for Ronald Reagan's first inaugural (#53 on Eloquence). While he occasionally nodded toward liberal values, conservative ideology lay just beneath the surface, steering listeners "beyond the chauvinistic to the jingoistic."[86] If Kennedy's door was half open, Reagan's was half closed, with the American dream constantly challenged by excessive governmental regulation, runaway inflation, and a dangerous, determined, communism. The "price of freedom" is high, said Reagan, but on his watch, "sovereignty is not for sale." While Kennedy opened things up, Reagan hunkered down. The "right to dream heroic dreams" was dogged by the "eve of our struggle" and the potential "fate that will fall on us." Reagan's dream was also rife with double negatives: We should not be limiting "ourselves to small dreams" but instead "removing the roadblocks" to the economy. To dream with Reagan was to dream furtively.

Two of the most famous speeches—FDR's first fireside address and Richard Nixon's "Checkers" speech—did poorly on my measures of Eloquence (#90 and #82, respectively), in part because they were narrow rather than broad. Both speeches did well, however, in the Importance survey (#31 and #6, respectively). Contrary though these judgments are, they make sense. FDR's speech was historic because it was electronic. Prior to that time, hearing the president's voice only happened via Movietone News at the local movie theater. Roosevelt's radio address changed things, letting him talk directly to people in a surprisingly intimate way. Listening to Roosevelt on one's own radio in one's own living room was to encounter the nation's First Teacher "who embarks on a profound lesson" versus "a president whose language assumes the high office he occupies."[87]

According to the rhetorical scholar Amos Kiewe, Roosevelt's fireside address "is not adorned with flourish, does not incorporate impressive metaphors, and does not carry memorable lines."[88] Unlike his first inaugural, Roosevelt's fireside chat was cramped, not visionary. He mostly ran the numbers, explaining why even "the soundest banks couldn't get enough currency" to meet consumers' demands. Roosevelt's images are technical ("the mechanics of the situation," "the wheels of industry") and forceful ("judgment that has dictated our course," "you must not be stampeded by rumors"). Roosevelt studiously avoided high-flying rhetoric: "I do not promise you that every bank will be reopened or that individual losses will not be suffered." His concluding statement was only modestly encouraging: "It is your problem, my friends, your problem no less than mine. Together we cannot fail." Sobriety from beginning to end.

There was accountancy in Richard Nixon's "Checkers" speech as well. According to Lawrence Rosenfield, Nixon's speech "reminds one of stone blocks cemented into an edifice" and yet the response was "immediate and fantastic: the public was virtually unanimous in its support of Nixon."[89] Nixon's remarks were "devoid of stylistic eloquence or grace," says Celeste Condit, but he built a bond with his audience nonetheless.[90] By sharing the details of his life, by "going small," Nixon altered the dynamics of the 1952 presidential campaign. Long-term, the private lives of politicians would never be the same again because of Nixon's speech.

Nixon sacrificed transcendence and poetic imagination for pragmatics and personal investment, but the trade-off was smart. By exposing the questions voters were already asking about his use of campaign funds, Nixon showed that he was listening.

- *What the press asks*: "Dick, what about this fund we hear about?"
- *What the people ask*: "Well, what did you use the fund for, Senator?"
- *Low-cost campaign expenses*: "Should the printing . . . of a speech be charged to the taxpayers?"
- *High-cost campaign expenses*: "Well, how do you pay for these and how can you do it legally?"
- *Clearly legal expenses*: "But have you got any proof?"
- *Under-the-table payments*: "Is there a possibility that maybe you got some sums in cash?"
- *His personal indebtedness*: "What do we owe?"[91]

Even by contemporary standards, the detail contained in Nixon's answers was remarkable. He talked about his wife's experience as a stenographer and, later, as a schoolteacher; about his time as an attorney in California; about the audit of his senatorial finances by

Price Waterhouse Inc.; and about his payments on the lecture circuit. There was more: the cost of his house in Whittier, California (where his parents now lived), how much life insurance he had, and what his GI policy was worth. He also mentioned his mortgage payments for his home in Washington, DC. Then, memorably, Nixon spoke of the "little cocker spaniel dog in a crate" he received from a man in Texas, a dog the Nixon girls would later name "Checkers." Gentle smiles all around.

Nixon ended his speech with a broadside against the Stevenson campaign, but that was really a footnote to his masterwork. Everything about Nixon's speech was actuarial, nothing expansive. In theological terms, all was confessional, nothing doctrinal. Nixon steeled his listeners against his tormentors, avoiding broad philosophical matters. Instead, he spoke of small things, of the humdrum of life. He made his listeners voyeuristic, and then he granted them absolution for their sins.

CONCLUSION

My way of measuring eloquence is ineluctably my own. It is no wiser than others' although it does have the advantage of being empirically demonstrable. That makes it useful, but Martin Luther King Jr. also helps. Had his "I Have a Dream" speech not ranked number 1 on Eloquence, my method would have been rightly suspect. King's metaphors alone made his speech special. He uses all the human senses—sight ("the beacon light of hope"), sound ("jangling discords of our nation"), taste ("thirst for freedom")," and touch ("heat of oppression")—to ground his ideas.[92] He uses cultural resonance too, blending geography with argument ("the prodigious hilltop of New Hampshire," "the heightening Alleghenies of Pennsylvania") to surround his listeners with the problems he identifies.

There is a relentlessness to King's speech, a steady marching forward: "one hundred years later, the Negro still is not free"; "nineteen sixty-three is not an end but a beginning"; "we have come here today to dramatize a shameful condition." The future King envisions is his people's future, but it is his as well: "I have a dream that my four little children will one day live in a nation where they will not be judged by the color of their skin but by the content of their character." King is present, available, throughout his text. "This is the faith that I will go back to the South with," says King, a sign that he is concerned for the nation generally but that he has a private life as well.

King's is not a speculative speech although it is filled with dreams. He mentions specific places ("Lookout Mountain of Tennessee," "Stone Mountain of Georgia"), specific people ("Jews and gentiles, Protestants and Catholics"), and specific experiences ("down in Alabama, with its vicious racists"). King engages our imaginations, but he is steadfastly historical too, interspersing snippets of patriotism ("My country ' tis of thee, sweet land of liberty, of thee I sing") with people's narratives ("Some of you have come from narrow jail cells"). King tells a big-but-small story. Ignoring it is not easy.

There is an unmistakable righteousness to King's speech. As Robert Cox notes, King teases out the moral implications of all he surveys.[93] The Constitution and the Declaration of Independence, King says, join together as a "promissory note" that every American inherits. Time, too, is moral, with the "tranquilizing drug of gradualism" no longer justified because of "the fierce urgency of now." King's background as a preacher lets him make law and religion a single thing: The Negro "finds himself in exile in his own land," but he nonetheless must continue "with the faith that unearned suffering is redemptive."

King has a brilliant way of cutting off our avenues of escape. Had we no eyes to see or ears to hear, we could turn away. Had we no sense of history, no capacity for imagination, we could resist his prayers and injunctions. King's eloquence negates those alternatives. Fifty years later, his speech lives on, doing what only eloquence can do: reminding us what is right and wrong, how we have failed one another, and how the breach can be repaired. King lived a life of eloquence. Justice was his heir.

8

ELOQUENCE TOMORROW

"It is the doctrine of the popular music-masters," Ralph Waldo Emerson once observed, "that whoever can speak can sing. So, probably, every man is eloquent once in his life."[1] Finally, a reprieve for George W. Bush! President Bush was not an eloquent man. He was earnest, to be sure, and he manfully navigated his way through the press corps thicket and the chicken dinners. But Bush was also given to malaprops and to humorous asides that made sense only to him. If Donald Trump was the Scylla of inelegance and George W. Bush its Charybdis, Barack Obama was the Odysseus sailing between these outcroppings on his way to glory.

But then came the twentieth anniversary of the 9/11 tragedy, and former President Bush found himself in Shanksville, Pennsylvania, alongside Vice President Kamala Harris, who delivered a perfectly banal remembrance of the tragedy. "The forty passengers and crew members of Flight 93," said Harris, "didn't know each other. They were different people from different places. They were on that particular flight for different reasons. But they did not focus on what may separate us. No. They focused on what we all share—the humanity we all share."[2] Harris groped her way through her eight-minute address, and then came the man who had led the nation on that fateful day in 2001, just nine months after becoming commander in chief. This time, he did not disappoint.

Bush began by recalling how Flight 93 had plummeted into the Pennsylvania countryside because a number of brave Americans had taken control of the plane, changing its trajectory and thereby averting an even greater disaster for the nation. After offering praise for the first responders, Bush's remarks took a philosophical turn. He mentioned "the brute randomness of death" and how, on some occasions, all we can hear is "God's terrible silence." "There is no simple explanation for the mix of providence and human will that sets the direction of our lives," Bush observed, although sometimes "after wandering long and lost in the dark, many have found they were actually walking, step by step, toward grace."[3]

Then, another quick turn. Describing domestic and international terrorists as "children of the same foul spirit," Bush connected the "day of trial and grief" he had witnessed twenty years earlier to the "malign forces," "religious bigotry," "nativism," and "designs of evil" rampant in the United States today. Although Bush never mentioned the January 6, 2021 insurrection in the nation's capital, it was clearly on his mind. His remarks accomplished a rare trifecta: honoring those who had died, indicting a new era of terrorism, and reinscribing the nation's most sacred values—self-sacrifice, courage under fire, and openness to diversity. Bush did a lot of work in ten minutes, and, at the very least, he got to the threshold of eloquence.

Was Bush's rhetoric important? That is this book's central question. Bush spoke. People listened. So what? In classical times, eloquence was seen as "a perfected human capacity," the unmistakable sign of "a virtuous nature," but that sounds like old talk today, irrelevant talk.[4] We now live in a hurry-up world where we have less time for speaking, less time for listening. We seem to care less about language too. "Over time," says one online poster, "eloquence has been elevated out of the expected. It almost feels baroque and suspect when it finds its way into print, into a speech, or worse, into ordinary conversation."[5] Today, we have other baubles to fascinate us: pixels, gaming, networks, onboarding, browsers, bandwidth, malware. Computers lure us into a quiet world where human speech is tolerated but not needed.

Nevertheless, special, set-aside assemblies where people come together still exist. People like George W. Bush can still summon up old memories on such occasions and connect them to present-day concerns. During such moments, the speaker seems to appropriate our own sensibilities, feelings we do not understand but cannot deny. The eloquent speaker anticipates our anticipations, capturing our inchoate senses of foreboding and possibility. The eloquent speaker describes the world just as we see it or, more accurately, as we see it just after the speaker has spoken. The eloquent speaker trades in mysteries we could ignore but cannot ignore.

This book has laid out a model of eloquence based on the American experience. It has done so in an empirical way, using computer-based measures to separate the wheat from the chaff, the eloquent from the ordinary. Throughout, however, I have treated these quantitative counts not as probative indices but as "pointers" that call our attention to language patterns that would otherwise have gone unnoticed. The more texts I examined, the more patterns I found and, as a result, the more questions that confronted me. Projects in the digital humanities are not important because they are digital but because they explore the human mystery.

This book has offered an assessment of eloquence, so now it is time to assess our assessment. Is eloquence still a viable construct? Is it still practiced, still powerful? Have traditional understandings of eloquence stood the test of time? How does eloquence affect us as citizens? How does it shape our attitudes and social practices? Can it still compel us in a world where people's attention shifts by the nanosecond? Can it call forth the best in us, or is it just another gimmick? If a wondrous new eloquence descended upon us tomorrow, would we notice it? Eloquence is an old thing. Is it still our thing?

THE VECTORS OF ELOQUENCE

The model of eloquence embraced in this book was built deductively by assuming that eloquence is the product of *cultural resonance,* which, in the United States, is the product of equal parts pragmatism ("you will reap tangible benefits by listening to me") and transcendence ("you and I share enduring beliefs and values"). A second component of eloquence is *personal investment,* whereby speakers use their personal beliefs and experiences to validate the case they are making. The third leg of the stool is *poetic imagination,* operationalized by examining how metaphors reframe ideas and spark new visions for society. Cultural resonance and personal investment were assessed by DICTION, a content-analytic program that searches a text with some fifty dictionaries or word lists. Because metaphors are so multidimensional, they were hand-coded by me to assure consistency.

Quantitative analyses like these are imperfect, so I have buttressed them with detailed textual study of the rhetoric under investigation. Overall, some fifty thousand texts were examined, but three corpora were studied in depth: classic American oratory (n = 154), twentieth-century public address (n = 655), and political campaign speeches (n = 6,036). These collections included a wide range of speakers, topics, and settings; the emotional and political circumstances surrounding them also varied, as did the media attention they received. Eloquence, it was assumed, requires many things: speakers' awareness of their own strengths and weaknesses; an understanding of their moment in history; the courage to take on controversial issues; an ear for an audience's needs and susceptibilities; and a feeling for the texture of language. Altogether, these compounds form the substrate of eloquence, a concept that Ralph Waldo Emerson has called a kind of "practical chemistry."[6]

Chapter 4 highlighted what has made American politics distinctive since the nation's founding—a constant wrangling between the pragmatic and the transcendent. As of this writing, for example, some Americans regard surgical masks not as a medical preventative against the coronavirus but as a noxious sign of governmental over-reach. "Politics is becoming religion in our country," complained Governor Spencer Cox of Utah when reflecting on the vaccine wars.[7] Even junior-high history classes have become corrupt, according to some, with critical race theory being foisted upon innocent twelve-year-olds to make them ashamed of their ancestors' roles in eighteenth-century slavery. Replacement theory, too, posits a threat to white Americans. As former Congressman Steve King of Iowa has declared, "we can't restore our civilization with somebody else's babies."[8]

But transcendence is only part of the story. Americans—not all of them, but most of them—quickly grow tired of ideology. That is even true in higher education circles from time to time. Rafael Walker, an English professor at Baruch College, recently declared himself finished with the "administrative statements" issued by university presidents when confronting racist or sexist incidents on campus. "What universities can do to console their communities in the wake of tragedies," says Walker, "is to explain what concrete steps they had taken in ensuring that these tragedies do not happen again." "They should detail their commitments not to abstractions," says Walker, but in the most American way imaginable: by announcing new "allocations of finances and personnel." "'Thoughts and prayers,'" says Walker, advance nothing.[9]

Professor Walker overstates things. As we saw in chapter 4, thoughts and prayers are sometimes all that is available in a politician's arsenal, so they use transcendence to add expansiveness, intensity, and a sense of community to their public appeals. Pragmatic arguments, in contrast, draw on materialist and populist sensibilities to make politics immediate, actional. This intertwining of the transcendent and the pragmatic distinguishes political discourse from the other genres I analyzed—religion, journalism, literature, social activism, entertainment, and corporate rhetorics alike. From time to time, uber-pragmatists like Donald Trump and Mitch McConnell hold sway, but eventually their rhetoric feels soulless, mercantile, self-serving. When that happens, new voices emerge to emphasize equal opportunity, freedom of speech, labor rights, and welcoming immigration laws. Soon enough, all of these airy theorizers are deemed tiresome, so some upstart calls for a new round of tax cuts. The cycle never stops.

"Instead of resolving our fundamental differences all at once," says Bryan Garsten, the American people "are left to struggle over them as they arise repeatedly in different forms in particular cases over a long period of time."[10] Nineteenth-century oratory "made objects larger," says Richard Weaver, but it did not make them clearer, and clarity is an American favorite.[11] "I propose that the surplus of all the big fortunes," said Huey Long, "above the few millions to any one person at the most, shall go into the United States ownership."[12] That sort of clarity works for a while, until it begins to sound, well, sacrilegious. Americans like their religions until, of course, they do not. Norman Vincent Peale struck the right balance, according to Donald Trump. "He would instill a very positive feeling about God," said Trump, "that also made me feel positive about myself."[13] God and country, God and the Self, nicely packaged. What American could ask for more?

Both transcendence and pragmatism can seem cold, distant, so personal investment warms things up. Chapter 5 shows how American eloquence today demands a direct, human interface. Americans demand *authorship*, not just word-saying, so personal investment becomes a "tell," an indicator of whether a speaker really lives with his or her beliefs. When delivering a speech from a teleprompter, for example, both Joe Biden and Donald Trump seem burdened. To read a text is to give it voice, but to speak a text is to make a bid for authenticity. Donald Trump hates words, so his body noticeably slumps and he uses a singsong voice when repeating what others have written for him. Biden, in contrast, is mystified by words, so he struggles when trying to connect ideas to the people seated before him.

Today's presidents speak in public far more often than they did before, so overexposure is a constant danger. Modern media complicate the picture. The more often we see someone on television, the more we read their tweets, the more we want to know them. Then, the more we know someone, the more complicated they become for us and the sooner issues of trust arise. But there is no stopping this runaway train: today's speakers refer to themselves far more often than they did in the past, especially during political campaigns, so voters spend much of their time second-guessing politicians' motives, which, of course, can never be seen.

Many years ago, the social scientist Wendell Johnson described what he called IFD disease, in which idealization leads to frustration and thence to demoralization.[14] So, for example, a new, attractive politician comes out of the shadows—Barack Obama, for example. He tours the country, taking on the issues of the day, and, because issues are issues—persistent, irresolvable—frustration follows. Eight years of issues, eight years of Obama, and the once Perfect Self is thrown onto the ash heap of history, only to be followed by a reality show host. The media love what is shiny and new, so the IFD cycle spins faster and faster, with replacement personalities constantly being auditioned—Cori Bush, perhaps, or maybe Matt Gaetz. They rise, they fall, they explain, they fade away. Leaders "forfeit their moral authority," says Saint Augustine, "when they lose sight of their own need for repentance and conversion."[15] Humility is important, but IFD has an iron will.

My studies show that personal investment increases when politicians are comparatively unknown, when they are under fire, and when the issues being addressed are important to them personally. Historically, presidents referred to themselves more frequently when campaigning than when speaking from the Oval Office, but that has changed in recent years, perhaps because of the special "intimacy" television affords. Interestingly, one study finds that, when running for the presidency, former governors used the token *we* considerably more often than the token *I*, perhaps because of their closer connections to people in their locales.[16] After becoming president, however, a different logic applies, with self-awareness and self-absorption often merging into one. Donald Trump made that maxim a billboard.

At its best, personal investment signals boldness, confidence, and the willingness to stand by one's commitments. People perk up their ears when speakers mention themselves, so sound bites on the nightly news often contain self-references. But too much personal investment can lead to preening when times are good and defensiveness when times are bad. Nonetheless, personal openness remains a prized American trait. In the past, eloquence demanded greater distance between speaker and listener. It was more formal, more considered, with speakers speaking not just for themselves but for the People Incarnate. We no longer trust such distance, so we now get a different kind of political leader.

Chapter 6 featured poetic imagination—how speakers used verbal imagery to do their bidding. Metaphors connect two things to one another and thus become a third, grand, thing. Even children make metaphors—"Mrs. Johnson is a monster," "this classroom is a zoo"—taking delight in their newfound talents. Even as adults, though, we stay connected to primitive things—to the human body, to nature, to the base emotions—and we remain interested in who is more powerful than whom, who works hard and who does not. As we mature, we grow into moral metaphors, into images of community, but their roots were with us in childhood. Adults differ from children only because they have more tools with which to work.

As we saw in chapter 6, metaphors help us imagine the unimaginable and define the hard-to-define. Metaphors extend us, letting us try out new ideas before investing in them fully ("America is a salad bowl, not a melting pot"). Metaphors hurry us along, quickening our decision making (e.g., Chuck Schumer on COVID: "We were looking at a freight train coming across the country but now we're looking at a bullet train"). Using metaphors is therefore a kind of delinquency, a willingness to go beyond the conventional. Because politics is an indeterminate sphere where agreements are usually tentative, where facts are misunderstood, and where the future is unclear, metaphors help us sound definitive when we are only guessing.

Great speakers, people like Winston Churchill and Martin Luther King Jr., breathed in metaphorical dust. Their eloquence came not from random images but from their mastery over metaphorical groupings (the earth, everyday tools, measures of time and temperature) that helped create a mosaic. Using metaphors therefore involves a kind of second-language learning. As John Burrows notes, in England of yore, British classical education "exerted a powerful influence on the ways boys wrote" while girls, who received their education in more local and unstructured venues, "continued to write something more like spoken English."[17] Many of the speeches analyzed in this book were fashioned by shockingly defiant women who violated rhetorical norms to usher in new ways of thinking. As Cynthia Ozick notes, "inspiration is an intruder, a kidnapper of reason, a burglar who shoots the watchdogs dead. Inspiration closes off sentries and censors and monitors, Inspiration instigates reckless cliff-walking."[18]

Chapter 7 brought together the various components of eloquence to assess the rhetoric of the twentieth century. If eloquence is anything, I argued, it is a confabulation, an assemblage of pieces and parts that, together, produce something magical. That is why John Burrows urges us to consider "the contrast between handwoven rugs where the russet tones predominate and those where they give way to the greens and blues. The principal point of interest is neither a single stitch, a single thread, or even a single color but the overall effect."[19]

The Eloquence Index I calculated for each speech follows Burrows's logic by giving equal weight to Transcendence, Pragmatism, Personal Investment, and Poetic Imagination. The more often each property is deployed in a text, the greater its eloquence. There is a crudeness here, but the results become more plausible when one looks closely at the texts themselves, which I have done throughout this book.

Notably, my measurements of eloquence differed substantially from a national survey of scholars who had been asked to identify the most important speeches of the twentieth century. The appendix of this book compares my findings to theirs and reports no meaningful relationship between these different modes of assessment. While I focused exclusively on a text's linguistic properties, the scholarly survey considered many things—a speaker's background, their preferred rhetorical habits, the audience they addressed, the speech's historical surroundings, how it was delivered, and, of course, the inventional, dispositional, and ethical features of the texts. In short, I looked only at language while the survey respondents considered a great range of things.

Interestingly, I found no systematic differences in eloquence attributable to gender, political party, genre, era, or rhetorical setting. Eloquence, I concluded, is individualistic (some have it and some do not) and situational (some have it sometimes but not at other times). I teased out these various manifestations, following up my computer-based leads by exploring the texts themselves. Eloquence, I determined, produces four bounties: it makes the world feel settled, better defined; it adds a sense of righteousness to public discussions, making them less cold and anomic; it also increases social availability, creating tighter connections between speaker and audience; and it expands the range of things worthy of public consideration.

I also compared the speeches' eloquence to how much press coverage they received (as measured by Google hits) and found a strong, positive correlation between those measures. Journalists have an "ear for eloquence," I concluded, while scholars (whose judgments were negatively associated with press coverage) have an "ear for history," the sort of judgment that can be made only at some remove. This conclusion is, of course, provisional. Studies in the digital humanities can do many things, but they cannot, they must not, make covering law statements. My way of measuring eloquence is but one way of operating. What I gained in precision I may have been lost in nuance, so there is still much to learn.

THE IMPORTANCE OF ELOQUENCE

Teddy Roosevelt was not a great orator. Edgar Lee Masters once said that Roosevelt "has nothing to say and says it as poorly as possible."[20] Henry Steele Commager observed that Roosevelt's speeches sounded "tinny," overly practiced, empty.[21] As a leader, Roosevelt was actional, not verbal, but words were definitely on his mind when striking out at the "muckrakers" of his day in April 1906. "There is nothing more distressing to every good patriot, to every good American, than the hard, scoffing spirit which treats the allegation of dishonesty in a public man as a cause for laughter," said Roosevelt. "Such laughter is worse than the crackling of thorns under a pot," he continued, "for it denotes not merely the vacant mind, but the heart in which high emotions have been choked before they could grow to fruition." Here, Roosevelt had in mind the smear-mongers of his day, tabloid writers overseen by people like publisher William Randolph Hearst. "There never was a time," said Roosevelt when defending the political enterprise, "when loftier and more disinterested work for the betterment of mankind was being done than now."[22]

Something about the cynicisms of the day made President Roosevelt stretch toward eloquence. "But why bother?" some might ask, since eloquence is "morally corrupt," "rotten with vanity," "self-regarding," and "complacently narcissistic."[23] Surely Roosevelt could have done something better with his time than to strike out at third-rate journalists. Besides, the art of eloquence can be needlessly provocative, sending people off in dangerous directions. Truth is all you need in politics—be honest, transparent, and the people will follow.

A contrary case can also be made. "Have you ever known a great society in the history of the world," asks Brian Snee, "in which the ability to use language well has been regarded as a character flaw?"[24] The first step in doing politics, says Seth Thompson, is to get citizens to see themselves "as part of some larger entity rather than as completely unique and individualized."[25] Eloquence produces "the common sense of a culture," says John Murphy, and that was especially important in the United States, a vast and often dangerous place when Europeans first arrived on its shores.[26] "There was no other route for power to take," says Christopher Looby, "than that of language stretched over time and space."[27] Some say that the United States spoke itself into being, but a better trope is that it rehearsed itself into being, repeating—often in public ceremonies—certain beliefs until they became common property. America was declared a nation in 1776 but it took considerably more time to make it an organic entity. As Kenneth Cmiel reminds us, eloquence had to become civic for it to become functional.[28]

At any given time, the people of a nation are likely to be confused. It they know what is going on, they may not know what it means. If they have a glimmer of meaning, that meaning may not be shared by others. To be eloquent is thus to enter the fray, to risk visibility. Sometimes eloquence responds to a memorial instinct—the need to preserve what is commonly loved, what is considered sacred. Eloquence also responds to a protective instinct—guarding the rights of groups and individuals—and to a projective instinct—imagining new pathways for a people to tread. Eloquence can also be the product of an insurgent instinct, counteracting the forces of evil. To give up on eloquence, then, is to give up on society itself. To give up on eloquence is also to give up on language, on our ability to put into words what is important to us.

Eloquence is a communal art. We see this during eulogies when the simultaneity of grief causes people to reflect on feelings they share but cannot easily label. The eloquent speaker taps into these feelings and reappropriates them for some new purpose. Timothy Luke argues, unkindly, that Ronald Reagan's D-Day address "remanufactured and renovated for sale an ideo-political commodity in the psychosocial markets of the 1980s."[29] Yes, but Reagan also celebrated the gallantry of thousands when he prayed: "Here, in this place where the West held together, let us make a vow to our dead. Let us show by our actions that we understand what they died for."[30] Ideopolitical commodity indeed.

Eloquence is also an art of reorientation that taps into "the raw consensual stuff in the rhetorical environment" and puts it to work.[31] Eloquence retheorizes things, providing fresh explanations for why things are the way they are. Eugene Debs assigned responsibility for social unfairness to the forces of capital. Caesar Chavez's opponent was an uncaring church; Barry Goldwater's was a spendthrift Congress. Eloquence trades in these oversize explanations, depending on an unknowable future to fix what needs to be fixed now. As Ted Kennedy said at his brother Robert's funeral, "Our future may lie beyond our vision, but it is not completely beyond our control. It is the shaping impulse of America that neither fate nor nature nor the irresistible tides of history, but the work of our own hands, matched to reason and principle, that will determine our destiny."[32]

Eloquence is a restorative art. Even though the past is gone, irretrievably gone, it still has hermeneutical value. As Martin Reisigl notes, there is a clear difference between our "common memories," events we remember seeing, and our "shared memories," those we have been taught but have not seen.[33] Both kinds of memory are powerful, and eloquence becomes our "ultimate resource of community expression."[34] When President Bill Clinton spoke to the people of Oklahoma City after the terrible bombing in 1995, he made the past thunderously present: "Let us teach our children that the God of comfort is also the God of righteousness. Those who trouble their own house will inherit the wind. Justice will prevail."[35]

Eloquence is also a socializing agent. The eloquent speaker speaks *within* an audience, not *to* them or *for* them. Listening to an eloquent speech is like listening to the best version of ourselves. That is especially true with populists. In an attempt to curb wartime hysteria and the suppression of free speech prior to America's entry into World War I, Senator Robert LaFollette of Wisconsin stood in the well of the Senate to add the people's voice to a conversation previously dominated by policy makers and military strategists. America may be justified in going to war, LaFollette said, but only if it retains all of its American values while so doing:

> Today and for weeks past, honest and law-abiding citizens of this country are being terrorized and outraged in their rights by those sworn to uphold the laws and protect the rights of the people. I have in my possession numerous affidavits establishing the fact that people are being unlawfully arrested, thrown into jail, held

incommunicado for days, only to be eventually discharged without ever having been taken into court, because they have committed no crime. Private residences are being invaded, loyal citizens of undoubted integrity and probity arrested, cross-examined, and the most sacred constitutional rights guaranteed to every American citizen are being violated. . . . Our government, above all others, is founded on the right of the people freely to discuss all matters pertaining to their government, in war not less than in peace.[36]

LaFollette is modestly eloquent here and showed considerable courage in defending free speech at a time of prewar panic. But he also stands back a bit, making a legal rather than an existential case. The women discussed in this book, in contrast, tended to humanize things. The pictures they painted were sharply etched, sometimes uncomfortably so, and they focused especially on the *experiences* of those they were trying to help.

- *Margaret Sanger on forced pregnancies and unwanted children*: "At the Grand Central Station of life, trainload after trainload of children are coming in, day and night—nameless refugees arriving out of the Nowhere into the Here. Trainload after trainload—many unwelcome, unwanted, unprepared for, unknown, without baggage, without passports, most of them without pedigrees. These unlimited hordes of refugees arrive in such numbers that the reception committee is thrown into a panic."[37]
- *Carrie Chatman Catt on the travails of women suffragists*: "Think upon Dr. Elizabeth Blackwell, snubbed and boycotted by other women because she proposed to study medicine. Behold Dr. Antoinette Brown Blackwell, standing in sweet serenity before an Assembly of howling clergymen, angry that she, a woman dared to attend a Temperance Convention as a delegate. Revere the intrepid Susan B. Anthony mobbed from Buffalo to Albany because she demanded fair play for women. These are they who built with others the foundation of political liberty for American women."[38]
- *Anna Howard Shaw on war, women, and their dead sons*: "In all the Universe of God there is nothing more sublimely wonderful than a

strong-limbed, clean-hearted, keen-brained, aggressive young man, standing as he does on the border line of life, ready to reach out and grapple with its problems. Oh how wonderful he is, and he is hers. She gave her life for him, and in an hour this country calls him out and in an hour he lies dead; that wonderful, wonderful thing lies dead; and sitting by his side, that mother looking into the dark years to come knows that when her son died her life's hope died with him, and in the face of that wretched motherhood, what man dare ask what a woman knows of war?"[39]

One can, of course, listen to Margaret Sanger and still be pro-life. One can listen to Carrie Chapman Catt and be opposed to staunch feminism. And one can listen to Anna Howard Shaw and be convinced that the nation must defend itself. One can also accuse all three of "cherry-picking" their data and of "stacking the deck." Still, their vignettes are disquieting, and their words linger. When Elizabeth Glaser gave her superb speech on the AIDS crisis in 1992, even Orrin Hatch, a rock-ribbed conservative, a Mormon, and then senator from Utah, was caught off guard. "I never really centered on the fact there were a significant number of children who suffered," said Hatch. "She brought that home to me."[40] A painful admission, but a brave one too.

Try as he might, Orrin Hatch could no longer think of AIDS as "the gay disease." He could no longer attribute it solely to wanton libertines who probably voted Democratic. AIDS was now a *human* disease for him. Orrin Hatch, a staunch antiabortionist who had seven brothers and sisters and who had fathered six children of his own, now had a problem. Elizabeth Glaser had created an "aha" moment for him. He had been sidelined by eloquence.

THE FUTURE OF ELOQUENCE

Today, new voices are emerging, new issues are dotting the public agenda, and new modes of human interaction are appearing daily. Someone, somewhere, is drawing a crowd, demanding that we offload our tired biases and become more inclusive. They are telling us to grow a conscience, to act immediately if not sooner. We may reject some of these voices and do so angrily. Over time, though, they will change us in some way. It has happened before. It will happen again.

But eloquence has its challenges in an age of cynicism. Why listen anew when we have been misled by rhetoric in the past? Why pay attention to speakers whose dreams seem barren, impractical, too costly, morally suspect? Surely by now we have earned the right to pull within ourselves, to declare a pox on all the political houses. Surely we must now become "calculating voters," treating politics as a game show and eloquence as a mere performance. Surely all the great men and women have now left us, taking their eloquence with them to the grave. Where is Dr. King these days? Where is Emma Goldman? Will Nancy Pelosi dislodge Eleanor Roosevelt? Surely not.

Suddenly, though, the replacements begin to emerge: Greta Thunberg on the environment; Bill Gates on global health; Bakari Sellers on civil rights; Deepak Chopra on alternative medicines; Malala Yousafzai on third-world children; Bono on human justice; Oprah Winfrey on life goals; Steve Jobs on modern technologies; Amanda Gorman on political insurrection; Robert Gates on world peace; Fareed Zakaria on international trade; William Barber on racial reconciliation; Michael Beschloss on political leadership; Brene Brown on social authenticity; Barack Obama on everything else.

Indeed, the signal/noise ratio is now so high in the United States that it is often hard to be heard. The issues, too, tumble forth: climate change, immigration policy, abortion rights, sexual predation, online disinformation, health-care injustice, gun control, gender identity, techno-colonialism, disability rights, vaccine mandates, First Amendment protections, religious freedom. "All the emotions we experience in life proper," says the critic Kenneth Burke, "are simply the material on which eloquence may feed."[41] On that score we need not worry: there are now plenty of emotions flitting about. What are we to do with them?

Some might argue that there is no longer a market for traditional understandings of eloquence because of new technologies.[42] Today's speech acts are doled out in mini-segments on Fox and MSNBC, providing just enough time for a smile, a grimace, two threats, and three outraged expostulations per encounter. In this Twitter-size environment, cultural resonance, personal investment, and poetic imagination become a distant memory. Talk is now atomized, with people's browsing histories, social networks, and even their credit reports being collected and analyzed so that "text packets" can be sent to them online, individually. In such an environment, says Rob Goodman, "representative thinking"—thoughts that apply equally well to all—becomes an impossibility.[43]

But let us pause for a moment. Yes, technologies are changing us, but much else remains the same. People are still born, and they still die. Wars still break out, and fiscal problems still defy easy solutions. People—and groups—still harbor their prejudices and, worse, share them with one another. Ceremonies are still being held, the United Nations still exists, and young people still graduate from college. Members of Congress still chatter, and the lecture circuit is more popular, and more lucrative, than ever before. Social activists, members of the clergy, corporate entrepreneurs, and all manner of worn-out pols still ascend the public stage each and every day.

And when the public speaking stops, more talk ensues. Radio and TV interviews reinforce what the speaker just said, after which the speaker follows up with a TED Talk, with blogs and podcasts, and perhaps with a book tour to generate regional appeal. While this is going on, the speakers' supporters and detractors—the second wave—battle it out on Facebook and Twitter, resending morsels of the original text across streaming platforms, hoping for the grandest of all things—virality. In a sense, the original speech never stops, so righteousness, definitiveness, expansiveness, and availability become more and more achievable. Eloquence, in a sense, can now be circulatory.

Technologies aside, any new eloquence will need what the old eloquence needed: the courage to stand out against the moral backdrop; the ingenuity to confront intractable issues like injustice and brutality; the inspiration to say something that has not been said before; the stamina to pursue a political project over time; the command of language needed to reach people emotionally. These requirements are unlikely to change. Why not eloquence today? Why not eloquence tomorrow?

Some say that eloquence is an elitist concept, but that argument is a canard. Why would someone with the capacity to speak not wish to speak well? Why would we not want to listen to better stories better told? Why not expand our imaginations and learn something new? Why would the supply of great orators have been exhausted in 1799 or 1899 or 1999 or yesterday? If political issues are no longer worthy of eloquence, are they really issues? Are they really worthy? And why lower our standards for eloquence? Why treat Donald Trump's animadversions as an acceptable personality quirk? Why not demand that Joe Biden practice what he is going to say before he says it? To cheat on eloquence is to cheat on ourselves. Why would we wish to do that?

CONCLUSION

Books are hard to write because they are long and must contain ideas. But, for me, writing this book has been inspiring. It has caused me to listen again to some of the most admirable Americans of the twentieth century and to appreciate the enormity of their tasks—to say something salvific about racial turmoil and human rights and to confront poverty, lawlessness, disease, and war head-on. None of these leaders had easy solutions to the problems they identified, but they confronted them nonetheless. Woodrow Wilson never got a functioning League of Nations, and Clarence Darrow lost when defending Leopold and Loeb at trial. Anita Hill saw Clarence Thomas serve on the Supreme Court, Shirley Chisholm failed to get the nation's wealth shared equitably, Stokely Carmichael did not end racism, and sexism outran Crystal Eastman and

Ann Richards. Ronald Reagan's presidency did not leave economic markets unfettered, and Catholic anguish about abortion rights outlived Mario Cuomo. Their collective eloquence changed things, but it was not a curative.

An underlying premise of this book is that we need to better understand eloquence to increase its supply. A second premise is that the world is better because of eloquence. Eloquence opens people up and gives them hope when they have none. Understanding the components of eloquence is a step toward making it more central in our lives. My analyses have teased out some of these factors, hopefully making eloquence less mysterious. Some speakers were, by my standards, more eloquent than others, but all used rhetoric to make the world better, and that too should be recognized. Eloquence, I believe, is an abiding human need, a need that becomes especially obvious when it goes unfulfilled.

My model of eloquence is only one model. We need to know more about how other cultures use public discourse to build common cause. To celebrate eloquence, as I have done in this book, is to celebrate the majesty of language. But it is also to celebrate a political system that lets people decide for themselves who will lead them and how. The poet Wallace Stevens said, "The words of things entangle and confuse / The plum survives its poems."[44] Plums may be magnificent enough that they need no rhetoric, but that is not true for democracies. A democracy needs all the words it can get to keep a people a people, to inspire them, and to nurse their wounds. A democracy thrives because of its eloquences.

APPENDIX

"IMPORTANCE" VERSUS "ELOQUENCE" RANKINGS FOR TWENTIETH-CENTURY SPEECHES

SURVEYED IMPORTANCE	CALCULATED ELOQUENCE		SPEECH
RANK	RANK	INDEX	
1	1	5.80	Martin Luther King: I Have a Dream (1968)
20	2	5.01	Douglas MacArthur: Duty, Honor, Country (1962)
56	3	3.42	Geraldine Ferraro: VP acceptance at DNC (1984)
79	4	3.26	Elizabeth Glaser: DNC address (1992)
64	5	2.93	Hubert Humphrey: DNC speech (1948)
51	6	2.88	Lyndon Johnson: Great Society (1964)
85	7	2.65	Gerald Ford: Taking the oath (1974)
54	8	2.52	Adlai Stevenson: 1952 DNC acceptance (1952)
22	9	2.28	John F. Kennedy: Ich Bin ein Berliner (1963)
2	10	2.21	John F. Kennedy: Inaugural address (1961)
49	11	2.14	Jesse Jackson: DNC keynote (1988)

(continued)

SURVEYED IMPORTANCE	CALCULATED ELOQUENCE		SPEECH
RANK	RANK	INDEX	
39	12	1.64	Richard Nixon: Resignation address (1974)
50	13	1.62	Mary Fisher: Whisper of AIDS (1992)
33	14	1.61	William Faulkner: Nobel acceptance (1950)
82	15	1.55	Ursula Le Guin: Mills College speech (1983)
4	16	1.23	FDR: Pearl Harbor attack (1941)
71	17	1.22	Lou Gehrig: Farewell (1939)
8	18	1.15	Ronald Reagan: Shuttle *Challenger* address (1986)
97	19	1.09	Joseph Welch: No Sense of Decency (1954)
94	20	1.07	Gerald Ford: Pardoning Nixon (1974)
9	21	1.05	John F. Kennedy: Houston Ministerial Association (1960)
12	22	0.97	Jesse Jackson: DNC speech (1984)
58	23	0.90	Ronald Reagan: D-Day anniversary (1984)
88	24	0.89	Jimmy Carter: Crisis of Confidence (1979)
74	25	0.83	Ted Kennedy: DNC address (1980)
21	26	0.72	Richard Nixon: Silent Majority (1969)
38	27	0.70	Ann Richards: DNC keynote (1988)
23	28	0.65	Clarence Darrow: Plea for mercy (1924)
62	29	0.47	Barry Goldwater: RNC acceptance (1964)
5	30	0.46	Barbara Jordan: DNC address (1976)
25	31	0.42	Ronald Reagan: Time for Choosing (1964)
34	32	0.41	Eugene Debs: Statement to the Court (1918)
80	33	0.40	Eugene Debs: The Issue (1908)

SURVEYED IMPORTANCE	CALCULATED ELOQUENCE		SPEECH
RANK	RANK	INDEX	
77	34	0.27	FDR: First inaugural address (1933)
11	35	0.19	Mario Cuomo: DNC keynote (1984)
73	36	0.06	Carrie Chapman Catt: U.S. Congress address (1917)
28	37	0.00	FDR: Arsenal of Democracy (1940)
29	38	−0.01	Ronald Reagan: Evil Empire (1983)
10	39	−0.04	Lyndon Johnson: We Shall Overcome (1965)
92	40	−0.08	Ronald Reagan: Brandenburg Gate (1987)
53	41	−0.22	Ted Kennedy: Truth and Tolerance (1983)
15	42	−0.24	Martin Luther King: Been to Mountaintop (1968)
69	43	−0.28	Anita Hill: Clarence Thomas hearing (1991)
42	44	−0.37	FDR: Four Freedoms (1941)
44	45	−0.45	William Jennings Bryan: Imperialism (1900)
96	46	−0.49	Lyndon Johnson: Let Us Continue (1963)
14	47	−0.50	Douglas MacArthur: Farewell to Congress (1951)
41	48	−0.58	Margaret C. Smith: Conscience Declaration (1950)
24	49	−0.60	Russell Conwell: Acres of Diamonds (1900–1925)
32	50	−0.65	Harry Truman: Truman Doctrine (1947)
57	51	−0.66	Robert LaFollette: Free Speech in Wartime (1917)
43	52	−0.71	Martin Luther King: Break the Silence (1967)
30	53	−0.74	Ronald Reagan: First inaugural address (1981)
75	54	−0.76	Lyndon Johnson: Will Not Run (1968)

(continued)

SURVEYED IMPORTANCE	CALCULATED ELOQUENCE		SPEECH
RANK	RANK	INDEX	
89	55	-0.78	Malcolm X: White Oppression (1963)
70	56	-0.79	Woodrow Wilson: League of Nations #2 (1919)
61	57	-0.82	John L. Lewis: Rights of Labor (1937)
17	58	-0.86	Robert F. Kennedy: MLK Assassination (1968)
86	59	-0.88	Cesar Chavez: Immigrants and Church (1968)
68	60	-0.89	Ted Kennedy: Robert Kennedy eulogy (1968)
95	61	-0.89	Woodrow Wilson: League of Nations #1 (1919)
84	62	-0.95	Huey P. Long: Share Our Wealth (1935)
47	63	-1.11	John F. Kennedy: Cuban missile crisis (1962)
45	64	-1.19	Barbara Bush: Wellesley commencement (1900)
90	65	-1.20	Bill Clinton: Oklahoma City bombing (1995)
7	66	-1.23	Malcolm X: Ballot or Bullet (1964)
36	67	-1.25	Dwight D. Eisenhower: Atoms for Peace (1953)
87	68	-1.25	Elizabeth Gurley Flynn: Smith Act trial (1953)
40	69	-1.27	Woodrow Wilson: Fourteen Points (1918)
46	70	-1.31	John F. Kennedy: Civil Rights (1963)
81	71	-1.39	Margaret Sanger: Children Era (1925)
13	72	-1.41	Barbara Jordan: Impeachment (1974)
52	73	-1.44	George Marshall: Marshall Plan (1947)
35	74	-1.49	Hillary Clinton: Human Rights (1995)
72	75	-1.52	Richard Nixon: Cambodian invasion (1970)
67	76	-1.56	Newton Minow: TV and Public Interest (1961)
60	77	-1.64	Ted Kennedy: Chappaquiddick (1969)
77	78	-1.67	Woodrow Wilson: First inaugural address (1933)

SURVEYED IMPORTANCE	CALCULATED ELOQUENCE		SPEECH
RANK	RANK	INDEX	
19	79	-1.69	Woodrow Wilson: War message (1917)
63	80	-1.73	Stokely Carmichael: Black Power (1966)
26	81	-1.75	Huey P. Long: Every Man a King (1934)
6	82	-1.79	Richard Nixon: Checkers (1952)
27	83	-1.79	Ann Howard Shaw: Principles of a Republic (1915)
78	84	-1.80	Mario Savio: Sproul Hall (1964)
100	85	-1.94	John Kerry: Senate Foreign Relations (1972)
76	86	-2.01	FDR: Commonwealth Club (1932)
48	87	-2.14	Spiro Agnew: TV news coverage (1969)
66	88	-2.17	Carrie Chatman Catt: The Crisis (1916)
55	89	-2.18	Eleanor Roosevelt: Adoption of Declaration (1948)
31	90	-2.21	FDR: First fireside chat (1933)
59	91	-2.27	Mario Cuomo: Faith and Morality (1984)
91	92	-2.46	Shirley Chisholm: Equal Rights Amendment (1970)
65	93	-2.55	Emma Goldman: Address to the Jury (1917)
99	94	-2.71	Robert F. Kennedy: Cape Town affirmation (1966)
93	95	-2.89	Elie Wiesel: Perils of indifference (1986)
18	96	-2.90	Dwight D. Eisenhower: Farewell address (1961)
98	97	-2.92	Eleanor Roosevelt: Human rights (1950)
83	98	-3.01	Crystal Eastman: Female suffrage (1920)
16	99	-3.31	Teddy Roosevelt: Man with a muckrake (1906)
37	100	-3.42	John F. Kennedy: American U. speech (1963)

ACKNOWLEDGMENTS

For a scholar, being a mentor is profoundly important, but eventually it seems to stop, with the mentee setting off to conquer the world or, at least, getting a tenure-track job somewhere. I have had the good fortune of sending thirty-three such young people on their way, and that is deeply satisfying. For the recipient, however, mentorship is a cursed thing. Writing this book has caused me to reflect repeatedly on those who helped make my scholarly life—hell, my life itself—possible. Those who opened up the world of ideas to me as an undergraduate—Jay Savereid, Bill Price, and Melvin Wolfe—abide with me today. But did I thank them sufficiently when they were among the living? Did they know how profoundly they had affected me? Could they realize how the mentee's debt grows larger over time, as radically new events force one to draw on older teachings, thereby leaving no practical way of paying off the balance . . . ever? Mentorship, a damnable thing.

In partial recompense, I have dedicated this book to two former teachers during my graduate program, persons whose memories lie trapped within me many years later. Dick Gregg was a brilliant phenomenologist with a way of discovering curiosities in the sorriest of texts, a man intrigued by political life, about why things were the way they were and how they could be made better. George Borden was not a phenomenologist, but he was a fine behavioral scientist, among the first in the field of communication to ask if computers might disclose interesting patterns in language, thereby revealing the seen-but-unnoticed. In this book, I draw deeply on what they taught me, which is not to say that they are responsible for any of the book's shortcomings.

I am also indebted to two career-long friends of mine, Professors Steve Lucas of the University of Wisconsin–Madison and the late Marty Medhurst of Baylor University. It was only through their kindness and professionalism that this book was made possible. They provided me with background information on their survey in 1999, a survey that identified what they considered to be the hundred most important speeches of the twentieth century. In my own fashion, I followed up on their work, sometimes arriving at different conclusions about political eloquence. This book and the Lucas-Medhurst survey epitomize what scholars are supposed to do—ask questions of one another and find new truths. Steve and Marty enthusiastically encouraged me to take on this project. For that, and for so much else, I am profoundly grateful.

Because this book delves into recent American history, writing it has made me think irretrievably of my doctoral mentor, Carroll Arnold, but also of several mentors-by-proxy who helped a younger version of me find his way in the academy, a group that includes Jeff Auer, Sam Becker, Jane Blankenship, John Waite Bowers, Wayne Brockriede, Ted Clevenger, Murray Edelman, Hank Ewbank, Walt Fisher, Doris Graber, Gerry Mohrmann, Larry Rosenfield, Tom Scheidel, Bob Scott, Herb Simons, Herm Stelzner, and especially Ed Black and Marie Hochmuth Nichols.

When writing this book, I also reflected on my contemporaries in the study of American public discourse, persons whose scholarship I deeply admire, a group that includes among others Barry Brummett, Tom Farrell, Dilip Gaonkar, Tom Goodnight, Bruce Gronbeck, Bob Hariman, Bob Ivie, David Kaufer, Andy King, Mike Leff, Mike

McGee, Mike Osborn, Martha Solomon Watson, David Zarefsky, and especially Karlyn Kohrs Campbell and Kathleen Hall Jamieson.

A younger cohort of rhetorical scholars has also inspired me and, even better, challenged me to think new thoughts, a group that includes among others Rob Asen, Vanessa Beasley, Denise Bostdorff, Dana Cloud, Celeste Condit, Lisa Corrigan, Nathan Crick, Jim Darsey, Bonnie Dow, Ron Greene, Josh Gunn, Mike Hogan, Davis Houck, Michael Lee, Kristy Maddux, Sam McCormick, Jennifer Mercieca, Pete Simonson, Robert Terrill, Kirt Wilson, and especially John Murphy and Mary Stuckey.

I am also indebted to my colleagues in political science who received me warmly over the years as I reached across the disciplinary boundaries, persons whose scholarship and professionalism are nonpareil, a group that includes among others Julia Azari, Lance Bennett, Jeff Cohen, Ann Crigler, George Edwards, Mo Fiorina, John Geer, Lori Cox Han, John Hibbing, Elvin Lim, Bruce Miroff, Diana Owen, Tom Patterson, Robert Shapiro, Daron Shaw, Stephen Skowronek, Bat Sparrow, Jeff Tulis, and especially David Paletz and Kathy Cramer.

This book and the memories that descended upon me when writing it show that the past abides, so to all of the preceding I am deeply grateful. I am also grateful for the support of Dean Jay Bernhardt and my department chair, Craig Scott, who supported the research leave needed to complete this project. I also appreciate the labors of my research assistants—Suzanne Burdick, Yujin Kim, Inbal Leibovits, and Clayton Terry—who removed obstacles from my path, as did the staff of the Annette Strauss Institute for Civic Life at U.T.–Austin. I also admire the herculean efforts of Dr. Michael Eidenmuller, whose website (AmericanRhetoric.com) consistently brings the concept of eloquence to life. Finally, I am indebted to my editor at Columbia University Press, Stephen Wesley, who supported this project from the very beginning and who, blessedly, likes the way I write. This, too, is a debt I cannot repay. Perhaps bitcoin?

RPH
March 2022

NOTES

1. ELOQUENCE: WHY?

1. Lloyd Steffen, "A Plea for Political Eloquence: A Reminder from Religion," *Huffington Post*, March 21, 2016, https://www.huffpost.com/entry/a-plea -for-political-eloq_b_9507836.
2. Quoted in Stephen Mailloux, "Rhetorical Ways of Proceeding: *Eloquentia Perfecta* in American Jesuit Colleges," in *Traditions of Eloquence: The Jesuits and Modern Rhetorical Studies*, ed. Cynthia Gannett and John C. Brereton (New York: Fordham University Press, 2016), 164.
3. Quoted in Adam S. Potkay, "Theorizing Civic Eloquence in the Early Republic: The Road from David Hume to John Quincy Adams," *Early American Literature* 34 (1999): 158.
4. Quoted in Potkay, "Theorizing Civic Eloquence," 161.
5. Theodore L. Glasser and James S. Ettema, "Ethics and Eloquence in Journalism: An Approach to Press Accountability," *Journalism Studies* 9, no. 4 (2008): 528.
6. Anderson Cooper, "360 Degrees," *CNN Transcripts*, July 14, 2020, http:// transcripts.cnn.com/TRANSCRIPTS/2007/14/acd.01.html.
7. Simon Sebag Montefiore, "What Makes a Great Speech?" *LitHub*, June 1, 2021, https://lithub.com/what-makes-a-great-speech/.
8. Kevin Liptak and Athena Jones, "With Latest Jabs, Trump-Obama Relationship Reaches Historic Nastiness," *CNN Politics*, September 3, 2017, https:// www.cnn.com/2017/06/28/politics/trump-obama-relationship/index .html.

9. Gabriel Sherman, "'With Obama He's Going for the Jugular': As Trump Goes After Obama, Some in Trumpworld See a 'Big Risk,'" *Vanity Fair*, May 19, 2020, https://www.vanityfair.com/news/2020/05/trump-goes-after-obama.

10. Trymaine Lee, as quoted in "The Relationship Between President Trump and Former President Obama," WBEZ Chicago, May 26, 2020, https://www.wbez.org/stories/the-relationship-between-president-trump-and-former-president-obama/d3c48596-22c6-457d-946f-5b51ad7056a8.

11. Charles M. Blow, "Trump's Obama Obsession," *New York Times*, June 29, 2017, https://www.nytimes.com/2017/06/29/opinion/trumps-obama-obsession.html.

12. See Chris Cillizza, "The 28 Most Outrageous Lines from Donald Trump's Mount Rushmore Speech," *CNN Politics*, July 4, 2020, https://www.cnn.com/2020/07/04/politics/donald-trump-mount-rushmore-south-dakota-speech-lines/index.html.

13. For more on the rhetoric of Donald Trump, see Roderick P. Hart, *Trump and Us: What He Says and Why People Listen* (New York: Cambridge University Press, 2020); Joshua Gunn, *Political Perversion: Rhetorical Aberration in the Time of Trumpeteering* (Chicago: University of Chicago Press, 2020); and Jennifer Mercieca, *Demagogue for President: The Rhetorical Genius of Donald Trump* (College Station: Texas A&M University Press, 2020).

14. Matthew Bevis, *The Art of Eloquence: Byron, Dickens, Tennyson, Joyce* (Columbus: Ohio State University Press, 2007), 205.

15. Marcus Priest, "Eloquence Has Left the Court, Your Honour," *Financial Review*, August 24, 2007, https://www.afr.com/companies/professional-services/eloquence-has-left-the-court-your-honour-20070824-j715w.

16. Danielle R. Pye, "Eloquence in a New Key: Toward a Theory of Presentational Communication" (PhD diss., University of Texas at Austin, 2016).

17. Quoted in Jerrold E. Seigel, *Rhetoric and Philosophy in Renaissance Humanism: The Union of Eloquence and Wisdom, Petrarch to Valla* (Princeton, NJ: Princeton University Press, 1968), 43.

18. Giambattista Vico, "Remarks on Eloquence" in *The Rhetorical Tradition: Readings from Classical Times to the Present*, ed. Patricia Bizzell and Bruce Herzberg (Boston: Bedford, 1990), 726.

19. John Locke, *An Essay Concerning Human Understanding*, book 3, chap. 10, 189, https://www.earlymoderntexts.com/assets/pdfs/locke1690book3.pdf.

20. Lynda E. Boose, "Scolding Brides and Bridling Scolds: Taming the Woman's Unruly Member," *Shakespeare Quarterly* 42 (1991): 204. For more on feminism and Shakespeare, see Ling Yu, "A Study of How Kate Is Portrayed as a Shrew in *The Taming of the Shrew* by Shakespeare," *Journal of Contemporary Educational Research* 5, no. 4 (2021).

21. Philip Arrington, *Eloquence Divine: In Search of God's Rhetoric* (Eugene, OR: Cascade, 2017), 208–9.

22. Quentin Skinner, "Moral Ambiguity and the Renaissance Art of Eloquence," *Essays in Criticism* 44, no. 4 (1994): 271; my italics.

23. Quoted in Don Paul Abbott, "'Eloquence Is Power': Hobbes on the Use and Abuse of Rhetoric," *Rhetorica* 32, no. 4 (2014) 400.

24. For more on eloquence and mistrust, see Mary E. Stuckey, *Slipping the Surly Bonds: Reagan's Challenger Address* (College Station: Texas A&M University Press, 2006), 20.

25. Hannah Gray, "Renaissance Humanism: The Pursuit of Eloquence," *Journal of the History of Ideas* 24, no. 4 (1963): 504, 507.

26. David Crystal, *The Gift of the Gab: How Eloquence Works* (New Haven, CT: Yale University Press, 2016).

27. Thomas Davis et al., *Treasury of Eloquence: Being a Compendium of Irish Oratory and Literature* (Boston: Murphy and McCarthy, 1882), v.

28. Helen F. North, "Emblems of Eloquence," *Proceedings of the American Philosophical Society* 137, no. 3 (1993): 406, 411–12.

29. Davis W. Houck, "FDR's Commonwealth Club Address: Redefining Individualism, Adjudicating Greatness," *Rhetoric & Public Affairs* 7, no. 3 (2004): 276.

30. Hugh Blair, "Lectures on Rhetoric and Belles Lettres," in *The Rhetorical Tradition: Readings from Classical Times to the Present*, ed. Patricia Bizzell and Bruce Herzberg (Boston: Bedford, 1990), 818.

31. As reproduced in Crystal, *The Gift of the Gab*, 119.

32. Peggy Noonan, *What I Saw at the Revolution: A Political Life in the Reagan Era* (New York: Random House, 2003), 69.

33. For more on how the public sphere can be colonized, see Tom Shachtman, *The Inarticulate Society: Eloquence and Culture in America* (New York: Free Press, 1995), 236.

34. Issues like those sketched out here are currently being explored in the field of rhetorical studies—and profitably so. New questions about how political leaders should address issues of diversity, equity, and inclusion are being regularly featured in the scholarly journals, although no easy answers have been forthcoming, a testament to the difficulty of saying anything conclusive about a nation that can choose Barack Obama and Donald Trump in successive elections. For a sampling of how scholars have been addressing such matters, see two wonderfully engaging collections: the centennial issue of the *Quarterly Journal of Speech* 101, no. 1 (February 2015); and the special issue of *Rhetoric and Public Affairs* 24, no. 1–2 (Spring–Summer 2021).

35. Quoted in Catherine Nicholson, *Uncommon Tongues: Eloquence and Eccentricity in the English Renaissance* (Philadelphia: University of Pennsylvania Press, 2014), 67.

36. Nicholson, *Uncommon Tongues*, 10.

2. ELOQUENCE: WHEN AND WHERE?

1. Susan Sontag, *As Consciousness Is Harnessed to Flesh: Journals & Notebooks, 1964–1980*, ed. David Rieff (New York: Farrar, Straus and Giroux, 1976).

2. https://www.brainyquote.com/quotes/meg_ryan_346716.

3. From then-candidate Bush's nomination acceptance address at the Republican National Convention, August 1988, https://www.entrepreneur.com /article/312638.

4. https://www.goodreads.com/quotes/371820-a-despot-doesn-t-fear -eloquent-writers-preaching-freedom-he-fears-a.

5. Erving Goffman, "On Face-Work: An Analysis of Ritual Elements in Social Interaction," *Psychiatry* 18, no. 3 (1955): 227.

6. https://www.goodreads.com/quotes/480041-you-must-speak-straight -so-that-your-words-may-go.

7. For more on the texture of orality, see Carroll C. Arnold, "Oral Rhetoric, Rhetoric, and Literature," *Philosophy and Rhetoric* 40, no. 1 (2007): 170–87.

8. For more on these differences in modality, see Sarah Liggett, "The Relationship Between Speaking and Writing: An Annotated Bibliography," *College Composition and Communication* 35, no. 3 (1984): 334–44; Wallace L. Chafe, "Linguistic Differences Produced by Differences Between Speaking and Writing," in *Literacy, Language and Learning: The Nature and Consequences of Reading and Writing*, ed. David R. Olson, Nancy Torrance, and Angela Hildyard (New York: Cambridge University Press, 1985), 105–23; and Karlyn K. Campbell, Susan S. Huxman, and Thomas A. Burkholder, *The Rhetorical Act: Thinking, Speaking, and Writing Critically* (Stamford, CT: Cengage, 2015).

9. Denis Donoghue, *On Eloquence* (New Haven, CT: Yale University Press, 2008), 41.

10. As quoted in James Perrin Warren, *Culture of Eloquence: Oratory and Reform in Antebellum America* (University Park: Pennsylvania State University Press, 1999), 115.

11. As quoted in Denis Donoghue, *The American Classics: A Personal Essay* (New Haven, CT: Yale University Press, 2005), 9.

12. Donoghue, *On Eloquence*, 41.

13. As quoted in Brian Vickers, *In Defence of Rhetoric* (Oxford: Clarendon, 1988), 1–2.

14. Bryan Garsten, *Saving Persuasion* (Cambridge, MA: Harvard University Press, 2006), 65.

15. Vickers, *In Defence of Rhetoric*, 4.

16. Garsten, *Saving Persuasion*, 141.

17. Kathy M. Houff, "François de Salignac de la Mothe-Fénelon: 1851–1715," in *Eighteenth-Century British and American Rhetoric and Rhetoricians and Sources*, ed. Michael G. Moran (Westport, CT: Greenwood, 1994), 84.

18. Beth Innocenti Manolescu, "Clerics Competing for and Against 'Eloquence' in Mid-Eighteenth-Century Britain," *Rhetoric Society Quarterly* 30, no. 1 (2000): 47.

19. Donoghue, *The American Classics*, 260.

20. Lars Leeten, "Kant and the Problem of 'True Eloquence,'" *Rhetorica* 37, no. 1 (2019): 61, 82.

21. Leeten, "Kant and the Problem of 'True Eloquence,'" 74.

22. Garsten, *Saving Persuasion*, 45, 52, 65.

23. As quoted in Garsten, *Saving Persuasion*, 200–201.

24. Donoghue, *On Eloquence*, 154. Eloquence has often been conceived of as having an "excess" of certain rhetorical features, but I find it more useful to concentrate on its normative features. That is especially true when examining *spoken* eloquence, an arena in which straying too far from the norms of a given speech community can make an audience suspicious of a speaker's sincerity and cultural sensitivity.

25. Thomas B. Farrell, *Norms of Rhetorical Culture* (New Haven, CT: Yale University Press, 1993), 266.

26. Olivier Morin and Alberto Acerbi, "Birth of the Cool: A Two-Centuries Decline in Emotional Expression in Anglophone Fiction," *Cognition and Emotion* 31, no. 8 (2017): 1663–75.

27. For reasons such as these, says James Fallows, "rhetorical polish . . . can be a staff-enhanced virtue" in a world in which rhetoric is constantly "manufactured" by persons and parties in positions of power. See James Fallows, "On Eloquence vs. Prettiness," *Atlantic*, May 18, 2009, https://www.theatlantic.com/technology/archive/2009/05/on-eloquence-vs-prettiness/17695/.

28. Nicholas Buttrick, Robert Moulder, and Shigehiro Oishi, "Historical Changes in the Moral Foundations of Political Persuasion," *Personality and Social Psychology Bulletin*, March 18, 2020, https://journals.sagepub.com/doi/abs/10.1177/0146167220907467.

29. Donoghue, *On Eloquence*, 153.

30. For a colorful discussion of memorability, see Bill Cunningham, "The Lost Power of Eloquence," *Justice Bill Cunningham's Blog*, February 14, 2016, https://justicebillcunningham.wordpress.com/2016/02/14/the-lost-power-of-eloquence/.

31. Kathleen Hall Jamieson, *Eloquence in an Electronic Age: The Transformation of Political Speechmaking* (New York: Oxford University Press, 1988).

32. Jamieson, *Eloquence in an Electronic Age*, 89. For a contemporary look at how new technologies affect presidential discourse, see Stephen J. Heidt and Damien Smith Pfister, "Trump, Twitter, and the Microdiatribe: The Short Circuits of Networked Presidential Public Address," in *Reading the Presidency: Advances in Presidential Rhetoric*, ed. Stephen J. Heidt and Mary E. Stuckey (Bern, Switzerland: Peter Lang, 2019), 171–87.

33. Peter Elbow, *Vernacular Eloquence: What Speech Can Bring to Writing* (New York: Oxford University Press, 2012), 373.

34. Celeste M. Condit, "In Praise of Eloquent Diversity: Gender and Rhetoric as Public Persuasion," *Women's Studies in Communication* 20, no. 2 (1997): 106.

35. Condit, "In Praise of Eloquent Diversity," 106.

36. Julius Lester, "The Singing Is Over: The Angry Children of Malcom X," *Sing Out* 16 (October–November 1961): 21–25.

37. Robert L. Caserio, "Eloquence: A Response to Harold Bloom's *The American Canon*," *Symplokē* 28, no. 1 (2020): 431, 441.

38. Quoted in Alan Brinton, "Hugh Blair and the True Eloquence," *Rhetoric Society Quarterly* 22, no. 3 (1992): 31.

39. Maurice Bloch, ed., *Political Language and Oratory in Traditional Society* (New York: Academic Press, 1975).

40. Aripova A. Khasanovna, "The Live Word Is an Important Tool That Constitutes the Content-Essence of the Oratory Art," *American Journal of Social Science and Education Innovations* 3 (2021): 427.

41. John Comaroff, "Talking Politics: Oratory and Authority in a Tswana Chiefdom," in *Political Language and Oratory in Traditional Society*, ed. Bloch, 152–53.

42. Anne Salmond, "Mana Makes the Man: A Look at Maori Oratory and Politics," in *Political Language and Oratory in Traditional Society*, ed. Bloch, 55.

43. Hannah Arendt, "Truth and Politics," in *Between Past and Future* (New York: Penguin, 2006), 237.

44. Andrew Strathern, "Veiled Speech in Mount Hagen," in *Political Language and Oratory in Traditional Society*, ed. Bloch, 193.

45. R. B. Parkinson, "Literary Form and the 'Tale of the Eloquent Peasant,'" *Journal of Egyptian Archaeology* 78 (1992): 163–78.

46. Lesley Rameka, Ruth Ham, and Linda Mitchell, "Pōwhiri: The Ritual Encounter," *Contemporary Issues in Early Childhood* (2021), https://journals.sagepub.com/doi/abs/10.1177/1463949121995591.

47. Rob Goodman, "Eloquence and Its Conditions" (PhD diss., Columbia University, 2018), 242, 258. Goodman has followed up on this work with

a marvelous book, *Words on Fire: Eloquence and Its Conditions* (New York: Cambridge University Press, 2022). His is more a conceptual work than an empirical one and thus provides a consistently interesting counterpoint to my own study.

48. Maurice Bloch, introduction to *Political Language and Oratory in Traditional Society*, ed. Bloch, 6.

49. Bloch, introduction, 17.

50. Ronald Greene, "John Dewey's Eloquent Citizen: Communication, Judgment, and Postmodern Capitalism," *Argumentation and Advocacy* 39 (2003): 194.

51. David B. Coplan, "Eloquent Knowledge: Lesotho Migrants' Songs and the Anthropology of Experience," *American Ethnologist* 14, no. 3 (1987): 419, 429, 431.

52. https://www.goodreads.com/quotes/4252974-half-drunken-poetry-is-the-most-honest-kind-of-poetry-too.

53. Edwin Black, *Rhetorical Questions: Studies of Public Discourse* (Chicago: University of Chicago Press, 1992), 101. See also Richard Weaver, *The Ethics of Rhetoric* (New York: Henry Regnery, 1953).

54. Donoghue, *On Eloquence*, 149.

55. Kenneth Cmiel, *Democratic Eloquence: The Fight Over Popular Speech in Nineteenth-Century America* (New York: William Morrow, 1990), 58.

56. Cmiel, *Democratic Eloquence*, 52, 95.

57. Cmiel, *Democratic Eloquence*, 60.

58. Black, *Rhetorical Questions*, 81.

59. Black, *Rhetorical Questions*, 148.

60. Roderick P. Hart, *Seducing America: How Television Charms the Modern Voter* (New York: Oxford University Press, 1994).

61. Genuinely pioneering work on metaphor has been done by Michael Osborn over a long and distinguished career. See especially *Michael Osborn on Metaphor and Style* (East Lansing: Michigan State University Press, 2018).

62. Black, *Rhetorical Questions*, 95.

63. Bill Jewett, "Obama Afghan Speech Eloquent, but Flawed," *Intelligencer Journal*, December 21, 2009, https://lancasteronline.com/opinion/letters_to_editor/obama-afghan-speech-eloquent-but-flawed/article_f7b571e7-a7aa-5ec9-8f7c-8e1c25d1404e.html.

64. Robert F. Dorr, "Advocates for Threatened Global Hawk Are Eloquent but Wrong-headed," *Air Force Times*, May 14, 2012.

65. Joel Yanofsky, "Left's Limbaugh: Eloquent but Crabby," *Gazette* (Montreal), August 26, 1995.

66. Felicity Hannah, "Pension Scam Victims Lose £82,000 Each in 24 Hours," *Independent*, November 8, 2019, https://www.independent.co.uk/money /spend-save/pensions-scams-theft-fraud-victims-pensioners-old-age -fca-a9194221.html.

67. Andrew Smith, "Sweden's Big Noise," *Sunday Times* (London), January 3, 1999.

68. Lois Gilbert, "Eloquent, but Perhaps Ultimately Pointless, Memoir," *Santa Fe New Mexican*, December 8, 2002.

69. Brad Wheeler, "Albums We Never Saw Coming," *Globe and Mail*, October 25, 2019, https://www.theglobeandmail.com/arts/music/article-albums-we -never-saw-coming/.

70. John Rockwell, "Wynton Marsalis's Abyssinian Mass Brings Joy to the Lincoln Center, New York," *Financial Times*, November 27, 2019, https:// www.ft.com/content/5f656804-0f7e-11ea-a7e6-62bf4f9e548a.

3. ELOQUENCE: HOW?

1. Dana Varinsky and Leanna Garfield, "7 Things Frank Lloyd Wright, One of the Most Iconic American Architects, Got Wrong About Design," *Business Insider*, June 8, 2017, https://www.businessinsider.com/frank-lloyd-wright -houses2017-6.

2. For an interesting take on the often paradoxical nature of movement rhetoric, see Don Waisanen and Judith Kafka, "Conflicting Purposes in U.S. School Reform: The Paradoxes of Arne Duncan's Educational Rhetoric," *Rhetoric and Public Affairs* 23, no. 4 (2020): 637–74.

3. Celeste M. Condit, "In Praise of Eloquent Diversity: Gender and Rhetoric as Public Persuasion," *Women's Studies in Communication* 20, no. 2 (1997): 106.

4. As reported in the *New York Times Magazine*, September 11, 1932, 2.

5. Denis Donoghue, *On Eloquence* (New Haven, CT: Yale University Press, 2008), 19.

6. Nathan Crick, *Democracy and Rhetoric: John Dewey on the Arts of Becoming* (Columbia: University of South Carolina Press, 2010), 177.

7. Simon Sebag Montefiore, "What Makes a Great Speech?" *Literary Hub*, June 1, 2021, https://lithub.com/what-makes-a-great-speech/.

8. For more on DICTION, including its structure and function as well as a comprehensive bibliography, see www.dictionsoftware.com.

9. John Barth, *Giles Goat-Boy* (New York: Doubleday, 1966), 61.

10. Stephen Marche, "Literature Is Not Data," *Los Angeles Review of Books*," October 28, 2012, https://lareviewofbooks.org/article/literature-is-not -data-against-digital-humanities.

11. Timothy Brennan, "The Digital-Humanities Bust," *Chronicle of Higher Education*, October 15, 2017, https://www.chronicle.com/article/the-digital-humanities-bust/.

12. Laurens W. M. Bod, "Who's Afraid of Patterns? The Particular Versus the Universal and the Meaning of Humanities 3.0," *Low Countries Historical Review* 128, no. 1 (2013): 171–80. Joseph Raben offers an interesting overview of how the digital humanities got started in "Humanities Computing Twenty-Five Years Later," *Computers and the Humanities* 25 (1991): 341–50.

13. For more on such matters, see Franco Moretti, *Distant Reading* (London: Verso, 2013).

14. Suguru Ishizaki and David Kaufer, "Computer-Aided Rhetorical Analysis," in *Applied Natural Language Processing: Identification, Investigation, and Resolution*, ed. Philip M. McCarthy and Chutima Boonthum-Denecke (Hershey, PA: IGI Global, 2012), 276–95.

15. Franco Moretti and Dominique Pestre, "Bankspeak: The Language of World Bank Reports, 1946–2012," *Pamphlet No. 9: Stanford Literary Lab*, March 2015, https://litlab.stanford.edu/LiteraryLabPamphlet9.pdf.

16. Ryan Light, "From Words to Networks and Back: Digital Text, Computational Social Science, and the Case of Presidential Inaugural Addresses," *Social Currents* 1, no. 2 (2014): 111–29.

17. John W. Black, Cleavonne S. Stratton, Alan C. Nichols, and Marian A. Chavez, *The Use of Words in Context: The Vocabulary of College Students* (Heidelberg: Springer, 1985).

18. Joshua C. Jackson et al., "Emotion Semantics Show Both Cultural Variation and Universal Structure," *Science*, December 20, 2019, https://science.sciencemag.org/content/366/6472/1517.

19. Graham Bowley, "Computers That Trade on the News," *New York Times*, December 22, 2010, https://dealbook.nytimes.com/2010/12/23/computers-that-trade-on-the-news/.

20. Jean-Baptiste Michel et al., "Quantitative Analysis of Culture Using Millions of Digitized Books," *Science*, January 14, 2011, https://science.sciencemag.org/content/331/6014/176.

21. John Burrows, "Textual Analysis," in *A Companion to Digital Humanities*, ed. Susan Schreibman, Ray Siemens, and John Unsworth (Malden, MA: Blackwell, 2004), 323–47.

22. Laura E. Wallace, Rebecca Anthony, Christian M. End, and Baldwin M. Way, "Does Religion Stave Off the Grave? Religious Affiliation in One's Obituary and Longevity," *Social Psychological and Personality Science* 10, no. 5 (2018): 662–70.

23. William J. Brady, Julian A. Wills, John T. Jost, Joshua A. Tucker, and Jay J. Van Bavel, "Emotion Shapes the Diffusion of Moralized Content in Social Networks," *PNAS* 114, no. 28 (2017): 7,313–18.

24. Lev Manovich, "Trending: The Promises and the Challenges of Big Social Data," in *Debates in the Digital Humanities*, ed. Matthew Gold (Minneapolis: University of Minnesota Press, 2012), 469.

25. Eric Slauter, "Revolutions in the Meaning and Study of Politics," *American Literary History* 22, no. 2 (2010): 325–40.

26. Dana Boyd and Kate Crawford, "Critical Questions for Big Data: Provocations for a Cultural, Technological, and Scholarly Phenomenon," *Information, Communication, and Society* 15, no. 5 (2012): 662–79.

27. Franco Moretti, "Literature Measured," *Pamphlet No. 12: Stanford Literary Lab*, April 2016, https://litlab.stanford.edu/LiteraryLabPamphlet12.pdf.

28. Stephen J. Ramsay, "Textual Behavior in the Human Male," paper presented at the Inaugural Symposium of the Institute of the Humanities and Global Cultures, Charlottesville, Virginia, November 9, 2011.

29. David Kaufer and Robert Hariman, "Discriminating Political Styles as Genres: A Corpus Study Exploring Hariman's Theory of Political Style," *Text & Talk* 28, no. 4 (2008): 491.

30. Lori Young and Stuart Soroka, "Affective News: The Automated Coding of Sentiment in Political Texts," *Political Communication* 29 (2012): 205. For more on how textual patterns recur through time, see Zoltan Majdik, "Five Considerations for Engaging with Big Data from a Rhetorical -Humanistic Perspective," *Poroi* 16, no. 1 (2021), https://doi.org/10.13008/2151-2957.1312.

31. Thomas Carlyle, *Latter Day Pamphlets*, ed. Michael K. Goldberg and Jules P. Seigel (Ottawa: Canadian Federation for the Humanities, 1983), 41, 263.

32. Portions of this discussion have been adapted from Roderick P. Hart, "Genre and Automated Text Analysis: A Demonstration," in *Rhetoric and the Digital Humanities*, ed. Jim Ridolfo and William Hart-Davidson (Chicago: University of Chicago Press, 2015), 152–68. For more on this matter of granularity, see Jussi Karlgren, Magnus Sahlgren, Fredrik Olsson, Fredrik Espinoza, and Ola Hamfors, "Usefulness of Sentiment Analysis," In *Proceedings of the Thirty-Fourth European Conference on IR Research, Barcelona, Spain* (Berlin: Springer, 2012).

33. Charles J. Brainerd and Valerie F. Reyna, "Memory Independence and Memory Interference in Cognitive Development," *Psychological Review* 100 (1993): 42–67.

34. G. Robert Boynton and Milton Lodge, "Voters' Images of Candidates," in *Presidential Campaigns and American Self-Image*, ed. Arthur H. Miller and Bruce E. Gronbeck (Boulder, CO: Westview, 1994), 176–89.

35. Susan Wittig, "The Computer and the Concept of Text," *Computers and the Humanities* 11 (1977): 211–15.

36. Rosanne G. Potter, preface to *Literary Computing and Literary Criticism: Theoretical and Practical Essays in Theme and Rhetoric*, ed. Rosanne G. Potter (Philadelphia: University of Pennsylvania Press, 1989), xvi.

37. Michael Gavin, "Is There a Text in My Data? (Part 1): On Counting Words," *Journal of Cultural Analytics*, January 25, 2020, 4 https://culturalanalytics .org/article/11830-is-there-a-text-in-my-data-part-1-on-counting-words.

38. Nan Z. Da, "The Computational Case Against Computational Literary Studies," *Critical Inquiry* 45 (2019): 601–39.

39. These are the types of studies Nan Za critiques in her survey of computer-based literary studies.

40. Walter Fisher, "Reaffirmation and Subversion of the American Dream," *Quarterly Journal of Speech* 47 (1973): 160–67.

41. Carroll C. Arnold, "Reflections on American Public Discourse," *Communication Studies* 28 (1977): 73–85.

42. Michael Sandel, *Democracy's Discontent: America in Search of a Public Philosophy* (Cambridge, MA: Belknap, 1996), 322.

43. George Core, "The Eloquence of Fact," *Virginia Quarterly Review* 54, no. 4 (1978): 738.

44. J. Lee Campbell, "'It Is as if a Green Bough Were Laid Across the Page': Thoreau on Eloquence," *Rhetoric Society Quarterly* 20, no. 1 (1990): 64.

45. Campbell, "Thoreau on Eloquence," 62.

46. Kenneth Cmiel, *Democratic Eloquence: The Fight Over Popular Speech in Nineteenth-Century America* (New York: William Morrow, 1990), 262.

47. Sandra M. Gustafson, *Eloquence in Power: Oratory and Performance in Early America* (Chapel Hill: University of North Carolina Press, 2000), 25.

48. For a statistical perspective on Trump's rhetoric, see Roderick P. Hart, *Trump and Us: What He Says and Why People Listen* (New York: Cambridge University Press, 2020).

49. James Spanier and Robert L. Wendzel, *Games Nations Play* (Washington, DC: Congressional Quarterly Press, 1996).

50. Steven Perry, "Rhetorical Functions of the Infestation Metaphor in Hitler's Rhetoric," *Central States Speech Journal* 34 (1983): 229–35.

51. Francis A. Beer, "The Epidemiology of Peace and War," *International Studies Quarterly* 23 (1979): 45–86.

52. Paul Chilton and Mikhail Ilyin, "Metaphor in Political Discourse: The Case of the 'Common European House,' " *Discourse and Society* 4 (1991): 7–31.

53. Garrett Hardin, "Living on a Lifeboat," in *Managing the Commons*, ed. Garrett Hardin and John Baden (New York: W. H. Freeman, 1977), 261–79.

54. Portions of this discussion draw upon Roderick P. Hart, Sharon E. Jarvis, William P. Jennings, and Deborah Smith-Howell, *Political Keywords: Using Language That Uses Us* (New York: Oxford University Press, 2005).

55. John M. Murphy, "Theory and Public Address: The Allusive Mr. Bush," in *The Handbook of Public Address*, ed. Shawn J. Parry-Giles and J. Michael Hogan (New York: Wiley-Blackwell, 2010), 276.

56. David Zarefsky, "Knowledge Claims in Rhetorical Criticism," *Journal of Communication* 58 (2008): 629.

57. Stanley Fish, "Computational Literary Studies: Participant Forum Responses," *Critical Inquiry*, April 1, 2019, https://critinq.wordpress.com/2019/04/01/computational-literary-studies-participant-forum-responses-3/.

58. Carl Bridenbaugh, "The Great Mutation," *American Historical Review* 68, no. 3 (1963): 326.

59. Daniel C. O'Connell and Sabine Kowal, "Political Eloquence," in *The Social Psychology of Politics*, ed. Victor C. Ottati et al. (New York: Kluwer/Plenum, 2002), 95.

60. Two recent works based on the Campaign Mapping Project are Roderick P. Hart, *Civic Hope: How Ordinary Americans Keep Democracy Alive* (Cambridge: Cambridge University Press, 2018); and Sharon E. Jarvis and Soo-Hye Han, *Votes That Count and Voters Who Don't: How Journalists Sideline Electoral Participation Without Even Knowing It* (State College: Pennsylvania State University Press, 2018).

61. For the complete corpus, see Stephen E. Lucas and Martin J. Medhurst, eds., *Words of a Century: The Top 100 American Speeches, 1900–1999* (New York: Oxford University Press, 2009).

62. James M. Hughes, James M., Nicholas J. Foti, David C. Krakauer, and Daniel N. Rockmore, "Quantitative Patterns of Stylistic Influence in the Evolution of Literature," *PNAS* 109 (May 15, 2012), https://www.pnas.org/content/109/20/7682.

63. Richard A. Lanham, *The Motives of Eloquence: Literary Rhetoric in the Renaissance* (Eugene, OR: Wipf & Stock, 1976), 22.

64. John Durham Peters, *Speaking Into the Air: A History of the Idea of Communication* (Chicago: University of Chicago Press, 1999), 264.

65. James Fallows, "On Eloquence vs. Prettiness," *Atlantic*, May 18, 2009, https://www.theatlantic.com/technology/archive/2009/05/on-eloquence-vs-prettiness/17695/.

66. Thomas B. Farrell, *Norms of Rhetorical Culture* (New Haven, CT: Yale University Press, 1993), 267.

4. CULTURAL RESONANCE

1. *The Federalist Papers*, ed. Jacob E. Cooke (Middletown, CT: Wesleyan University Press, 1961), 9.
2. For more on these matters, see Vincent Parrillo, *Diversity in America*, 4th ed. (New York: Routledge, 2013), 44.
3. As quoted in Christopher Looby, *Voicing America: Language, Literary Form, and the Origins of the United States* (Chicago: University of Chicago Press, 1996), 24.
4. Looby, *Voicing America*, 224–25.
5. Looby, *Voicing America*, 228, 278.
6. As quoted in Looby, *Voicing America*, 276.
7. As quoted in Loooby, *Voicing America*, 21.
8. Daniel T. Rodgers, *Contested Truths: Keywords in American Politics Since Independence* (Cambridge, MA: Harvard University Press, 1987), 217.
9. Walter Bagehot, *The English Constitution*, with an introduction by R. H. S. Crossman (Ithaca, NY: Cornell University Press, 1867/1966), 61.
10. David A. Graham, "The President Who Doesn't Read," *Atlantic*, January 5, 2018, https://www.theatlantic.com/politics/archive/2018/01/americas-first-post-text-president/549794/; Viet Thanh Nguyen, "The Post-Trump Future of Literature," *New York Times*, December 22, 2020, https://www.nytimes.com/2020/12/22/opinion/fiction-poetry-trump.html; Amy B. Wang, "Donald Trump Says He's a Big Fan of History. But He Doesn't Seem to Trust Historians," *Washington Post*, May 4, 2017, https://www.washingtonpost.com/news/the-fix/wp/2017/05/04/donald-trump-says-hes-a-fan-of-history-but-he-doesnt-seem-to-trust-historians/; Ian Frazier, "Donald Trump and Uses and Misuses of the Bible," *New Yorker*, June 15, 2020, https://www.newyorker.com/news/daily-comment/donald-trump-and-uses-and-misuses-of-the-bible; Pat Ralph, "Ten Celebrities, CEOs, and Conservative Provocateurs We Know Have Been Dinner Guests at Trump's White House," *Business Insider*, May 4, 2018, https://www.businessinsider.com/trump-dinner-guests-at-white-house-2018-4.
11. For more on these matters, see Dan Balz, "A Bipartisan Deal, an Angry GOP Reaction and the (Still) Long Road Ahead for Biden's Agenda," *Washington Post*, June 26, 2021, https://www.washingtonpost.com/politics/a-bipartisan-deal-an-angry-gop-reaction-and-the-still-long-road-ahead-for-bidens-agenda/2021/06/26/d4ff45c8-d622-11eb-ae54-515e2f63d37d_story.html; Katie Shepherd, "Biden Apologizes for Snapping at CNN Reporter Over

Putin Questions: 'I Shouldn't Have Been Such a Wise Guy,'" *Washington Post*, June 17, 2021, https://www.washingtonpost.com/nation/2021/06/17/biden -putin-cnn-kaitlan-collins/; Adrian Horton, "How Will Joe Biden's Presidency Affect Arts and Culture in America?," *Guardian*, November 13, 2020, https://www.theguardian.com/culture/2020/nov/13/joe-biden-arts -culture-us-president; Helen Stoilas, "With Powerful Poem, Amanda Gorman Sets the Tone for Biden's Presidency," *Art Newspaper*, January 20, 2021, https://www.theartnewspaper.com/news/with-powerful-poem-amanda -gorman-sets-the-tone-for-biden-s-presidency.

12. The data reported here are drawn largely from the materials housed in the Campaign Mapping Project (https://moody.utexas.edu/centers/strauss /campaign-mapping-project). *Pragmatic Style* for Citizens' Letters = 9.6871, for Religious Sermons = 7.8104, for Corporate Advocacy = 9.2477, for Social Protest = 9.4010, for Classic Oratory = 7.6151, for Notable Literature = 7.9656, for Political Ads = 10.4401, for Print Journalism = 10.2094, for Broadcast Journalism = 10.1957, for Popular Entertainment = 9.0915, for White House Remarks = 9.6731, for Campaign Speeches = 10.4754; $F[1,48877] = 133.071$, $p < .000$; *Transcendent Style* for Citizens' Letters = 10.7483, for Religious Sermons = 14.8065, for Corporate Advocacy = 9.9249, for Social Protest = 11.3449, for Classic Oratory = 13.0242, for Notable Literature = 10.0780, for Political Ads = 11.4507, for Print Journalism = 9.1567, for Broadcast Journalism = 9.5545, for Popular Entertainment = 9.8749, for White House Remarks = 12.3750, for Campaign Speeches = 11.9491; $F[1,48877] = 637.732$, $p < .000$.

13. Roderick P. Hart, *The Political Pulpit* (West Lafayette, IN: Purdue University Press, 1977).

14. Jeremy Engles provides a rich and detailed exegesis of how themes of resentment resurfaced powerfully in the second half of the twentieth century in the United States, although he does not focus particularly on religiopolitical discourses. See *The Politics of Resentment: A Genealogy* (University Park: Penn State University Press, 2015).

15. Quoted in Jessica Estepa, "Note to President Trump: Andrew Jackson Wasn't Alive for the Civil War," *USA Today*, May 1, 2017, https://www .usatoday.com/story/news/politics/onpolitics/2017/05/01/note-president -trump-andrew-jackson-wasnt-alive-civil-war/101149060/.

16. Andrew Jackson, "First Inaugural Address," *Miller Center*, March 4, 1829, https://millercenter.org/the-presidency/presidential-speeches/march-4 -1829-first-inaugural-address.

17. Denis Donoghue, *On Eloquence* (New Haven, CT: Yale University Press, 2008).

18. Thus far, the Clinton-Patterson team has produced two novels: *The President Is Missing* (New York: Grand Central, 2019) and *The President's Daughter* (New York: Little, Brown, 2021).

19. For more on these matters, see Roderick P. Hart, *Civic Hope: How Ordinary Americans Keep Democracy Alive* (New York: Cambridge University Pres, 2018).

20. The data reported here are from the speeches housed in the Campaign Mapping Project (https://moody.utexas.edu/centers/strauss/campaign -mapping-project). By political party: *Pragmatic Style* for Democrats = 9.8545, for Republicans = 10.2915; $F[1, 7675] = 83.990$, $p < .000$; *Transcendent Style* for Democrats = 11.4640, Republicans = 11.8463; $F[1, 7675] = 28.947$, $p < .000$. By incumbency: *Pragmatic Style* for sitting presidents =10.4728, for challengers = 10.0994; $F[1, 6596] = 42.457$, $p < .000$; *Transcendent Style* for sitting presidents = 11.8745, for challengers = 11.4253; $F[1, 6596] = 34.925$, $p < .000$. By campaign outcome: *Pragmatic Style* for winners =10.3073, for losers = 9.8829; $F[1, 7640] = 81.418$, $p < .000$; *Transcendent style* for winners = 11.6600, for losers = 11.6563; $F[1, 7640] = .003$, $p < .975$.

21. Gary Wills, *Lincoln at Gettysburg: The Words That Remade America* (New York: Simon & Schuster, 2006), 37.

22. Sandra M. Gustafson, *Eloquence in Power: Oratory and Performance in Early America* (Chapel Hill: University of North Carolina Press, 2000), 268.

23. Richard Weaver, *The Ethics of Rhetoric* (New York: Henry Regnery, 1953), 182–83.

24. Weaver, *The Ethics of Rhetoric*, 168, 170.

25. Weaver, *The Ethics of Rhetoric*, 185.

26. Kenneth Cmiel, *Democratic Eloquence: The Fight Over Popular Speech in Nineteenth-Century America* (New York: William Morrow, 1990), 28.

27. Robert L. Ivie, "Democracy, War, and Decivilizing Metaphors of American Insecurity," in *Metaphorical World Politics*, ed. Francis A. Beer and Christ'l De Landtsheer (East Lansing: Michigan State University Press, 2004), 86.

28. John M. Murphy, "The Sunshine of Human Rights: Hubert Humphrey at the 1948 Democratic Convention," *Rhetoric and Public Affairs* 23, no. 1 (2020): 96.

29. Murphy, "The Sunshine of Human Rights," 98.

30. Hubert H. Humphrey, "The Sunshine of Human Rights," July 14, 1948, in *Words of a Century: The Top 100 American Speeches, 1900-1999*, ed. Stephen E. Lucas and Martin J. Medhurst (New York: Oxford University Press, 2009), 279–92.

31. Ralph Brauer, "The Tragedy of Citizen Humphrey," *Midwest Quarterly* 32, no. 3 (1991): 346.

32. Martha Solomon, "Ideology as Rhetorical Constraint: The Anarchist Agitation of 'Red Emma' Goldman," *Quarterly Journal of Speech* 74, no. 2 (1988): 184–200.

33. Cesar Chavez, "Speech on Breaking His Fast," March 10, 1968, in *Words of a Century*, ed. Lucas and Medhurst, 464–65.

34. For more on this matter of religious iconography, see Luis D León, "Cesar Chavez in American Religious Politics: Mapping the New Global Spiritual Line," *American Quarterly* 59, no. 3 (2007): 857–81. See also John C. Hammerback and Richard J. Jensen, "Ethnic Heritage as Rhetorical Legacy: The Plan of Delano," *Quarterly Journal of Speech* 80 (1994): 53–70.

35. G. Thomas Goodnight, "Ronald Reagan's Re-formulation of the Rhetoric of War: Analysis of the 'Zero Option,' 'Evil Empire,' and 'Star Wars' Addresses," *Quarterly Journal of Speech* 72, no. 4 (1986): 401.

36. Robert C. Rowland and John M. Jones, "Reagan's Strategy for the Cold War and the Evil Empire Address," *Rhetoric and Public Affairs* 19, no. 3 (2016): 441.

37. Rowland and Jones, "Reagan's Strategy," 430.

38. Ronald Reagan, "Evil Empire," March 8, 1983, in *Words of a Century*, ed. Lucas and Medhurst, 554–61.

39. Hilary Carey, "Religion and the 'Evil Empire,' "*Journal of Religious History* 32, no. 2 (2008): 185.

40. William F. Lewis, "Telling America's Story: Narrative Form and the Reagan Presidency," *Quarterly Journal of Speech* 73, no. 3 (1987): 288.

41. Lewis, "Telling America's Story," 285.

42. Barry Goldwater, "Speech Accepting the Republican Presidential Nomination," July 16, 1964, in *Words of a Century*, ed. Lucas and Medhurst, 409–15.

43. For more on this, see Mark P. Moore, "Rhetorical Criticism of Political Myth: From Goldwater Legend to Reagan Mystique," *Communication Studies* 42, no. 3 (1991): 295–308.

44. Kristy Maddux, "Fundamentalist Fool or Populist Paragon? William Jennings Bryan and the Campaign Against Evolutionary Theory," *Rhetoric and Public Affairs* 16, no. 3 (2013): 494.

45. Harold Barrett, "Scott of the *Oregonian* vs. William Jennings Bryan," *Quarterly Journal of Speech* 48, no. 2 (1962): 172.

46. William Jennings Bryan, "Against Imperialism," August 8, 1900, in *Words of a Century*, ed. Lucas and Medhurst, 10–24.

47. Mary E. Stuckey, "Legitimating Leadership: The Rhetoric of Succession as a Genre of Presidential Discourse," *Rhetoric Society Quarterly* 22, no. 2 (1992): 25–38.

48. Gerald R. Ford, "Our Long National Nightmare Is Over," August 9, 1974, in *Words of a Century*, ed. Lucas and Medhurst, 527–29.

49. Edward M. Kennedy, "Tolerance and Truth in America," October 3, 1983, in *Words of a Century*, ed. Lucas and Medhurst, 565–71.

50. Bryan Garsten, *Saving Persuasion* (Cambridge, MA: Harvard University Press, 2006). 1.

51. For more on Trump's curious relationship with religion, see Daniel Burke, "The Guilt-Free Gospel of Donald Trump," *CNN Politics*, October 24, 2016, https://www.cnn.com/2016/10/21/politics/trump-religion-gospel /index.html; Eugene Scott, "Trump Believes in God, but Hasn't Sought Forgiveness," *CNN Politics*, July 18, 2015, https://www.cnn.com/2015/07/18 /politics/trump-has-never-sought-forgiveness/index.html; and McKay Coppins, "Trump Secretly Mocks His Christian Supporters," *Atlantic*, September 19, 2020, https://www.theatlantic.com/politics/archive/2020/09 /trump-secretly-mocks-his-christian-supporters/616522/.

52. Carolyn Eastman, *A Nation of Speechifiers: Making an American Public After the Revolution* (Chicago: University of Chicago Press, 2009), 3–4.

53. Eastman, *A Nation of Speechifiers*, 209.

54. Marissa Gemma, Frederic Glorieux, and Jean-Gabriel Ganascia, "Operationalizing the Colloquial Style: Repetition in Nineteenth-Century American Fiction," *Digital Scholarship in the Humanities* 33, no. 2 (2017): 312–35.

55. Gemma, Glorieux, and Ganascia, "Operationalizing the Colloquial Style," 313.

56. Robert A Ferguson, "Hearing Lincoln and the Making of Eloquence," *American Literary History* 21, no. 4 (2009): 698, 699.

57. As quoted in Ross Posnock, "American Sophistication," *Oxford Research Encyclopedia: Literature*, December 17, 2020, https://oxfordre.com/literature /search?siteToSearch=literature&q=posnock&searchBtn=Search&isQuick Search=true.

58. Posnock, "American Sophistication."

59. Kenneth Tynan, "Diary Entry on October 19, 1971," *The Diaries of Kenneth Tynan* (London: Bloomsbury, 2002).

60. Lyndon B. Johnson, "The Great Society," May 22, 1964, in *Words of a Century*, ed. Lucas and Medhurst, 405–8.

61. Michael Weiler, "The Rhetoric of Neoliberalism," *Quarterly Journal of Speech* 70, no. 4 (1984): 366; David Zarefsky, "The Great Society as a Rhetorical Proposition," *Quarterly Journal of Speech* 65, no. 4 (1979): 368.

62. Dennis Merrill, "The Truman Doctrine: Containing Communism and Modernity," *Presidential Studies Quarterly* 36, no. 1 (2006): 27.

63. Russell Conwell, "Acres of Diamonds," 1900–1925, in *Words of a Century*, ed. Lucas and Medhurst, 1–9.

64. Malcolm X, "The Ballot or the Bullet," April 3, 1964, in *Words of a Century*, ed. Lucas and Medhurst, 392–405.

65. Robert E. Terrill, "Protest, Prophecy, and Prudence in the Rhetoric of Malcolm X," *Rhetoric & Public Affairs* 4, no. 1 (2001): 40.

66. Thomas Alan Schwartz, "He Was Trump Before Trump: VP Agnew Attacked the News Media 50 Years Ago," *Conversation*, November 8, 2019,

https://theconversation.com/he-was-trump-before-trump-vp-spiro-agnew
-attacked-the-news-media-50-years-ago-122980.

67. Spiro T. Agnew, "Television News Coverage," November 13, 1969, in *Words of a Century*, ed. Lucas and Medhurst, 496–503.

68. Rollin W. Quimby, "Agnew, the Press, and the Rhetorical Critic," *Western Journal of Communication* 39, no. 3 (1975): 146.

69. Peter B. Levy, "Spiro Agnew, the Forgotten Americans, and the Rise of the New Right," *Historian* 75, no. 4 (2013): 714.

70. Ernest G. Bormann, "A Rhetorical Analysis of the National Radio Broadcasts of Senator Huey Pierce Long," *Communication Monographs* 24, no. 4 (1957): 246.

71. J. Michael Hogan and L. Glen Williams, "The Rusticity and Religiosity of Huey P. Long," *Rhetoric & Public Affairs* 7, no. 2 (2004): 160.

72. Hogan and Williams, "The Rusticity and Religiosity of Huey P. Long," 165.

73. Huey P. Long, "Share Our Wealth," March 7, 1935, in *Words of a Century*, ed. Lucas and Medhurst, 237–48.

74. John Stuart Mill, "What Is Poetry?" in *Collected Works of John Stuart Mill*, ed. John M. Robinson and Jack Stillinger (London: Routledge & Kegan Paul, 1833, 1996), 1:348.

75. Paul Greenberg, "The Decline of American Eloquence," *Tulsa World*, February 24, 2019, https://tulsaworld.com/archive/the-decline-of-american
-eloquence/article_e9e03d3d-a0df-57e3-84c8-fb3faba6bbf0.html.

76. Greenberg, "The Decline of American Eloquence."

77. Patrick Leahy, "Comment on the House Vote to Impeach President Donald J. Trump," Press Release, December 18, 2019, https://www.leahy.senate.gov
/press/comment-on-the-house-vote-to-impeach-president-donald-j
-trump.

78. Senator John Cornyn, Twitter, December 19, 2019, https://twitter.com
/johncornyn/status/1207634972816953344?lang=en.

79. John F. Kennedy, "Ich Bin ein Berliner," June 26, 1963, in *Words of a Century*, ed. Lucas and Medhurst, 373–74.

80. Ed Bryan, "The Geopolitics of Improvised Language: President John F. Kennedy's 'Ich Bin Ein Berliner' Address," *AREA: Royal Geographical Society*, October 2020, https://rgs-ibg.onlinelibrary.wiley.com/doi/abs/10.1111
/area.12678. For more on Kennedy's modernism, see Isabel Fay and Jim A. Kuypers, "Transcending Mysticism and Building Identification Through Empowerment of the Rhetorical Agent: John F. Kennedy's Berlin Speeches on June 26, 1963," *Southern Communication Journal* 77, no. 3 (2012): 198–215.

81. For more on this matter, see Christoph Schubert, "Cognitive Categorization and Prototypicality as Persuasive Strategies: Presidential Rhetoric in the USA," *Journal of Language and Politics* 13, no. 2 (2014): 313–35.

82. Ronald Reagan, "Speech at the Brandenburg Gate," June 12, 1987, in *Words of a Century*, ed. Lucas and Medhurst, 613–18. For a thoughtful analysis of Reagan's joint use of the pragmatic and transcendent, see Robert C. Rowland and John M. Jones. "Reagan at the Brandenburg Gate: Moral Clarity Tempered by Pragmatism," *Rhetoric & Public Affairs* 9, no. 1 (2006): 21–50.

83. Mark Vail, "The' Integrative' Rhetoric of Martin Luther King Jr.'s 'I Have a Dream' Speech," *Rhetoric & Public Affairs* 9, no. 1 (2006): 54.

84. Alexandra Alvarez, "Martin Luther King's 'I Have a Dream': The Speech Event as Metaphor," *Journal of Black Studies* 3 (1998): 349.

85. Robert Sitkoff, *The Struggle for Black Equality: 1954–1980* (New York: Hill and Wang, 1981).

86. Edwin Black, "The 'Vision' of Martin Luther King," in *Literature as Revolt and Revolt as Literature: The Proceedings of the Fourth Annual University of Minnesota Spring Symposium in Speech-Communication* (Minneapolis: University of Minnesota, 1970), 9.

87. As quoted in Garth E. Pauley, *LBJ's American Promise: The 1965 Voting Rights Address* (College Station: Texas A&M University Press, 2006), 15.

88. Lyndon B. Johnson, "We Shall Overcome," March 15, 1965, in *Words of a Century*, ed. Lucas and Medhurst, 554–61.

89. Pauley, *LBJ's American Promise*, 145.

90. Steven R. Goldzwig, "LBJ, the Rhetoric of Transcendence, and the Civil Rights Act of 1968," *Rhetoric & Public Affairs* 6, no. 1 (2003): 43.

91. For more on how Jackson mentioned, but finessed, the factional strife in the Democratic Party, see Lesley A. Di Mare, "Functionalizing Conflict: Jesse Jackson's Rhetorical Strategy at the 1984 Democratic National Convention," *Western Journal of Communication* 51, no. 2 (1987): 218–26. For an interesting discussion of how Jackson often used a "Midwestern populist sensibility," see Charles P. Henry, "Jesse Jackson and the Decline of Liberalism in Presidential Politics," *Black Scholar* 20, no. 1 (1989): 2–11.

92. Jesse Jackson, "The Rainbow Coalition," July 18, 1984, in *Words of a Century*, ed. Lucas and Medhurst, 584–93.

93. Eugene V. Debs, "The Issue," May 23, 1908, in *Words of a Century*, ed. Lucas and Medhurst, 30–40.

94. Ronald Lee and James R. Andrews, "A Story of Rhetorical-Ideological Transformation: Eugene Debs as Liberal Hero," *Quarterly Journal of Speech* 77 (1991): 20–37.

95. Lee and Andrews, "A Story of Rhetorical-Ideological Transformation," 28.

96. Nick Salvatore, *Eugene V. Debs: Citizen and Socialist* (Urbana: University of Illinois press, 1982).

97. Mario Cuomo, "Religious Belief and Public Morality," September 13, 1984, in *Words of a Century*, ed. Lucas and Medhurst, 597–610.

98. Thomas B. Farrell, *Norms of Rhetorical Culture* (New Haven, CT: Yale University Press, 1993), 217.

99. Calvin L. Troup, "Cuomo at Notre Dame: Rhetoric Without Religion," *Communication Quarterly* 43, no. 2 (1995): 179.

100. Gary D. Glenn, "Rhetoric and Religion in the 1984 Campaign," *Political Communication* 5, no. 1 (1988): 1–13.

101. Tammy L. Brown, " 'A New Era in American Politics': Shirley Chisholm and the Discourse of Identity," *Callaloo* 31, no. 4 (2008): 1013–25. Anastasia Curwood makes a similar case in "Black Feminism on Capitol Hill: Shirley Chisholm and Movement Politics, 1968–1984," *Meridians* 13, no. 1 (2015): 204–32.

102. Leroy G. Dorsey, "Woodrow Wilson's Fight for the League of Nations: A Reexamination," *Rhetoric and Public Affairs* 2, no. 1 (1999): 131.

103. A. Duane Litfin, "Eisenhower on the Military-Industrial Complex: Critique of a Rhetorical Strategy," *Communication Studies* 25, no. 3 (1974): 205. Martin Medhurst offers a more generous interpretation of Eisenhower's strategy in "Reconceptualizing Rhetorical History: Eisenhower's Farewell Address," *Quarterly Journal of Speech* 80, no. 2 (1994): 195–218.

104. John M. Murphy, " 'A Time of Shame and Sorrow': Robert F. Kennedy and the American Jeremiad," *Quarterly Journal of Speech* 76, no. 4 (1990): 411.

105. Roderick P. Hart, "Culture, Rhetoric, and the Tragedy of Jimmy Carter," B. Aubrey Fisher Memorial Lecture (Salt Lake City: University of Utah, 1992), https://communication.utah.edu/_resources/documents/fisher-memorial-lectures/1991-fisher-lecture.pdf, 1.

106. Todd A. Berger, "Jimmy Carter's Malaise Speech, Social Desirability Bias, and the Yuppie Nuremberg Defense: The Real Reason Why Law Students Say They Want to Practice Public Interest Law, Yet So Few Actually Do," *Kansas Journal of Law and Public Policy* 2, no. 1 (2012): 141.

107. Jimmy Carter, "Energy and the Crisis of Confidence," July 15, 1979, in *Words of a Century*, ed. Lucas and Medhurst, 536–42.

108. Ronald Lee, "Electoral Politics and Visions of Community: Jimmy Carter, Virtue, and the Small Town Myth," *Western Journal of Communication* 59, no. 1 (1995): 58.

109. Hermann G. Stelzner, " 'War Message,' December 8, 1941: An Approach to Language," *Communication Monographs* 33, no. 4 (1966): 423.

110. Franklin D. Roosevelt, "War Message," December 8, 1941, in *Words of a Century*, ed. Lucas and Medhurst, 269–70.

111. Herbert L. Carson, "War Requested: Wilson and Roosevelt," *Communication Studies* 10, no. 1 (1958): 29, 30.

112. Jason C. Flanagan, "Woodrow Wilson's 'Rhetorical Restructuring': The Transformation of the American Self and the Construction of the German Enemy," *Rhetoric & Public Affairs* 7, no. 2 (2004): 127.

113. Robert W. Tucker, "A Benediction of the Past: Woodrow Wilson's War Address," *World Policy Journal* 17, no. 2 (2000): 78.
114. Woodrow Wilson, "War Message," April 2, 1917, in *Words of a Century,* ed. Lucas and Medhurst, 73–79.
115. Edward M. Kennedy, "Chappaquiddick," July 25, 1969, in *Words of a Century,* ed. Lucas and Medhurst, 485–88.
116. Grant C. Cos, "Chappaquiddick Revisited: Scandal and the Modern-Mediated Apologia," in *Scandal in a Digital Age,* ed. Hinda Mandell and Gina Masullo Chen (London: Palgrave Macmillan, 2016), 41–42.
117. Martin E. P. Seligman, Peter Railton, Roy F. Baumeister, and Chandra Sripada, *Homo Prospectus* (New York: Oxford University Press, 2016).
118. Robert L. Tsai, *Eloquence and Reason: Creating a First Amendment Culture* (New Haven, CT: Yale University Press, 2008), 6.
119. William Butler Yeats, "Anima Hominis," reproduced in *Mythologies* (London: Macmillan, 1959), 331.
120. Laurel V. Cortés, "Mining the English Language in Search of True Eloquence," *Press-Enterprise,* September 24, 2918, https://www.pe.com/2018/09/24/mining-the-english-language-in-search-of-true-eloquence/.
121. Diana Schaub, "The Greatness and Decline of American Oratory: The Democratization of American Political Oratory," *Claremont Review of Books* 7, no. 3 (2007), https://claremontreviewofbooks.com/the-greatness-and-decline-of-american-oratory/.

5. PERSONAL INVESTMENT

1. This and all subsequent extracts from Lincoln's speech can be found at Abraham Lincoln, "Gettysburg Address," *Abraham Lincoln Online,* November 19, 1863, http://www.abrahamlincolnonline.org/lincoln/speeches/gettysburg.htm.
2. Joseph Biden, "Memorial Day Speech," May 20, 2021, New Castle, Delaware. https://www.whitehouse.gov/briefing-room/speeches-remarks/2021/05/30/remarks-by-president-biden-at-an-annual-memorial-day-service/
3. Sojourner Truth, "Ain't I a Woman?," Akron, Ohio, 1851, https://www.nps.gov/articles/sojourner-truth.htm.
4. Joyce I. Middleton, "Echoes from the Past: Learning How to Listen Again," in *Sage Handbook of Rhetorical Studies,* ed. Andrea A. Lumsford, Kirt W. Wilson, and Rosa A. Eberly (Thousand Oaks, CA: Sage, 2009), 361.
5. Jay Fliegelman, *Declaring Independence: Jefferson, Natural Language, and the Culture of Performance* (Palo Alto, CA: Stanford University Press, 1993), 5, 95.

6. Fliegelman, *Declaring Independence*, 95.

7. Fliegelman, *Declaring Independence*, 190.

8. Patrick Henry, " 'Give Me Liberty or Give Me Death,' " *Colonial Williamsburg*, March 3, 2020, https://www.colonialwilliamsburg.org/learn/deep-dives/give-me-liberty-or-give-me-death/.

9. Robert Dodaro, *Christ and the Just Society in the Thought of Augustine* (Cambridge: Cambridge University Press, 2005), 196.

10. Thomas M. Carr, "Voltaire's Concept of Enlightened Eloquence," *Nottingham French Studies* 19, no. 1 (1980): 22.

11. Carr, "Voltaire's Concept of Enlightened Eloquence," 23.

12. Denis Donoghue, *The Practice of Reading* (New Haven, CT: Yale University Press, 1998), 43.

13. Self-references for classic orators = 6.2412, for twentieth-century speakers = 9.9946, for modern campaign speeches = 13.2841; $F [2, 6842] = 79.250$, $p < .000$.

14. Frederick Douglass, "A Plea for Freedom of Speech in Boston" (December 9, 1860), *Law and Liberty*, August 21, 2019, https://lawliberty.org/frederick-douglass-plea-for-freedom-of-speech-in-boston/.

15. These data are roughly divided across the respective presidencies as follows: Self-references for 1948–1956 = .5012, for 1960–1964 = .5170, for 1968–1976 = .7600, for 1980–1988 = .5126, for 1992–1996 = .8091, for 2000–2004 = .8901, for 2008–2012 = .7844, for 2016 = .8566, for 2020 = .9978; $F [8, 7816] = 20.963$, $p < .000$. My findings in this regard are corroborated by other scholars; see especially Daniel C. O'Connell and Sabine Kowal, "Political Eloquence," in *The Social Psychology of Politics*, ed. Victor C. Ottati et al. (New York: Kluwer/Plenum, 2002), 89–103.

16. Joshua Scacco and Kevin Coe have also called attention to this increasing "personalization" of the presidency, which they attribute in part to the now numerous sites for rhetorical engagement—local politicking, entertainment TV, White House ceremonies, and a plethora of websites and social media outlets. See Joshua M. Scacco and Kevin Coe, *The Ubiquitous Presidency: Presidential Communication and Digital Democracy in Tumultuous Times* (New York: Oxford University Press, 2021).

17. As quoted in J. Lee Campbell, " 'It Is as if a Green Bough Were Laid Across the Page: Thoreau on Eloquence," *Rhetoric Society Quarterly* 20, no. 1 (1990): 64, 65.

18. See "The Second Clinton-Bush-Perot Presidential Debate," Richmond, Virginia, October 15, 1992, https://www.debates.org/voter-education/debate-transcripts/october-15-1992-second-half-debate-transcript/.

19. Henry M. Day, "The Art of Discourse," in *The Rhetorical Tradition: Readings from Classical Times to the Present*, ed. Patricia Bizzell and Bruce Herzberg (Boston: Bedford, 1990), 865.

20. Kenneth Burke, *Counter-Statement* (Berkeley: University of California Press, 1968), 171.
21. Catherine l. Langford, "George Bush's Struggle with the 'Vision Thing,'" in *The Rhetorical Presidency of George H. W. Bush*, ed. Martin J. Medhurst (College Station: Texas A&M University Press, 2006), 20–21.
22. Simon M. Luebke, "Political Authenticity: Conceptualization of a Popular Term," *International Journal of Press/Politics*, August 12, 2020, https://journals.sagepub.com/doi/full/10.1177/1940161220948013.
23. Domenico Montanaro, "Trump Derails First Presidential Debate with Biden," NPR, September 30, 2020, https://www.npr.org/2020/09/30/918500976/trump-derails-first-presidential-debate-with-biden-and-5-other-takeaways.
24. Christal Hayes, "Jake Tapper Calls First Presidential Debate a 'Hot Mess Inside a Dumpster Fire After Trump, Biden Clash," *USA Today*, September 29, 2020, https://www.usatoday.com/story/news/politics/elections/2020/09/29/presidential-debate-called-train-wreck-after-trump-biden-clash/3583646001/; Shane Goldmacher, "Six Takeaways from the First Presidential Debate," *New York Times*, September 30, 2020, https://www.nytimes.com/2020/09/30/us/politics/debate-takeaways.html; Aris Folley, "CNN's Dana Bash on First Debate: 'That Was a S—show,'" *The Hill*, September 29, 2020, https://thehill.com/homenews/media/518878-cnns-dana-bash-on-first-debate-that-was-a-s-show.
25. Eve Fairbanks, "Actually, the First Presidential Debate Was Terrific," *Washington Post*, October 1, 2020, https://www.washingtonpost.com/outlook/2020/10/01/presidential-debate-was-good/.
26. Hannah Arendt, *The Human Condition* (Chicago: University of Chicago Press, 1958).
27. Arendt, *The Human Condition*, 38.
28. Arendt, *The Human Condition*, 186.
29. Arendt, *The Human Condition*, 51–52.
30. For this measure, a pragmatic/transcendent ratio (PTR) was calculated for each speech and then compared to the number of self-references used. Self-references for high PTR = 9.9301, for mid PTR = 12.9969, for low PTR = 13.3765; $F [2, 7725] = 56.627$, $p < .000$.
31. Edwin Black, "The Invention of Nixon," in *Beyond the Rhetorical Presidency*, ed. Martin J. Medhurst (College Station: Texas A&M University Press, 1996) 107–8.
32. Black, "The Invention of Nixon," 121.
33. Anita Hill, "Statement to the Senate Judiciary Committee," October 11, 1991, in *Words of a Century: The Top 100 American Speeches, 1900–1999*, ed. Stephen E. Lucas and Martin J. Medhurst (New York: Oxford University Press, 2009), 637–41.

34. Alison Regan, "Rhetoric and Political Process in the Hill-Thomas Hearings," *Political Communication* 11 (1994): 277–85; Roderick P. Hart, "Politics and the Virtual Event: An Overview of the Hill-Thomas Hearings," *Political Communication* 11 (1994): 272–73.

35. Vanessa Beasley, "The Logic of Power in the Hill-Thomas Hearings: A Rhetorical Analysis," *Political Communication* 11 (1994): 292.

36. Self-references for governing speeches = 8.9780, for campaign speeches = 13.6646; F [1, 4375] = 177.227, p < .000.

37. See Andrew R. Flint and Joy Porter, "Jimmy Carter: The Re-emergence of Faith-Based Politics and the Abortion Rights Issue," *Presidential Studies Quarterly* 35, no. 1 (2005): 28.

38. G. Thomas Goodnight, "Ronald Reagan's Re-formulation of the Rhetoric of War: Analysis of the 'Zero Option,' 'Evil Empire,' and 'Star Wars' Addresses," *Quarterly Journal of Speech* 72, no. 4 (1986): 390–414.

39. Garth E. Pauley, *LBJ's American Promise: The 1965 Voting Rights Address* (College Station: Texas A&M University Press, 2006), 13.

40. Lyndon B. Johnson, "We Shall Overcome," March 16, 1965, *Words of a Century*, ed. Lucas and Medhurst, 427–33.

41. Mark S. Massa, "Catholic for President?: John F. Kennedy and the 'Secular' Theology of the Houston Speech, 1960," *Journal of Church and State* 39, no. 2 (1997): 298, 300.

42. Massa, "Catholic for President?," 30.

43. Harold Barrett, "John F. Kennedy Before the Greater Houston Ministerial Association," *Communication Studies* 15, no. 4 (1964): 260.

44. For more on this delicate balance, see Barbara Warnick, "Argument Schemes and the Construction of Social Reality: John F. Kennedy's Address to the Houston Ministerial Association," *Communication Quarterly* 44, no. 2 (1996): 188.

45. John F. Kennedy, "Speech to the Greater Houston Ministerial Association," September 12, 1960, in *Words of a Century*, ed. Lucas and Medhurst, 333–36.

46. Joseph Welch, "Defense of Fred Fisher at the Army-McCarthy Hearings," June 9, 1954, in *Words of a Century*, ed. Lucas and Medhurst, 328–32.

47. James Darsey, "Joe McCarthy's Fantastic Moment," *Communication Monographs* 62, no. 1 (1995): 74.

48. Thomas B. Farrell, *Norms of Rhetorical Culture* (New Haven, CT: Yale University Press, 1993), 44.

49. James Darsey, "The Legend of Eugene Debs: Prophetic Ethos as Radical Argument," *Quarterly Journal of Speech* 74, no. 4 (1988): 434, 446.

50. Michael J. Lee, "The Populist Chameleon: The People's Party, Huey Long, George Wallace, and the Populist Argumentative Frame," *Quarterly Journal of Speech* 92, no. 4 (2006): 360–61.

51. John M. Murphy, "The Sunshine of Human Rights: Hubert Humphrey at the 1948 Democratic Convention," *Rhetoric and Public Affairs* 23, no. 1 (2020): 95.

52. Robert E. Terrill, "Protest, Prophecy, and Prudence in the Rhetoric of Malcolm X," *Rhetoric & Public Affairs* 4, no. 1 (2001): 67, 68.

53. Bethany Keeley, "I May Not Get There with You: 'I've Been to the Mountaintop' as Epic Discourse," *Southern Communication Journal* 73, no. 4 (2008): 283, 287.

54. Bonnie J. Dow and Mari Boor Tonn, "'Feminine Style' and Political Judgment in the Rhetoric of Ann Richards," *Quarterly Journal of Speech* 79, no. 3 (1993): 294.

55. Patricia A. Sullivan, "Signification and African-American Rhetoric: A Case Study of Jesse Jackson's 'Common Ground and Common Sense' Speech," *Communication Quarterly* 41, no. 1 (1993): 4, 7.

56. For more on this theme, see Joshua Gunn, "Hystericizing Huey: Emotional Appeals, Desire, and the Psychodynamics of Demagoguery," *Western Journal of Communication* 71, no. 1 (2007): 1–27.

57. Elizabeth Glaser, "AIDS: A Personal Story," July 14, 1922, in *Words of a Century*, ed. Lucas and Medhurst, 642–47.

58. Darsey, "The Legend of Eugene Debs," 434.

59. Amy Aronson, "Recovering the 'Most Neglected Feminist Leader of the Twentieth Century': Crystal Eastman, Historical Memory, and the Bequest of an Intersectional Inheritance," *Women's Studies Quarterly* 48, no. 1 (2020): 150.

60. Aronson, "Recovering the 'Most Neglected Feminist Leader of the Twentieth Century,'" 150.

61. Aronson, "Recovering the 'Most Neglected Feminist Leader of the Twentieth Century,'" 154.

62. Crystal Eastman, "Now We Can Begin," September 10, 1920, in *Words of a Century*, ed. Lucas and Medhurst, 152–55.

63. Elvin T. Lim, "The Lion and the Lamb: De-mythologizing Franklin Roosevelt's Fireside Chats," *Rhetoric and Public Affairs* 6, no. 3 (2003): 451.

64. Lim, "The Lion and the Lamb," 440.

65. Franklin D. Roosevelt, "Arsenal of Democracy," December 29, 1940, in *Words of a Century*, ed. Lucas and Medhurst, 256–62.

66. David Henry, "The Rhetorical Dynamics of Mario Cuomo's 1984 Keynote Address: Situation, Speaker, Metaphor," *Southern Speech Communication Journal* 53, no. 2 (1988): 106.

67. Henry, "The Rhetorical Dynamics of Mario Cuomo's 1984 Keynote Address," 110.

68. Henry, "The Rhetorical Dynamics of Mario Cuomo's 1984 Keynote Address," 110.

69. Mario Cuomo, "A Tale of Two Cities," July 17, 1984, in *Words of a Century*, ed. Lucas and Medhurst, 576–83.
70. Hermann G. Stelzner, "The Quest Story and Nixon's November 3, 1969 Address," *Quarterly Journal of Speech* 5, no. 2 (1971): 165, 167.
71. Stelzner, "The Quest Story," 167.
72. Richard M. Nixon, "Address on the Cambodian Incursion," April 30, 1970, in *Words of a Century*, ed. Lucas and Medhurst, 503–9.
73. For more on this, see Robert A. Vartabedian, "Nixon's Vietnam Rhetoric: A Case Study of Apologia as Generic Paradox," *Southern Speech Communication Journal* 50, no. 4 (1985): 380.
74. Richard M. Nixon, "Address Resigning the Presidency," August 8, 1974, in *Words of a Century*, ed. Lucas and Medhurst, 523–26.

6. POETIC IMAGINATION

1. All of the foregoing have been reprised by Caitlin Schneider, "17 Poets' Quotes About Poetry," *Mental Floss*, April 2, 2015, https://www.mentalfloss.com/article/62623/17-poets-quotes-about-poetry.
2. Portions of this paragraph have been repurposed from Roderick P. Hart, "Make Politics Your Passion," in *Fixing American Politics: Solutions for the Media Age*, ed. Roderick P. Hart (New York: Routledge, 2022), 3.
3. John F. Kennedy, "Remarks at the Book and Authors' Club Luncheon," Cleveland, Ohio, February 20, 1958, https://www.jfklibrary.org/archives/other-resources/john-f-kennedy-speeches/cleveland-oh-19580220.
4. Michael Silverstein, "The Poetics of Politics: 'Theirs' and 'Ours,'" *Journal of Anthropological Research* 61, no. 1 (2005): 2.
5. Silverstein, "The Poetics of Politics."
6. Robert E. Brown, "Conjuring Unity: The Politics of the Crowd and the Poetics of the Candidate," *American Behavioral Scientist* 54, no. 4 (2010): 383.
7. Brown, "Conjuring Unity," 383.
8. Alex Gallo-Brown, "What Can Poetry Do That Politics Can't?," *ElectricLit*, October 18, 2017, https://electricliterature.com/what-can-poetry-do-that-politics-cant/.
9. Margaret Chase Smith, "Declaration of Conscience," June 1, 1950, in *Words of a Century: The Top 100 American Speeches, 1900–1999*, ed. Stephen E. Lucas and Martin J. Medhurst (New York: Oxford University Press, 2009), 294–98.
10. Nathan Crick, "The Rhetorical Singularity," *Rhetoric Review* 28, no. 4 (2009): 378.
11. Smith, "Declaration of Conscience."

12. Ralph Waldo Emerson, "Eloquence," in *Society and Solitude* (Boston: Houghton-Mifflin, 1870/1904), 92–93.

13. Cynthia Ozick, "The Moral Necessity of Metaphor: Rooting History in a Figure of Speech," *Harper's*, May 1986, 68.

14. Ozick, "The Moral Necessity of Metaphor," 67.

15. Martin Luther King Jr., "I Have a Dream," August 28, 1963, in *Words of a Century*, ed. Lucas and Medhurst, 375–78.

16. Joseph Grady, "Using Metaphor to Influence Public Perceptions and Policy: How Metaphors Can Save the World," in *Routledge Handbook of Metaphor and Language*, ed. Elena Semino and Zsófia Demjén (Oxfordshire: Taylor & Francis, 2020), 443, 448.

17. Grady, "Using Metaphor," 448.

18. Friedrich Nietzsche, "On Truth and Lying in an Extra-Moral Sense," in *Friedrich Nietzsche on Rhetoric and Language*, ed. and trans. Sandra L. Gilman, Carole Blair, and David J. Parent (Oxford: Oxford University Press, 1989).

19. Nietzsche, "On Truth and Lying," 250.

20. Michael Osborn, *Michael Osborn on Metaphor and Style* (East Lansing: Michigan State University Press, 2018), 207.

21. Andrew Goatly, *The Language of Metaphors* (London: Routledge, 1997), 107.

22. Goatly, *The Language of Metaphors*, 152; Eva F. Kittay, *Metaphor: Its Cognitive Force and Linguistic Structure* (Oxford: Clarendon, 1987), 316.

23. Shelly Chaiken and Charles Stangor, "Attitudes and Attitude Change," *Annual Review of Psychology* 38 (1987): 593.

24. For more along these same lines, see Bruce Cumings, "The World Shakes China," *National Interest* 43 (1996): 28–41.

25. For additional insight, see Cornelius Puschmann and Jean Burgess, "Metaphors of Big Data," *International Journal of Communication* 8 (2014): 1690–1709; Irina Raicu, "Metaphors of Big Data," *Vox.com*, November 6, 2015, https://www.vox.com/2015/11/6/11620416/metaphors-of-big-data.

26. Vinodkumar Prabhakaran, Marek Rei, and Ekaterina Shutova, "How Metaphors Impact Political Discourse: A Large-Scale Topic-Agnostic Study Using Neural Metaphor Detection," occasional paper, Association for the Advancement of Artificial Intelligence, 2021, https://arxiv.org/pdf/2104.03928.pdf.

27. Danica Škara, "Body Metaphors—Reading the Body in Contemporary Culture," *Journal of the Croatian Anthropological Society* 28, no. 1 (2004): 189.

28. For more on this notion of struggle, see Otto Santa Ana, *Brown Tide Rising: Metaphors of Latinos in Contemporary American Public Discourse* (Austin: University of Texas Press, 2002), 35.

29. George Lakoff and Mark Johnson, *Metaphors We Live By* (Chicago: University of Chicago Press, 1980), 236–37.

30. For more on these two metaphors, see Yaron Ezrahi, "The Theatrics and Mechanics of Action: The Theater and the Machine in Political Metaphors," *Social Research* 12 (1995): 299–322.
31. See Roderick P. Hart and Kathleen E. Kendall, "Lyndon Johnson and the Problem of Politics," in *The Future of the Rhetorical Presidency*, ed. Martin Medhurst (College Station: Texas A&M University Press, 1996), 77–103.
32. Pauline Heyvaert, François Randour, Jérémy Dodeigne, Julien Perrez, and Min Reuchamps, "Metaphors in Political Communication: A Case Study of the Use of Deliberate Metaphors in Non-institutional Political Interviews," *Journal of Language and Politics* 19, no. 2 (2021): 201–25.
33. Mirya R. Holman, "Gender, Political Rhetoric, and Moral Metaphors in State of the City Addresses," *Urban Affairs Review* 52, no. 4 (2016): 501–30.
34. Jonathan Charteris-Black, *Politics and Rhetoric: The Persuasive Power of Metaphor* (New York: Palgrave Macmillan, 2011).
35. Mary Lowenthal Felstiner, "Family Metaphors: The Language of an Independence Revolution," *Comparative Studies in Society and History* 25, no. 1 (1983): 154–80.
36. Harry Berger, *Figures of a Changing World: Metaphors and the Emergence of Modern Culture* (New York: Fordham University Press, 2015).
37. Sally Wyatt, "Metaphors in Critical Internet and Digital Media Studies," *New Media and Society* 23, no. 7 (2021): 408.
38. Martha C. Nussbaum, *Poetic Justice: The Literary Imagination and Public Life* (Boston: Beacon, 2005), 2.
39. Nussbaum, *Poetic Justice*, xviii.
40. Seth Thompson, "Politics Without Metaphors Is Like a Fish Without Water," in *Metaphor: Implications and Applications*, ed. Jeffery S. Mio and Albert N. Katz (New York: Erlbaum, 1996), 195.
41. Robert Maslen, "Finding Systematic Metaphors," in *Routledge Handbook of Metaphor and Language*, ed. Semino and Demjén, 88–101.
42. Andreas Musolff, "Metaphor and Persuasion in Politics," in *Routledge Handbook of Metaphor and Language*, ed. Semino and Demjén, 309–23.
43. Nathan P. Kalmoe, "Mobilizing Voters with Aggressive Metaphors," *Political Science Research and Methods* 7, no. 3 (2019): 411–29.
44. Barbara H. Rosenwein, *Reading the Middle Ages: Sources from Europe, Byzantium, and the Islamic World* (Toronto: University of Toronto Press, 2018), 206.
45. Jan Dumolyn, "Justice, Equity and the Common Good: The State Ideology of the Councillors of the Burgundian Dukes," in *The Ideology of Burgundy: The Promotion of National Consciousness, 1364–1565*, ed. Jonathan Boulton and Jan Veenstra (Leiden: Brill, 2006), 12–13.

46. Eugene Debs, "The Issue," March 23, 1908, in *Words of a Century*, ed. Lucas and Medhurst, 30–40.

47. Eugene Debs, "Statement to the Court," September 14, 1918, in *Words of a Century*, ed. Lucas and Medhurst, 129–33.

48. Robert F. Kennedy, "Day of Affirmation," June 6, 1966, in *Words of a Century*, ed. Lucas and Medhurst, 434–40.

49. Emma Goldman, "Address to the Jury," July 9, 1917, in *Words of a Century*, ed. Lucas and Medhurst, 79–87.

50. Martha Solomon, "Ideology as Rhetorical Constraint: The Anarchist Agitation of 'Red Emma' Goldman," *Quarterly Journal of Speech* 74, no. 2 (1988): 192.

51. Joshua Gunn, "Hystericizing Huey: Emotional Appeals, Desire, and the Psychodynamics of Demagoguery," *Western Journal of Communication* 71, no. 1 (2007): 13.

52. Huey P. Long, "Every Man a King," February 23, 1934, in *Words of a Century*, ed. Lucas and Medhurst, 229–36.

53. Richard M. Rothman, "On the Speaking of John L. Lewis," *Communication Studies* 14, no. 3 (1963): 184.

54. John L. Lewis, "Labor and the Nation," September 3, 1937, in *Words of a Century*, ed. Lucas and Medhurst, 249–54.

55. Carrie Chapman Catt, "The Crisis," September 7, 1916, in *Words of a Century*, ed. Lucas and Medhurst, 57–73. For an especially insightful analysis of Catt's rhetoric and that of her contemporaries, see Susan S. Huxman, "Perfecting the Rhetorical Vision of Woman's Rights: Elizabeth Cady Stanton, Anna Howard Shaw, and Carrie Chapman Catt," *Women's Studies in Communication* 23, no. 3 (2000): 307–36.

56. Jennifer J. McGee, "A Pilgrim's Progress: Metaphor in the Rhetoric of Mary Fisher, AIDS Activist," *Women's Studies in Communication* 26, no. 2 (2003): 192.

57. Mary Fisher, "A Whisper of AIDS," July 14, 1992, in *Words of a Century*, ed. Lucas and Medhurst, 644–47.

58. Daniel S. Lucks, "Martin Luther King Jr.'s Riverside Speech and Cold War Civil Rights," *Peace and Change* 40, no. 3 (2015), 396; Frederick J. Antczak, "When 'Silence is Betrayal': An Ethical Criticism of the Revolution of Values in the Speech at Riverside Church," in *Martin Luther King Jr. and the Sermonic Power of Public Discourse*, ed. Carolyn Calloway-Thomas and John L. Lucaites (Tuscaloosa: University of Alabama Press, 1993), 146.

59. Martin Luther King Jr., "Speech at Riverside Church," April 4, 1967, in *Words of a Century*, ed. Lucas and Medhurst, 453–63.

60. Stephen P. Depoe, "Requiem for Liberalism: The Therapeutic and Deliberative Functions of Nostalgic Appeals in Edward Kennedy's Address to the

1980 Democratic National Convention," *Southern Journal of Communication* 55, no. 2 (1990): 187–88; Timothy R. Stanley, "'Sailing Against the Wind': A Reappraisal of Edward Kennedy's Campaign for the 1980 Democratic Party Presidential Nomination," *Journal of American Studies* 43, no. 2 (2009): 235.

61. Edward M. Kennedy, "The Dream Shall Never Die," August 12, 1980, in *Words of a Century*, ed. Lucas and Medhurst, 542–48.

62. Metaphorical density was measured by calculating the number of metaphors used, dividing by the total number of words in a speech, and then multiplying by 100.

63. Jonathan A. Cowden, "Self-Effacing and Self-Defeating Leadership: Adlai E. Stevenson," *Political Psychology* 20, no. 4 (1999): 845–74.

64. John M. Murphy, "Civic Republicanism in the Modern Age: Adlai Stevenson in the 1952 Presidential Campaign," *Quarterly Journal of Speech* 80, no. 3 (1994): 322.

65. Murphy, "Civic Republicanism in the Modern Age," 324.

66. Cowden, "Self-Effacing and Self-Defeating Leadership," 853.

67. Adlai Stevenson, "Let's Talk Sense to the American People," July 26, 1952, in *Words of a Century*, ed. Lucas and Medhurst, 306–9.

68. Ellen Reid Gold, "Ronald Reagan and the Oral Tradition," *Communication Studies* 39, no. 3 (1988): 164.

69. Ronald Reagan, "A Time for Choosing," October 27, 1964, in *Words of a Century*, ed. Lucas and Medhurst, 415–23.

70. Ronald Reagan, "Address on the Fortieth Anniversary of D-Day," June 6, 1984, in *Words of a Century*, ed. Lucas and Medhurst, 572–75.

71. Allison M. Prasch, "Reagan at Pointe du Hoc: Deictic Epideictic and the Persuasive Power of 'Bringing Before the Eyes,' " *Rhetoric and Public Affairs* 18, no. 2 (2015): 260.

72. Dennis Merrill, "The Truman Doctrine: Containing Communism and Modernity," *Presidential Studies Quarterly* 36, no. 1 (2006): 27–37.

73. Martin J. Medhurst, "Truman's Rhetorical Reticence, 1945–1947: An Interpretive Essay," *Quarterly Journal of Speech* 74, no. 1 (1988): 65.

74. Stephen M. Underhill, "Prisoner of Context: The Truman Doctrine Speech and J. Edgar Hoover's Rhetorical Realism," *Rhetoric and Public Affairs* 20, no. 3 (2017): 478.

75. Denise M. Bostdorff, *Proclaiming the Truman Doctrine: The Cold War Call to Arms* (College Station: Texas A&M University Press, 2008), 126.

76. Harry Truman, "The Truman Doctrine," March 12, 1947, in *Words of a Century*, ed. Lucas and Medhurst, 271–75.

77. Charles J. Stewart, "The Evolution of a Revolution: Stokely Carmichael and the Rhetoric of Black Power," *Quarterly Journal of Speech* 83, no. 4 (1997): 435.

78. Stokely Carmichael, "Black Power," October 29, 1966, in *Words of a Century,* ed. Lucas and Medhurst, 441–52.

79. For more on this aspect of Clinton's trip, see Kenneth V. Anderson, "Hillary Rodham Clinton as 'Madonna': The Role of Metaphor and Oxymoron in Image Restoration," *Women's Studies in Communication* 25, no. 1 (2002): 1–24.

80. Rose Helens-Hart, "Heeding the Call: Hillary Clinton's Rhetoric of Identification and Women's Human Rights at the Fourth World Conference on Women," *Ohio Communication Journal* 53 (2015): 75.

81. Mark Bennister, "The Oratory of Hillary Clinton," in *Democratic Orators from JFK to Barack Obama,* ed. Andrew S. Crines, David S. Moon, and Robert Lehrman (Heidelberg: Springer, 2016), 246.

82. Hillary Clinton, "Women's Rights Are Human Rights," September 5, 1995, in *Words of a Century,* ed. Lucas and Medhurst, 650–54.

83. Charles J. G. Griffin, "New Light on Eisenhower's Farewell Address," *Presidential Studies Quarterly* 22 (1992): 476–77.

84. For more on this concept of balance, see Martin J. Medhurst, "Reconceptualizing Rhetorical History: Eisenhower's Farewell Address," *Quarterly Journal of Speech* 80, no. 2 (1994): 195–218.

85. Dwight D. Eisenhower, "Farewell Address," January 17, 1961, in *Words of a Century,* ed. Lucas and Medhurst, 337–40.

86. See Karlyn Kohrs Campbell, *The Great Silent Majority: Nixon's 1969 Speech on Vietnamization* (College Station: Texas A&M University Press, 2014), 60–61.

87. Robert A. Vartabedian, "Nixon's Vietnam Rhetoric: A Case Study of Apologia as Generic Paradox," *Southern Speech Communication Journal* 50, no. 4 (1985): 371.

88. Richard M. Nixon, "The Great Silent Majority," November 3, 1969, in *Words of a Century,* ed. Lucas and Medhurst, 488–96.

89. Norman P. Lewis, "The Myth of Spiro Agnew's 'Nattering Nabobs of Negativism,'" *American Journalism* 27, no. 1 (2010): 105.

90. Spiro T. Agnew, "Television News Coverage," November 13, 1969, in *Words of a Century,* ed. Lucas and Medhurst, 496–503.

91. Bonnie J. Dow and Mari Boor Tonn, "'Feminine Style' and Political Judgment in the Rhetoric of Ann Richards," *Quarterly Journal of Speech* 79, no. 3 (1993): 290.

92. Diane M. Martin, "Balancing on the Political High Wire: The Role of Humor in the Rhetoric of Ann Richards," *Southern Journal of Communication* 69, no. 4 (2004): 286.

93. Ann Richards, "Keynote Speech at the Democratic National Convention," June 18, 1988, in *Words of a Century,* ed. Lucas and Medhurst, 618–23.

94. Robert E. Terrill, "Protest, Prophecy, and Prudence in the Rhetoric of Malcolm X," *Rhetoric & Public Affairs* 4, no. 1 (2001): 31; Robert E. Terrill, "Colonizing the Borderlands: Shifting Circumference in the Rhetoric of Malcolm X," *Quarterly Journal of Speech* 86, no. 1 (2000): 67, 68.

95. Malcolm X, "Message to the Grassroots," November 10, 1963, in *Words of a Century*, ed. Lucas and Medhurst, 379–88.

96. Mark LaVoie, "William Faulkner's 'Speech Accepting the Nobel Prize in Literature': A Language for Ameliorating Atomic Anxiety," *Rhetoric & Public Affairs* 17, no. 2 (2014): 200.

97. LaVoie, "William Faulkner's 'Speech Accepting the Nobel Prize in Literature,'" 216–17; Donald M. Kartiganer, "'Listening to the Voices': Public and Fictional Language in Faulkner," *Southern Quarterly* 45, no. 2 (2008): 30–31.

98. William Faulkner, "Speech Accepting the Nobel Prize in Literature," December 10, 1950, in *Words of a Century*, ed. Lucas and Medhurst, 298–99.

99. Edward deVooght, Sarah Van Leuven, and Liselot Hudders, "Figuring Out Political Rhetoric: A Quantitative Content Analysis of the Use of Rhetorical Figures on the 2018 Flemish Municipal Election Day," *Acta Politica*, 2021, https://biblio.ugent.be/publication/8646675.

100. deVooght, Lerven, and Hudders, "Figuring Out Political Rhetoric."

101. Ana Chkhaidza, Parla Buyruk, and Lera Boroditsky, "Linguistic Metaphors Shape Attitudes Toward Immigration," Proceedings of the Annual Meeting of the Cognitive Science Society, 2021, https://psyarxiv.com/qyhgr/.

102. Crick, "The Rhetorical Singularity," 377.

7. ELOQUENCE ASSESSED

1. Ralph Waldo Emerson, "Success," in *Society and Solitude: Twelve Chapters* (Boston: Osgood, 1876), 259.

2. Emerson, "Eloquence," in *Society and Solitude*, 56.

3. Emerson, "Eloquence," 58.

4. Emerson, "Eloquence," 81.

5. Emerson, "Eloquence," 83.

6. Emerson, "Eloquence," 87.

7. Emerson, "Eloquence," 75–76.

8. Emerson, "Eloquence," 80–81.

9. Emerson, "Eloquence," 83.

10. Elizabeth Glaser, "AIDS: A Personal Story," July 14, 1992, in *Words of a Century: The Top 100 American Speeches, 1900–1999*, ed. Stephen E. Lucas and Martin J. Medhurst (New York: Oxford University Press, 2009), 642–44.

11. For additional detail on the Lucas-Medhurst study, see Stephen E. Lucas and Martin J. Medhurst, "The Top 100 American Speeches of the Twentieth Century," paper presented at the annual convention of the National Communication Association, Seattle, November 2000.

12. Lucas and Medhurst, "The Top 100 American Speeches," 7.

13. Patterns by speech length for Eloquence Index: one segment = 1.2144, 2-3 segments = .7030; 4–6 segments = –2.898; 7–9 segments = –.9824; 10 or more segments = –.9674. F [4, 96] = 4.047, p < .004.

14. Patterns by speech length for Google hits: short speech = 1,771,918; midrange speech = 1,522,827; long speech = 4,258,900. F [2, 652] = 24.853, p < .000.

15. Patterns by gender for Google hits: male = 1,742,158; female = 2,872,461. F [1,653] = 12.878, p < .000.

16. Patterns by situation for Google hits: judicial arguments = 5,504,416; campaign speeches = 956,707; inspirational rituals = 2,804,732; international commentary = 1,921,035; crisis management = 932,277; rights declaration = 964,620. F [5, 649] = 30.796, p < .000.

17. As quoted in Frederick W. Haberman, "General MacArthur's Speech: A Symposium of Critical Comment," Quarterly Journal of Speech 37, no. 3 (1951): 326.

18. As quoted in Haberman, "General MacArthur's Speech," 321.

19. Robert P. Newman, "Lethal rhetoric: The Selling of the China Myths," Quarterly Journal of Speech 61, no. 2 (1975): 124.

20. As quoted in Haberman, "General MacArthur's Speech," 326.

21. Samuel P. Perry, "Douglas MacArthur as Frontier Hero: Converting Frontiers in MacArthur's Farewell to Congress," Southern Communication Journal 77, no. 4 (2012): 265.

22. Douglas MacArthur, "Old Soldiers Never Die," April 19, 1951, in Words of a Century, ed. Lucas and Medhurst, 300–305.

23. Quoted in Bernard K. Duffy and Ronald H. Carpenter, "The Case Against 'Extempore' Eloquence in MacArthur's Farewell to Cadets at West Point," ANQ: A Quarterly Journal of Short Articles, Notes and Reviews 30, no. 1 (2017): 52.

24. Quoted in Richard A. Behrenhausen, "Duty, Honor, Country," Naval War College Review 23, no. 1 (1970): 91.

25. Herbert L. Carson, "War Requested: Wilson and Roosevelt," Communication Studies 10, no. 1 (1958): 31.

26. Franklin Delano Roosevelt, "War Message," December 8, 1941, in Words of a Century, ed. Lucas and Medhurst, 269–79.

27. Hermann G. Stelzner, "'War Message' December 8, 1941: An Approach to Language," Communication Monographs 33, no. 4 (1966): 425.

28. Stelzner, "'War Message,'" 434.

29. Cindy L. Griffin, "Women as Communicators: Mary Daly's Hagiography as Rhetoric," *Communication Monographs* 60, no. 2 (1993): 174.

30. Ursula Le Guin, "A Left-Handed Commencement Address," May 22, 1983, in *Words of a Century*, ed. Lucas and Medhurst, 562–64.

31. Barbara Jordan, "Statement on the Articles of Impeachment Against Richard M. Nixon," July 25, 1974, in *Words of a Century*, ed. Lucas and Medhurst, 518–22.

32. Barbara Johnstone and Judith Mattson are more forgiving of Jordan's prose, noting that "linguistic consistency was for Jordan a sign of moral constancy," which is not to say it was elegant. See "Self-Expression and Linguistic Variation," *Language in Society* 26, no. 2 (1997): 221–46.

33. For more on this matter, see Ferald J. Bryan, "George C. Marshall at Harvard: A Study of the Origins and Construction of the 'Marshall Plan' Speech," *Presidential Studies Quarterly* 21, no. 3 (1991): 489–502.

34. James J. Kimble, "John F. Kennedy, the Construction of Peace, and the Pitfalls of Androgynous Rhetoric," *Communication Quarterly* 57, no. 2 (2009): 164; Denise M. Bostdorff and Shawna H. Ferris, "John F. Kennedy at American University: The Rhetoric of the Possible, Epideictic Progression, and the Commencement of Peace," *Quarterly Journal of Speech* 100, no. 4 (2014): 419.

35. Theodore O. Windt Jr., "Administrative Rhetoric: An Undemocratic Response to Protest," *Communication Quarterly* 30, no. 3 (1982): 247.

36. Dominic Manthey, "Mario Savio, 'An End to History': December 2, 1964," *Voices of Democracy* 10 (2015): 46.

37. Richard B. Gregg, "The Ego-Function of the Rhetoric of Protest," *Philosophy & Rhetoric* 4, no. 2 (1971): 78–79.

38. Gregg, "The Ego-Function," 78–79.

39. Mario Savio, "An End to History," in *Words of a Century*, ed. Lucas and Medhurst, 423-26.

40. Barbara Jordan, "Who Then Will Speak for the Common Good?," July 12, 1976, in *Words of a Century*, ed. Lucas and Medhurst, 532–35.

41. Brian T. Kaylor, "A New Law: The Covenant Speech of Barbara Jordan," *Southern Communication Journal* 77, no. 1 (2012): 14.

42. For more on Jackson's curious political appeal, see Charles P. Henry, "Jesse Jackson and the Decline of Liberalism in Presidential Politics," *Black Scholar* 20, no. 1 (1989): 2–11.

43. Jesse Jackson, "The Rainbow Coalition," June 18, 1984, in *Words of a Century*, ed. Lucas and Medhurst, 584–93.

44. Not everyone liked Jackson's speech. James McDaniel, for example, is put off by the logical inconsistencies and political compromises evident in

Jackson's remarks. What I describe as rhetorically intoxicating, McDaniel describes as irreparably corrupted by moral diddling. See James P. McDaniel, "Liberal Irony: A Program for Rhetoric," *Philosophy & Rhetoric* 35, no. 4 (2002): 297–327.

45. Jedediah Purdy, "Presidential Popular Constitutionalism," *Fordham Law Review* 77, no. 4 (2009): 1849.
46. Quoted in Robert T. Oliver, "Wilson's Rapport with His Audience," *Quarterly Journal of Speech* 27, no. 1 (1941): 81.
47. Oliver, "Wilson's Rapport," 79.
48. Woodrow Wilson, "First Inaugural Address," March 4, 1913, in *Words of a Century*, ed. Lucas and Medhurst, 40–43.
49. Jeffrey K. Tulis, *The Rhetorical Presidency* (Princeton, NJ: Princeton University Press, 2016), 135.
50. As quoted in Leroy G. Dorsey, "Woodrow Wilson's Fight for the League of Nations: A Reexamination," *Rhetoric and Public Affairs* 2, no. 1 (1999): 109.
51. Dorsey, "Woodrow Wilson's Fight," 110.
52. J. Michael Hogan, *Woodrow Wilson's Western Tour: Rhetoric, Public Opinion, and the League of Nations* (College Station: Texas A&M University Press, 2006), 23.
53. Hogan, *Woodrow Wilson's Western Tour*, 151.
54. Woodrow Wilson, "Final Address for the League of Nations," September 25, 1919, in *Words of a Century*, ed. Lucas and Medhurst, 143–52.
55. Richard Sandomir, *The Pride of the Yankees: Lou Gehrig, Gary Cooper, and the Making of a Classic* (New York: Hachette, 2017), 207.
56. Sandomir, *The Pride of the Yankees*, 199.
57. Sandomir, *The Pride of the Yankees*, 199, 201.
58. Denise M. Bostdorff, "Vice-Presidential Comedy and the Traditional Female Role: An Examination of the Rhetorical Characteristics of the Vice-Presidency," *Western Journal of Communication* 55, no. 1 (1991): 1–27.
59. Karlyn Kohrs Campbell and E. Claire Jerry, "Women and Speech: A Conflict in Roles," in *Seeing Female: Social Roles and Personal Lives*, ed. Sharon E. Brehm (New York: Greenwood, 1988), 123–34.
60. Catherine A. Dobris, "The 'Feisty' Feminist from Queens: A Feminist Rhetorical Analysis of the Autobiographies of Geraldine Ferraro," in *Telling Political Lives: The Rhetorical Autobiographies of Women Leaders in the United States*, ed. Brenda D. Marshall and Molly A. Mayhead (Lanham, MD: Lexington, 2008), 73–94.
61. Geraldine Ferraro, "Speech Accepting the Democratic Vice-Presidential Nomination," July 19, 1984, in *Words of a Century*, ed. Lucas and Medhurst, 593–97.

62. Mary E. Stuckey, "Legitimating Leadership: The Rhetoric of Succession as a Genre of Presidential Discourse," *Rhetoric Society Quarterly* 22, no. 2 (1992): 25–38.

63. Robert L. King, "Transforming Scandal Into Tragedy: A Rhetoric of Political Apology," *Quarterly Journal of Speech* 71, no. 3 (1985): 289–301.

64. James F. Klumpp and Jeffrey K. Lukehart, "The Pardoning of Richard Nixon: A Failure in Motivational Strategy," *Western Journal of Communication* 42, no. 2 (1978): 116–23.

65. Alexander Reger, "Following Ford: Reassessing the Pardon of Richard M. Nixon," *White House Studies* 13, no. 1 (2013): 83–108.

66. Gerald R. Ford, "Address on Pardoning Richard M. Nixon," September 8, 1974, in *Words of a Century*, ed. Lucas and Medhurst, 529–31.

67. Mary E. Stuckey, *Slipping the Surly Bonds: Reagan's Challenger Address* (College Station: Texas A&M University Press, 2006), 14.

68. Steven M. Mister, "Reagan's *Challenger* Tribute: Combining Generic Constraints and Situational Demands," *Central States Speech Journal* 37, no. 3 (1986): 158–65.

69. Richard A. Katula, "The Apology of Richard M. Nixon," *Communication Quarterly* 23, no. 4 (1975): 1–5.

70. James W. Hamilton, "Some Reflections on Richard Nixon in the Light of His Resignation and Farewell Speeches," *Journal of Psychohistory* 4, no. 4 (1977): 491–511.

71. Gerald L. Wilson, "A Strategy of Explanation: Richard M. Nixon's August 8, 1974 Resignation Address," *Communication Quarterly* 24, no. 3 (1976): 20.

72. Elie Wiesel, "The Perils of Indifference," April 12, 1999, in *Words of a Century*, ed. Lucas and Medhurst, 655–58.

73. Bradford Vivian, "Witnessing Time: Rhetorical Form, Public Culture, and Popular Historical Education," *Rhetoric Society Quarterly* 44, no. 3 (2014): 204–19.

74. As quoted in John Roper, "The Oratory of John Kerry," in *Democratic Orators from JFK to Barack Obama*, ed. Andrew S. Crines, David S. Moon, and Robert Lehrman (Heidelberg: Springer, 2016), 199.

75. Roper, "The Oratory of John Kerry," 194, 200.

76. John Kerry, "Vietnam Veterans Against the War," April 22, 1971, in *Words of a Century*, ed. Lucas and Medhurst, 512–17.

77. Denis Donoghue, *On Eloquence* (New Haven, CT: Yale University Press, 2008), 103.

78. Matthew Bevis, *The Art of Eloquence: Byron, Dickens, Tennyson, Joyce* (Columbus: Ohio State University Press, 2007), 3.

79. Davis W. Houck, *FDR and Fear Itself: The First Inaugural Address* (College Station: Texas A&M University Press, 2002), 73. For more on this notion of

Roosevelt's holy war, see Suzanne M. Daughton, "Metaphorical Transcendence: Images of the Holy War in Franklin Roosevelt's First Inaugural," *Quarterly Journal of Speech* 79, no. 4 (1993): 427–46.

80. Franklin D. Roosevelt, "First Inaugural Address," March 14, 1933, in *Words of a Century*, ed. Lucas and Medhurst, 221–24.

81. Thomas B. Farrell, *Norms of Rhetorical Culture* (New Haven, CT: Yale University Press, 1993), 93.

82. Farrell, *Norms of Rhetorical Culture*, 83.

83. Houck, *FDR and Fear Itself*, 108.

84. John F. Kennedy, "Inaugural Address," January 20, 1961, in *Words of a Century*, ed. Lucas and Medhurst, 341–44.

85. For more on Kennedy's use of antitheses, see Sara Ann Mehltretter, "John F. Kennedy, 'Inaugural Address' (20 January 1961)" *Voices of Democracy* 4 (2009): 41–59, https://voicesofdemocracy.umd.edu/john-f-kennedy-inaugural-address-20-january-1961/; Ronald H. Carpenter, "On Allan Nevins, Grand Style in Discourse, and John F. Kennedy's Inaugural Address: The Trajectory of Stylistic Confluence," *Style* 46, no. 1 (2012): 1–26; Meena Bose, "Words as Signals: Drafting Cold War Rhetoric in the Eisenhower and Kennedy Administrations," *Congress & the Presidency* 25, no. 1 (1998): 23–41; and Edward B. Kenny, "Another Look at Kennedy's Inaugural Address," *Communication Quarterly* 13, no. 4 (1965): 17–19.

86. Roderick P. Hart, "Of Genre, Computers, and the Reagan Inaugural," in *Form, Genre, and the Study of Political Discourse*, ed. Herbert Simons and Adam Aghazarian (Columbia: University of South Carolina Press, 1986), 292.

87. Amos Kiewe, *FDR's First Fireside Chat: Public Confidence and the Banking Crisis* (College Station: Texas A&M University Press, 2007), 83.

88. Kiewe, *FDR's First Fireside Chat*, 9.

89. Lawrence W. Rosenfield, "A Case Study in Speech Criticism: The Nixon-Truman Analog," *Communications Monographs* 35, no. 4 (1968): 435–50.

90. Celeste M. Condit, "Nixon's 'Fund': Time as Ideological Resource in the 'Checkers' Speech," in *Texts in Context: Critical Dialogues on Significant Episodes in American Political Rhetoric*, ed. Michael C. Leff and Fred J. Kauffeld (Davis, CA: Hermagoras, 1989), 222, 236.

91. Richard M. Nixon, "Checkers," September 23, 1952, in *Words of a Century*, ed. Lucas and Medhurst, 309–17.

92. Martin Luther King Jr., "I Have a Dream," August 28, 1963, in *Words of a Century*, ed. Lucas and Medhurst, 375–78.

93. J. Robert Cox, "The Fulfillment of Time: King's 'I Have a Dream' Speech," in *Texts in Context*, ed. Leff and Kauffeld, 181–204.

8. ELOQUENCE TOMORROW

1. Ralph Waldo Emerson, *Society and Solitude: Twelve Chapters* (Boston: Osgood, 1876), 55.

2. Kamala Harris, "Address in Shanksville, Pennsylvania," September 11, 2011, https://www.nytimes.com/2021/09/11/nyregion/kamala-harris-speech-shanksville-911.html.

3. George W. Bush, "Speech at the 9/11 Memorial in Shanksville," September 11, 2021, https://www.washingtonpost.com/video/national/george-w-bushs-full-speech-at-911-memorial-in-shanksville/2021/09/11/cbaaba95-863f-48d8-826a-13685ad3d46a_video.html.

4. S. Michael Halloran, "Eloquence in a Technological Society," *Communication Studies* 29 (1978): 266.

5. Inotivity, "The Decline of Eloquence," *Baker Muse Essays*, July 10, 2011, https://bakermuse.com/2011/07/10/the-decline-of-eloquence/.

6. As quoted in James Perrin Warren, *Culture of Eloquence: Oratory and Reform in Antebellum America* (University Park: Pennsylvania State University Press, 1999), 47.

7. Nick Niedzwiadek, "Utah's Governor: 'Politics Is Becoming Religion in Our Country,'" *Politico*, July 4, 2021, https://www.politico.com/news/2021/07/04/utah-governor-cox-politics-becoming-religion-498038.

8. As quoted in Nellie Bowles, "'Replacement Theory,' a Racist, Sexist Doctrine, Spreads in Far-Right Circles," *New York Times*, March 18, 2019, https://www.nytimes.com/2019/03/18/technology/replacement-theory.html.

9. Rafael Walker, "The Emptiness of Administrative Statements," *Chronicle of Higher Education*, June 23, 2020, https://www.chronicle.com/article/the-emptiness-of-administrative-statements.

10. Bryan Garsten, *Saving Persuasion* (Cambridge, MA: Harvard University Press, 2006), 210.

11. Richard Weaver, *The Ethics of Rhetoric* (New York: Henry Regnery, 1953), 175.

12. Huey P. Long, "Share Our Wealth," March 7, 1935, in *Words of a Century: The Top 100 American Speeches, 1900–1999*, ed. Stephen E. Lucas and Martin J. Medhurst (New York: Oxford University Press, 2009), 237–48.

13. Daniel Burke, "The Guilt-Free Gospel of Donald Trump," *CNN*, October 24, 2016, https://www.cnn.com/2016/10/21/politics/trump-religion-gospel/index.html.

14. Wendell Johnson, *People in Quandaries: The Semantics of Personal Adjustment* (New York: Harper, 1946).

15. Robert Dodaro, *Christ and the Just Society in the Thought of Augustine* (Cambridge: Cambridge University Press, 2005), 202.

16. Jacques Savoy, "Analysis of the Style and the Rhetoric of the 2016 U.S. Presidential Primaries," *Digital Scholarship in the Humanities* 33, no. 1 (2018): 143–59.

17. John Burrows, "Textual Analysis," in *A Companion to Digital Humanities*, ed. Susan Schreibman, Ray Siemens, and John Unsworth (Malden, MA: Blackwell, 2004), 344.

18. Cynthia Ozick, "The Moral Necessity of Metaphor: Rooting History in a Figure of Speech," *Harper's*, May 1986, 63.

19. Burrows, "Textual Analysis," 324.

20. As quoted in Kenneth Cmiel, *Democratic Eloquence: The Fight Over Popular Speech in Nineteenth-Century America* (New York: William Morrow, 1990), 249.

21. As quoted in Cmiel, *Democratic Eloquence*, 250.

22. Theodore Roosevelt, "The Man with the Muckrake," April 14, 1906, in *Words of a Century*, ed. Lucas and Medhurst, 24–29.

23. Denis Donoghue, *On Eloquence* (New Haven, CT: Yale University Press, 2008), 146.

24. "How the Virtue of Eloquence Became a Vice," *TedxWCC Talk*, April 5, 2017, https://www.youtube.com/watch?v=A-rgrj6mkWM.

25. Seth Thompson, "Politics Without Metaphors Is Like a Fish Without Water," in *Metaphor: Implications and Applications*, ed. Jeffery S. Mio and Albert N. Katz (New York: Erlbaum, 1996), 185–201.

26. John M. Murphy, "Theory and Public Address: The Allusive Mr. Bush," in *The Handbook of Public Address*, ed. Shawn J. Parry-Giles and J. Michael Hogan (New York: Wiley-Blackwell, 2010), 277.

27. Christopher Looby, *Voicing America: Language, Literary Form, and the Origins of the United States* (Chicago: University of Chicago Press, 1996), 67.

28. Cmiel, *Democratic Eloquence*, 24.

29. Timothy W. Luke, "History as an Ideo-Political Commodity: The 1984 D-day Spectacle," *New Political Science* 5, no. 1 (1984), 49.

30. Ronald Reagan, "Address on the Fortieth Anniversary of D-Day," June 6, 1984, in *Words of a Century*, ed. Lucas and Medhurst, 572–75.

31. Kathleen Hall Jamieson, *Eloquence in an Electronic Age: The Transformation of Political Speechmaking* (New York: Oxford University Press, 1988), 94.

32. Edward M. Kennedy, "Eulogy to Robert F. Kennedy," June 8, 1968, in *Words of a Century*, ed. Lucas and Medhurst, 482–85.

33. Martin Reisigl, "The Semiotics of Political Commemoration," in *The Routledge Handbook of Language and Politics*, ed. Ruth Wodak and Bernhard Forchtner (New York: Routledge, 2018), 369.

34. Robert L. Caserio, "Eloquence: A Response to Harold Bloom's *The American Canon*," *Symplokē* 28, no. 1 (2020): 431.

35. Bill Clinton, "Speech for Victims of the Oklahoma City Bombing," April 23, 1995, in *Words of a Century*, ed. Lucas and Medhurst, 648–50.
36. Robert M. LaFollette, "Free Speech in Wartime," October 6, 1917, in *Words of a Century*, ed. Lucas and Medhurst, 87–109.
37. Margaret Sanger, "The Children's Era," March 30, 1925, in *Words of a Century*, ed. Lucas and Medhurst, 208–11.
38. Carrie Chapman Catt, "The Crisis," September 7, 1916, in *Words of a Century*, ed. Lucas and Medhurst, 57–73.
39. Anna Howard Shaw, "The Fundamental Principles of a Republic," June 21, 1915, in *Words of a Century*, ed. Lucas and Medhurst, 43–56.
40. Orrin Hatch quoted in Kathleen M. German and Jeffrey L. Courtright, "Politically Privileged Voices: Glaser and Fisher Address the 1992 Presidential Nominating Conventions," in *Power in the Blood: A Handbook on AIDS, Politics, and Communication*, ed. William Elwood (Philadelphia: Routledge, 1999), 70.
41. Kenneth Burke, *Counter-Statement* (Berkeley: University of California Press, 1968), 40–41.
42. Rebecca Ottman has written a thoughtful dissertation in which she argues that eloquence must be reimagined in light of new technologies like TikTok and, more importantly, in light of the increasingly diverse young people who are boldly experimenting with new forms of language use. As Ottman notes, "the traditional essay tends to treat students as a tabula rasa when they enter the classroom, assuming they have no sense of their own writing process or awareness of audience. Ironically, many of the students entering our classrooms today are also putting together rhetorically compelling TikToks as a way of sending a message to a larger audience through manipulation of an algorithm. Our students are more rhetorically savvy than we often give them credit for being." See Rebecca D. Ottman, "Theorizing Eloquence as a Means-Driven Process of Recursive Invention" (PhD diss., Indiana University, 2021), 185.
43. Rob Goodman, "Eloquence and Its Conditions" (PhD diss., Columbia University, 2018).
44. Wallace Stevens, "The Comedian as the Letter C: A Nice Shady Home," *Poetry Foundation*, https://www.poetryfoundation.org/poems/47428/the-comedian-as-the-letter-c.

INDEX

Page numbers in *italics* indicate figures or tables.

Acerbi, Alberto, 21
"Acres of Diamonds" (Conwell), 74
activism: by African Americans,
    82–83; for African Americans,
    37–38; Black Lives Matter, 57, 139;
    Me Too, 57, 139; movement, 172;
    in politics, 34–35; rhetoric in,
    62–63; social, 62–63
Adams, John, 2
Africa, 22–26, 126–27
African Americans, 8–9, 37–38, 82–83,
    152
Agnew, Spiro, 77, 151–52, 164
AIDS, 115, 157
"Ain't I a Woman?" (Truth), 95–96
algorithms, 260n42
Allen, Robert S., 166
Amazon Prime, 1
anarchy, 67
Andrews, James, 85
Angelou, Maya, 124
annunciatory events, 164

Anthony, Susan B., 54, 59
Antifa, 46
apologies, 32, 121–22
appropriateness, 20–23
architecture, 36–37
Ardern, Jacinda, 4
Arendt, Hannah, 24–25, 104
Aristotle, 19
Arnold, Carroll, 18, 45–46
Aronson, Amy, 117
art, 19–20, 26, 36–37
artistry, 161
Asians, 22, 127
assessment: of availability, 178–82;
    of definitive eloquence, 168–73;
    of eloquence, 155–58, *158*,
    166–68, 182–85, 189–93, 208–9;
    of expansive eloquence, 185–89;
    importance and, 162–66, *163*; of
    Lucas-Medhurst Study, 158–62; of
    righteous eloquence, 173–78
attorneys, 54

Augustine (saint), 10, 45, 98, 197
Austen, Jane, 54
authenticity, 47–48, 102–3
autonomy, *29*
availability, 168, 178–82

Bacon, Francis, 8
Bagehot, Walter, 58
balance, 79–87, 244n44
Baldwin, Doug, 4
Barber, William, 62, 206
Barth, John, 40
Beecher, Henry Ward, 32
behavior, 1–2, 6
bemusement, 63
Berlin Wall, 80–81
Beschloss, Michael, 206
Bevis, Matthew, 7, 185
Bible, 5, 8–9
Biden, Beau, 93–95
Biden, Jill, 93–94
Biden, Joe, 48–52, 59, 93–95, 103, 109,
    196, 208
Big Data, 42, 127
bigotry, 83–84
Birkerts, Sven, 35
Black, Edwin, 32–34, 81, 106
Black Lives Matter, 57, 139
Blair, Hugh, 11, 23
Bliss, Panti, *28*
Bloch, Maurice, 23–25
Bod, Laurens, 41
boldness, 84–87
Bolivia, 1
Bonds, Barry, 179
Boor-Tonn, Mari, 152
Boose, Lynda, 8
Bostdorff, Denise, 171, 179–80
Boyd, Dana, 42
Boynton, Robert, 44

Brainerd, Charles, 44
Brauer, Ralph, 66
bravery, *28*
breadth, 66–67
Brennan, Timothy, 40
Bridenbaugh, Carl, 53
Brown, Brene, 206
Brown, Robert, 124
Brown, Tammy L., 86
Browning, Robert, 54
Bryan, William Jennings, 54, 69–70,
    131
Buckley, William F., 160
Burke, Kenneth, 206
Burrows, John, 199
Bush, Cori, 197
Bush, George H. W., 16, 102–3, 106,
    152
Bush, George W., *31*, 109, *110*, 178,
    191–93
Butts, Calvin O., 35

campaigns, 53, *108*, 108–9, 232n60
Campbell, George, 19
Campbell, Karlyn, 180
Campbell Soup Company, 84
candor, *28*
Carey, Hillary, 68
Carmichael, Stokely, 148–49, 164, 208
Carroll, Lewis, 54
Carson, Herbert, 89, 168
Carter, Gloria, *28*
Carter, Jimmy, 19, 87–88, *88*, 109, *110*;
    Gehrig and, 165; opponents of,
    143; Wilson and, 164
Casiero, Robert, 23
Cather, Willa, 54
Catt, Carrie Chapman, 141–42, 204–5,
    249n55
Chaiken, Shelly, 127

Challenger explosion, 181
challenging, 129–31
Charteris-Black, Jonathan, 129
Chavez, Caesar, 67, 202–3
Chavez, Hugo, 76
"Checkers" speech (Nixon), 160–61, 162, 187–89
children, 6–7, 198, 204–5
China, 11, 127
Chisholm, Shirley, 86, 161, 208
Chkhaidza, Ana, 154
choice, 17
Chopra, Deepak, 206
Churchill, Winston, 12, 168, 199–200
climate change, 13–14
Clinton, Bill, 48, 63; Nixon and, 103; on Oklahoma City bombing, *88*, 89, 203; Patterson and, 234n18; Reagan and, 101; in Watergate scandal, 2
Clinton, Hillary, 48, 79, 109, 148–49
closure, 180–81
Cmiel, Kenneth, 32, 46, 65, 202
Cochise (chief), 17
Cockburn, Bruce, 35
Coe, Kevin, 242n16
Cold War, 67–68
Coleridge, Samuel Taylor, 19–20
Collins, Kaitlan, 59
Collins, Susan, 48
colonialism, 56–57
Commager, Henry Steele, 68, 200–201
community, 70–72, 175, 225n24
concern, 62–63
Condit, Celeste, 22, 38, 188
consumers, 1
context, 44
controversy, 164
conversations, 32–33
Conwell, Russell, 74–75, 78

Coolidge, Calvin, 132
Cooper, Anderson, 5
Coplan, David, 26
Core, George, 46
Cornyn, John, 79
corporate advocacy, *60*, 64
corroboration, 42–43
cosmopolitanism, 7–8
COVID-19, 7, 13–14, 48, 65–66, 198
Cox, Robert, 190
Cox, Spencer, 195
Craft, Robert, 59
Crawford, Kate, 42
creativity, 80–81, 129
Crick, Nathan, 39, 125, 154
criticism: of culture, 15; of eloquence, 34–35, 225n24; of JFK, 171; of Jordan, 254n32; of MLK, 142–43
Cruz, Ted, 11, 48, 173
Crystal, David, 10
Cuban, Mark, 109
cultural resonance: balance in, 79–87; eloquence from, 3, 14–15, 91–92; history of, 27, 32, 56–58; importance in, 162–63; lexical properties of, 53; in politics, 58–64, *60*, 87–91, *88*; pragmatism and, 72–78; scholarship on, 45–47; transcendence and, 65–72
culture: art in, 26; criticism of, 15; cultural anthropology, 23–24; existentialism in, 104, *105*, 106–7; immediacy in, 75–76; intimacy in, 100–101, *101*; judgments in, 4; materialism in, 73–75; in modernity, 26–27; rhetoric in, 23–26; secularism in, 42; speech and, 26–27, *28–31*, 32–34; of UK, 129; of United States, 5, 7, 11–13; Western, 8, 11, 22; of Zoom, 1

Cuomo, Mario, 85–86, *118*, 119–21, 164, 209

Da, Nan, 45
Darrow, Clarence, 208
Darsey, James, 113, 116
Day, Henry, 102
Debs, Eugene, 84–86, 114, 116, 139–40
début events, 165
Declaration of Independence, 97, 190
deference, 62
defining, 127–29
definitive eloquence, 168–73
democracy, 20, 66, 72
Democrats: Cuomo for, 120–21; ideology of, 73; J. Jackson and, 239n91; T. Kennedy for, 143; Republicans and, 1–2, 69, *108*, 108–9, 160, 173–74; working-class votes for, 77
Depoe, Steven, 143
DeWine, Mike, *31*
dialect, 152
Dickinson, Emily, 5
DICTION: for cultural resonance, 46–47; on discourse, 43–44, 59–60, *60*; on metaphors, *50–51*, 50–52, 194; text with, 39–40
digital humanities, 40, 229n12
digital scholarship, 41–42
diligence, *31*
Dimon, Jamie, 59
diplomacy, 25, 172
disciplined emotions, 19–20
discourse, of presidents, 226n32
Disney Corporation, 64
disruption, 175
dogmatism, 113
Dole, Bob, *30*
Donne, John, 119

Donoghue, Denis, 19–21, 32, 39, 63, 98, 185
Doocy, Peter, 59
Dos Passos, John, 119
Douglass, Frederick, 59, 98, *99*, 100
Dow, Bonnie, 152
Drudge, Matt, 59
Dubois, W. E. B., 98
Dukakis, Michael, 48
Duncan, Robert, 124
Dylan, Bob, 145

Eastman, Crystal, 117, *118*, 119, 208–9
education, 7–8, 13–14, *28*, 40, 57
Edwards, Jonathan, 46, 91
efficiency, *30*
Egypt, 25
Ehrenreich, Barbara, 34–35
Eifler, John, 36
Eisenhower, Dwight, 86–87, 150, 179, 240n103
Elbow, Peter, 22
Eliot, T. S., 5
elitism, 12, 78
elliptical policy proposals, 88
eloquence. *See specific topics*
Emancipation Proclamation, 73
Emerson, Ralph Waldo, 10, 18–19, 40, 54, 125–26; on oratory, 191; on practical chemistry, 194; rhetoric of, 155–57
emotions, 2, 152
England. *See* United Kingdom
Engles, Jeremy, 234n14
English language, 22
entertainment, 1, 13
entrepreneurs, *108*, 108–13, *110*
Ettema, James, 2
Europe, 56–57, 80–81, 89, 182–83
evangelism, 113–14

"Every Man a King" (Long), 141
Evjue, William, 167
existentialism, 104, *105*, 106–7
expansive eloquence, 168, 185–89

Facebook, 101–2, 127, 207
facts, 5
Fairbanks, Eve, 103–4
Fallingwater (Pennsylvania), 36
Fallows, James, 55, 225n27
Falwell, Jerry, 71
Farrell, Thomas, 21, 55, 186
Faulkner, William, 153
FDR. *See* Roosevelt, Franklin
Federalist papers, 20, 56
feelings, 2
Felstiner, Mary, 129
feminism, 13, 95–96
Fénelon, François, 19
Ferguson, Robert, 73
Ferraro, Geraldine, 164, 179–80
Ferris, Shawna, 171
Fiorina, Carly, 109
Fish, Stanley, 53
Fisher, Mary, *105*, 106, 142
Fisher, Walter, 45
Flanagan, Jason, 89
Fliegelman, Jay, 97
Floyd, George, 2
Ford, Gerald, 70–71, *88*, 89, 160, 165, 180–81
Franklin, Ben, 49
frustration, 197
fury, *29*
future, of eloquence, 205–8

Gaetz, Matt, 197
Gaines, Chip, 74–75
Gaines, Joanna, 74–75
Gallo-Brown, Alex, 124

Garsten, Bryan, 71, 196
Gates, Bill, 206
Gates, Robert, 206
Gavin, Michael, 44–45
gay rights, 64
Gehrig, Lou, *105*, 106, 165, 179
Gemma, Marissa, 73
gender, *29*, 200
generalizations, 52–53
geolocation, 26
George III (king), 57–58
Germany, 80–81, 89, 182–83
Gettysburg Address (Lincoln), 65, 73, 93–96
Ginsberg, Allen, 124
Glaser, Ariel, 157
Glaser, Elizabeth, *105*, 106, 115–16, 157, 205
Glaser, Jake, 157
Glasser, Theodore, 2–3
Goatly, Andrew, 127
Goffman, Erving, 17
Goldman, Emma, 67, 140, 164, 206
Goldwater, Barry, 69–70, 146–47, 202–3
Goldzwiz, Steve, 83
Goodman, Rob, 207, 226n47
Goodnight, Thomas, 67, 109, 111
Google, 165, 253n16
Gorbachev, Michael, 81
Gorman, Amanda, 206
government, 57–58
Grady, Joseph, 126
Graham, Lindsey, *31*
granularity, 230n32
Gray, Hannah, 9
Great Depression, 77–78
Great Society, 73–74
Greek philosophy, 11
Greenberg, Paul, 79
Greene, Marjorie Taylor, 8, 66

Greene, Ronald, 25–26
Gregg, Richard, 172
Grey, Zane, 54
grief, 181
Griffin, Cindy, 169
Guggenheim Museum (New York City), 36
Gunn, Joshua, 141
Gunther, John, 167–68
Gustafson, Sandra, 48

Hancock, John, 54
Hannity, Sean, 59
Hargis, Billy James, 46
Hariman, Robert, 43
Harris, Kamala, 191–92
Hart, Gary, 83
Hatch, Orrin, 205, 260n40
hegemony, 25–26
Hemingway, Ernest, 12
Henry, David, 119
Henry, Patrick, 54, 57, 58, 96–98
Heyvaert, Pauline, 128–29
hierarchies, 25
Higginson, Thomas Wentworth, 18–19
Hill, Anita, 105, 106–7, 165, 208
hip hop music, 3
history: of cultural resonance, 27, 32, 56–58; education from, 13–14; of eloquence, 3, 3–4, 7–9, 18–20; of League of Nations, 45; modernity and, 54; of oratory, 3; of personal investment, 93–96; of poetic imagination, 123–25; of rhetoric, 15
HIV, 115, 157
Hobbes, Thomas, 20
Hogan, Michael, 176–77
Hollyhock House (Los Angeles), 36
Holmes, Oliver Wendell, 9
Holocaust, 182–83

Homer, 19, 104
Hoover, Herbert, 148
hostility, 61
Houck, Davis, 11, 185–86
humanists, 42–43
humility, 31, 179, 197
humor, 16, 27, 30
Humphrey, Hubert, 66, 114, 165
Hutchinson, Anne, 48
Huxley, Aldous, 54
hyperpersonalization, 117

iconography, in religion, 236n34
idealization, 197
identity, 29, 33, 47–48
ideology, 45–46, 73, 75
"I Have a Dream" (MLK), 37–38, 38, 81, 164, 189–90
imagery, 156
imagination, 23, 126–27, 198. See also poetic imagination
immediacy, 75–76
impeachment, 29
importance, 162–66, 163, 192–93, 200–205, 211–15
inaugural addresses, 185–87, 256n79
incongruity, 182
individuality, 140–44
inspiration, 30
Instagram, 1
integrity, 31
intelligence, 13, 54
intensity, 69–70
intimacy, 100–101, 101
introspection, 28, 88
irritation, 63–64

Jackson, Andrew, 62
Jackson, Jesse, 83–84, 114, 239n91, 254n42, 254n44; eloquence of, 100; rhetoric of, 45–46, 174–75

Jackson, Mahalia, 79
Jackson, Reggie, 179
James (king), 8
Jamieson, Kathleen Hall, 22
Japan, 11
Jay, John, 56–57
Jefferson, Thomas, 97
Jerry, Claire, 180
JFK. See Kennedy, John F.
John Birch Society, 46
John of Salisbury, 132
Johnson, Ben, 10
Johnson, Hugh, 78
Johnson, Lyndon, 73–74, 78, 82–83, *88*,
    89; to Carmichael, 149; Nixon and,
    151; Reagan and, 160; on Voting
    Rights Act, *110*, 110–11
Johnson, Mark, 128
Johnson, Wendell, 197
Jordan, Barbara, 79, 161, 170–71,
    173–74, 254n32
Joyce, James, 7
Judaism, 182–83
judgment, *3*, 3–7, *6*, 8

Kant, Immanuel, 19–20
Kaufer, David, 43
Kaylor, Brian, 174
Kemp, Louie, 145
Kennedy, John F. (JFK), 4, 34, 80–81;
    assassination of, 89, 160, 178;
    criticism of, 171; eloquence of,
    143–44, 163, *163*, 163–64; FDR
    and, 161; inaugural address of,
    186–87; on poetry, 124; psychology
    of, 111–12; Reagan and, 132; on
    religion, *105*, 106
Kennedy, Robert, 87, 139, 161, 203
Kennedy, Ted, 70–71, *88*, 89–90,
    105, 106; for Democrats, 143;
    eloquence of, *163*; at funerals, 203;

Goldman and, 164; on JFK, 178;
    Reagan and, 165
Kerry, John, 161, 183–84
Khrushchev, Nikita, 61
Kiewe, Amos, 187
Killer Mike (rapper), *28*
King, Martin Luther, Jr. (MLK), 81–82,
    87, 114, 126, 161; criticism of, 142–
    43; eloquence of, *8-9*, *163*, 199–200,
    206; MacArthur and, 168; Malcolm
    X and, 62, 75–76; speeches of,
    37–39, *38*, 131, 164, 189–90
King, Steve, 195
Kirchner, Néstor, 76
Klumpp, James, 180
Kopechne, Mary Jo, 89–90
Kopff, Christian, 167
Kowal, Sabine, 53
Krauthammer, Charles, 160
Ku Klux Klan, 46

LaFollette, Robert, 203–4
Lakoff, George, 128
Langford, Catherine, 102
language, 12–13, 16–20, 32, 72,
    226n47; English, 22; of leadership,
    62–63; metaphors, 33–34; politics
    and, 2–5, 23–26
Lanham, Richard, 55
Lankford, James, 63
Lawrence, D. H., 54
leadership, 25–26, 38–39, 62–63
Leahy, Patrick, 79
Lee, Ronald, 85, 88
Leeten, Lars, 20
Le Guin, Ursula, 168–70
Le Pen, Marine, 76–77
Lester, Julius, 22
Levy, Peter, 77
Lewis, John L., 141–42
Lewis, William, 68–69

lilting observations, 153
Lincoln, Abraham, 7, 12, 54, 65, 73, 91, 93–96
linguistic consistency, 254n32
linguistics, 10–11
literature, 41, 54, 60, 63
Locke, John, 8
Lodge, Milton, 44
logic, 19
Long, Huey, 77–78, 114, 141–42, 164, 196
Looby, Christopher, 57, 201
Lucas, Stephen, 158–59
Lucas-Medhurst Survey: corpus described, 54; importance vs. eloquence rankings, 163–66, 211–15; intellectual assumptions, 160–62; methodology used, 158–60.
Luebke, Simon, 102
Lukeheart, Jeffrey, 180

MacArthur, Douglas, 105, 106, 161, 166–68
Madagascar, 25
Maddux, Kristy, 69–70
Madison, James, 20
Malcolm X, 22, 78, 114, 161, 164; MLK and, 62, 75–76; strong dialect of, 152; on white oppression, 105, 106
Mandela, Nelson, 40
Manovich, Lev, 42
Manthey, Dominic, 172
manufactured rhetoric, 225n27
Maori, 24
March, Stephen, 40
Markle, Meghan, 28, 58
Marshall, George, 164, 171
Marx, Groucho, 33–34
Maslem, Robert, 130
Masters, Edgar Lee, 200

materialism, 73–75
McCain, John, 30
McCarthy, Joe, 112–13, 125
McConnell, Mitch, 195–96
McDaniel, James, 254n44
McGee, Jennifer, 142
mechanics, 174
Medhurst, Martin, 158–59, 240n103
media, 196–97, 207
Melpa, 25
memorability, 21
men, 165
Mencken, H. L., 61, 70
Merina, 25
Merrill, Dennis, 148
metaphors, 41, 157, 198, 227n61, 250n62; choosing, 144–50, 145; DICTION on, 50–51, 50–52, 194; effects of, 150–53; functions of, 125–31; by J. Jackson, 174–75; in politics, 49–52, 50–51; psychology of, 33–34; types of, 131–32, 133–34, 135–36, 137–38, 139–40
Me Too, 57, 139
Middleton, Joyce, 96
migrants, 26
militarism, 69, 86
Mill, John Stuart, 78
Minaj, Nicki, 11
Mister, Steven, 181
mistrust, 9
MLK. See King
modernity, 26–27, 54, 55, 65–66, 146, 196–97, 206–8
modesty, 163
Mondale, Fritz, 120, 180
Mondale, Walter, 83
Montefiore, Simon, 5, 39
Morales, Evo, 76
morality, 8, 79, 85–88, 197, 254n32
moral leadership, 38–39

moral refinement, 19–20, 27
Moretti, Franco, 41–42
Morin, Olivier, 21
movement activism, 172
Murdoch, Rupert, 59
Murkowski, Lisa, 48
Murphy, John, 52–53, 66, 145, 201
music, 3, 35
Musoff, Andreas, 130

nationality, 23–24
natural simplicity, 19–20, 27
nature, 174
Netflix, 1
New Left, 46
Newman, Robert, 167
New Zealand, 4, 24
Nicholson, Catherine, 15
Nietzsche, Friedrich, 3, 126
9/11, 178, 191–93
Nixon, Richard, 32–33, 71, 103, 106,
    182; "Checkers" speech by, 160–61,
    162, 187–89; eloquence of, 100,
    150–51, 163; Ford and, 180; Hill
    and, 165; impeachment of, 170;
    personal investment to, 121–22
Noonan, Peggy, 11–12, 181
novel circumstances, 164
novelty, 179–80
Nussbaum, Martha, 130

Obama, Barack, 8, 34, 124; eloquence
    of, 109, 110, 197, 206; Trump and,
    5–6, 14, 223n34
observations, 153
Ocasio-Cortez, Alexandria, 8
O'Connell, Daniel, 53
O'Donnell, Rosie, 109
Oklahoma City bombing, 88, 89, 203
Oliver, Robert, 175
ontology, 33

oral speech, 17–18, 45–46, 225n24
oratory, 3, 10–11, 53–54, 124, 191;
    scholarship on, 23–24, 39–43; in
    United States, 37–39, 38, 194
Orbán, Viktor, 76
Orwell, George, 61
Osborn, Michael, 126–27, 227n61
Osteen, Joel, 46
Ottman, Rebecca, 260n42
Oxford University Press, 159–60
Ozick, Cynthia, 126, 199

pairings, of metaphors, 136, 137–38,
    139
Palin, Sarah, 59, 101
Papua New Guinea, 25
partisanship, 160
Pascal, Blaise, 10
passion, 165
patriarchy, 11
Patterson, James, 63, 234n18
Patudi, Mansur Ali Kahn, 4
Pauley, Garth, 83
Peale, Norman Vincent, 196
Pearl Harbor attack, 168–70
Pearson, Drew, 166
Pelosi, Nancy, 66, 206
Perry, Samuel, 167
personal influence, 24
personal investment: in
    conversations, 32–33; eloquence
    from, 96–98, 99, 100–104, 101,
    121–22; by entrepreneurs, 108,
    108–13, 110; existentialism and,
    104, 105, 106–7; history of, 93–96;
    poetic imagination and, 3, 14–15,
    53, 194, 199; by politicians,
    197; prophecies and, 113–16;
    scholarship on, 47–48; sovereignty
    in, 116–17, 118, 119–21
personalization, 242n16

Peters, John, 55
Petrarca, Francesco, 7–8
Petrarch, 7–8
philosophical statements, 165
Picasso, Pablo, 33
poetic imagination: of children, 198; history of, 123–25; individuality and, 140–44; personal investment and, 3, 14–15, 53, 194, 199; scholarship on, 48–52, *50–51*, 153–54; truth and, 33–34. *See also* metaphors
poetry, 123–24, 154
poignancy, 143
Political Language and Oratory in Traditional Society (Bloch), 23–24
politics: activism in, 34–35; behavior in, 1–2; breadth in, 66–67; campaigns, 53; of community, 70–72; of COVID-19, 7, 65, 66; cultural resonance in, 58–64, *60*, 87–91, *88*; eloquence in, 47, 200; government and, 57–58; hegemony in, 25–26; humor in, 27; impeachment, *29*; intensity in, 69–70; J. Jackson in, 254n42; language and, 2–5, 23–26; in Lucas-Medhurst Corpus, 54; metaphors in, 49–52, *50–51*; in modernity, 55; partisanship in, 160; philosophy and, 10–14; poetry and, 123, 154; political hierarchies, 25; politicians, 48–49, 104, *105*, 106, 197; popularity in, 46; populism, 69–70, 76–79, 114, 141; pragmatism in, 64, 195–96; progressive, 164; psychology of, 87–88, *88*; of Reagan, 115; religion and, 234n14; of Republicans, 84; rhetoric in, 17, 90–91; secrecy in, 32–33; in United States, 24, 56–57;

vision in, 67–69. *See also specific topics*
populism, 69–70, 76–79, 114, 141, 239n91
Potter, Rosanne, 44–45
practical chemistry, 194
pragmatism: cultural resonance and, 72–78; Emerson on, 156; of E. Glaser, 157; of MLK, 81; in politics, 64, 195–96; transcendence and, 45–47, 59–60, *60*, 87–92, *88*, *158*, 194–96, 199, 239n82, 243n30
precocity, *28*
presidents: campaigns by, 53; discourse of, 226n32; eloquence of, 5–7, *6*, 185–89; inaugural addresses, 185–87, 256n79; psychology of, 58–59; rhetoric of, 87–88, *88*; scholarship on, 242n15; self-references by, 197; A. Stevenson on, 146. *See also specific presidents*
Priest, Marcus, 7
progressive politics, 164
prophecies, 113–16
Proust, Marcel, 33–34
prudence, 82–84
public apologies, 32, 121–22
public discourse, 45–46
public figures, 116–21
public personalities, 27, *28–31*, 32
public virtue, 20
Pueblo speech (Wilson), 177–78
Puttenham, George, 14
Pye, Danielle, 7

Quintilianus, Marcus Fabius, 19

Raben, Joseph, 229n12
race, 13, 22–24, 83–84, 114, 195
Rainbow Coalition, 84

Ramsay, Stephen, 43
Rapinoe, Megan, *29*
Reagan, Ronald, 22, 67–69, 80–81,
202, 209; administration, 84;
B. Clinton and, 101; eloquence
of, 109, *110*, 148, *163*, 239n82; on
Goldwater, 146–47; inaugural
address of, 186–87; JFK and, 132;
L. Johnson and, 160; T. Kennedy
and, 165; Noonan and, 181;
politics of, 115
Reisigl, Martin, 203
religion: Bible, 5, 8–9; conflict in, 152;
evangelism, 113–14; iconography
in, 236n34; to J. Jackson, 174; JFK
on, *105*, 106; Judaism, 182–83;
politics and, 234n14; prophets
in, 113–16; to Reagan, 67–68;
reform in, 48; rhetoric in, 77–78;
secularism, 42; sermons, 23, *38*;
theology, 20, 23; to Trump, 237n51;
in United States, 61–62, 85–86
Republicans: Democrats and, 1–2, 69,
108, 108–9, 160, 173–74; politics of,
84; populism to, 77; A. Stevenson
on, 146
resentment, 61–62, 234n14
resignation speech (Nixon), 182
resistance, to socialization, 7–9
resolve, *29*
Reyna, Valerie, 44
rhetoric: in activism, 62–63;
of attorneys, 54; boldness
in, 84–87; of Catt, 249n55;
concepts of, 19–20; in culture,
23–26; in education, 57; of
Emerson, 155; gender and, 200;
generalizations in, 52–53; history
of, 15; importance of, 192–93; of
J. Jackson, 45–46, 174–75; from
leadership, 25–26; manufactured,

225n27; metaphors in, 141–42; in
modernity, 206–8; movement in,
228n2; personalization in, 242n16;
in politics, 17, 90–91; power of,
22; of presidents, 87–88, *88*; of
public personalities, 27, *28–31*,
32; in religion, 77–78; rhetorical
clusters, 59–60, *60*; rhetorical
decisions, 87; rhetorical dexterity,
41; rhetorical intoxication,
254n44; scholarship on, 37–39, *38*,
52–54, 223n34; transcendence in,
91, 157; of Trump, 5–7, 34, 91; in
United States, 57–58, 160, 201–2;
of women, 204–5
Rich, Adrienne, 124
Richards, Ann, 101, 114, 152, 164,
208–9
righteous eloquence, 168, 173–78
Robie House (Chicago), 36
Rodgers, Daniel, 58
Rodriguez, Alex, 179
Rogers, Will, 60–61
Romney, Mitt, *29–30*
Roosevelt, Eleanor, 164, 206
Roosevelt, Franklin (FDR), 38–40, *88*,
88–89, 161, 164; eloquence of,
163, *163*; fireside chats by, 187–88;
inaugural address of, 185–86,
256n79; on Pearl Harbor attack,
168–70; persona of, *118*, 119
Roosevelt, Theodore, 16, 200–201
Rosenfield, Lawrence, 188
Rosenwein, Barbara, 132
Rothman, Richard, 141
Rousseau, Jean-Jacques, 19
Rovere, Richard, 167
ruminative language, 32
Rush, Benjamin, 57–58
Ruth, George Herman "Babe," 179
Ryan, Meg, 16

Sandel, Michael, 46
Sandomir, Richard, 179
Sanger, Margaret, 161, 204–5
Santayana, George, 10
Saturday Night Live (TV show), 63
Savio, Mario, 172–73
Scacco, Joshua, 242n16
scholarship: on cultural resonance, 45–47; digital, 41–42; on eloquence, 36–37, 43–45, 55, 102; on metaphors, 227n61, 250n62; on oratory, 23–24, 39–43; on personal investment, 47–48; on poetic imagination, 48–52, *50–51*, 153–54; on presidents, 242n15; on rhetoric, 37–39, *38*, 52–54, 223n34
Schumer, Chuck, 198
secrecy, 32–33
secularism, 42
self-attachment, 95, 116
self-disclosure, 95, 116
selfhood, 156
self-references. *See* personal investment
self-risk, 165
Seligman, Martin, 90
Sellers, Bakari, 206
sentimentality, 27, 32
sermons, 23, *38*
sexism, 195
sexual orientation, *28*, 64
Shaw, Anna Howard, 204–5
Short, Dewey, 167
Silverstein, Michael, 124
sincerity, *30*, 102–3
Škara, Danica, 127–28
Skinner, Quentin, 9
Slauter, Eric, 42
smartphones, 13
Smith, Al, 111

Smith, Margaret Chase, 124–25
Snee, Brian, 201
Soarez, Cyprian, 2
social activism, 62–63
social harmony, 24–25
socialism, 84–85
socialization, 1, 7–9
social media, 1, 101–2, 127, 207, 260n42
social memory, 3
Society and Solitude (Emerson), 155–56
Solomon, Martha, 140
Sontag, Susan, 16–17
Soroka, Stuart, 43
Sound and the Fury, The (Faulkner), 153
South Africa, 24, 26
sovereignty, 116–17, *118*, 119–21
speech: in Africa, 23–26; concepts of, 20–23; creativity with, 80–81; culture and, 26–27, *28–31*, 32–34; disciplined emotions in, 19; oral, 17–18, 45–46, 225n24; power of, 9, 24; prudence with, 82–84; psychology of, 1–2, 14–15, 18–20; sentimentality in, 27, 32; technology and, 37–38, *38*; tone in, 12; as transitory, 18; written, 17–18, 46, 54. *See also* rhetoric
speeches. *See specific topics*
spirituality, 174
spoken eloquence, 225n24
Stamp Act, 96–97
Stangor, Charles, 127
Stelzner, Herman, 169
Stevens, Wallace, 209
Stevenson, Adlai, 145–46, 148
Stevenson, Robert Louis, 40
Stewart, Charles, 148
strong dialect, 152
Stuckey, Mary, 70, 180
suffrage, 204–5

Swaggart, Jimmy, 46
Sykes, Sam, 27

Taliesin West (Arizona), 36
Tanden, Neera, 48–49
Tea Party, 46
technology, 22, 36–38, *38*, 207, 260n42.
    See also DICTION
TED Talks, 207
televangelism, 9
Tennant, Gilbert, 65
Teresa, Mother, 40
Terrill, Robert, 76, 152
thematic unity, 151–52
theology, 20, 23
Thiel, Peter, 59
Thomas, Clarence, *105*, 106–7, 208
Thompson, Seth, 201
Thoreau, Henry David, 101–2
Thunberg, Greta, 206
Tik Tok, 260n42
Tlaib, Rashida, 173
Tocqueville, Alexis de, 60–61, 73
tone, in speech, 12
transcendence: cultural resonance
    and, 65–72; Emerson on, 156;
    pragmatism and, 45–47, 59–60, *60*,
    87–92, *88*, *158*, 194–96, 199, 239n82,
    243n30; in rhetoric, 91, 157
transformation, 115
Treasury of Eloquence, 10–11
Truman, Harry, 114, 148, 166–67, 171
Truman Doctrine, 148
Trump, Donald: Joe Biden and, 103,
    196, 208; Cooper and, 5; COVID-19
    to, 48; on efficiency, *30*; eloquence
    of, 19, 58–59, 100, 197; Hutchinson
    compared to, 48; impeachment
    of, 79; irritation by, 63; A. Jackson
    and, 62; L. Johnson compared

to, 74; language of, 18, 72; Le
    Pen compared to, 76–77; Long
    compared to, 78; McConnell
    and, 195–96; Obama and, 5–6,
    14, 223n34; psychology of, 73,
    109; religion to, 237n51; rhetoric
    of, 5–7, 34, 91; A. Stevenson
    compared to, 145; on Twitter, 1
truth, 3, 5, 8–9, 33–34
Truth, Sojourner, 54, 91, 95–96, 98, *99*
Tsai, Robert, 91
Tswana, 24
Tucker, Robert, 89
Twitter, 1, 101–2, 207
Tynan, Kenneth, 73

United Kingdom (UK), 11, 57–58, 129
United States: African Americans in,
    8–9; American Fiction corpus, 54;
    architecture in, 36–37; creativity
    in, 129; culture of, 5, 7, 11–13;
    Declaration of Independence,
    97, 190; eloquence in, 2–3, 26–27,
    28–31, 32–34; Emerson and, 156–57;
    entrepreneurs in, *108*, 108–13,
    110; Germany and, 80–81; Great
    Depression in, 77–78; Great Society
    in, 73–74; ideology in, 75; language
    in, 13; in modernity, 65–66; morality
    in, 79; oratory in, 37–39, *38*, 194;
    politics in, 24, 56–57; populism
    in, 69–70, 76–79, 114, 141, 239n91;
    public discourse in, 45–46; religion
    in, 61–62, 85–86; resentment in,
    234n14; rhetoric in, 57–58, 160,
    201–2; Stamp Act in, 96–97; truth in,
    9; in Vietnam War, 124, 131, 142–44,
    150–52, 160, 173–74, 183–84; Voting
    Rights Act, *110*, 110–11
utilitarian appropriateness, 21

vectors, of eloquence, 194–200
vernacular appropriateness, 22
Vietnam War, 124, 131, 142–44,
    150–52, 160, 173–74, 183–85
violence, 2, 83–84
virtue, 85–86
vision, 67–69
Vivian, Brad, 183
Voltaire, 98
Voting Rights Act, 110, 110–11

Walker, Rafael, 195
Wall Street Journal, 3
Warnock, Ralph, 63
Washington, George, 91, 98, 99
Watergate scandal, 2
wealth, 78
Weaver, Richard, 27, 32, 65, 196
Weber, Max, 124, 172–73
Webster, Daniel, 57
Weiler, Michael, 74
Welch, Joseph, 105, 106, 113, 160
"We Shall Overcome" (Johnson, L.),
    82–83
Wesley, John, 46
Western culture, 8, 11, 22
White, E. B., 16, 123
White, William S., 176
Whitehead, Alfred North, 19
Whitfield, George, 65
Whitman, Walt, 124
Whittier, John Greenleaf, 124

Wiesel, Elie, 161, 182–83
Will, George, 160
William (prince), 58
Williams, Michelle, 29
Wilson, Woodrow, 16, 45, 86–87,
    88, 89, 208; J. Carter and, 164;
    Eisenhower and, 179; eloquence
    of, 163, 175–78; to Nixon, 151
Windt, Theodore, 172
Winfrey, Oprah, 58, 206
Wittig, Susan, 44–45
women: H. Clinton on, 149; feminism,
    13, 95–96; to Le Guin, 169–70; men
    compared to, 165; rhetoric of, 204–5;
    Richards on, 114; sexism, 195
word choice, 12, 43–44
Words of a Century (Oxford University
    Press), 159–60, 177
Words on Fire (Goodman), 226n47
World War II, 80–81, 88–89, 140,
    168–70
Wright, Fanny, 73
Wright, Frank Lloyd, 36–37, 40
written speech, 17–18, 46, 54
Wyatt, Sally, 129–30

Young, Lori, 43
Yousafzai, Malala, 206

Zakaria, Fareed, 206
Zarefsky, David, 52–53, 74
Zoom, 1